ON INFORMATION TECHNOLOGY

Video education courses are available on these topics through National Education Training Group, 1751 West Deihl Road, Naperville, IL 60563-9099 (tel: 800-526-0452 or 708-369-3000).

Database	Telecommunications	Networks and Data Communications	Society
AN END USER'S GUIDE TO DATABASE	TELECOMMUNICATIONS AND THE COMPUTER (third edition)	PRINCIPLES OF DATA COMMUNICATION	THE COMPUTERIZED SOCIETY
PRINCIPLES OF DATABASE MANAGEMENT (second edition)	COMMUNICATIONS SATELLITE SYSTEMS	TELEPROCESSING NETWORK ORGANIZATION	TELEMATIC SOCIETY: A CHALLENGE FOR TOMORROW
COMPUTER DATABASE ORGANIZATION (third edition)	**Distributed Processing**	SYSTEMS ANALYSIS FOR DATA TRANSMISSION	TECHNOLOGY'S CRUCIBLE
MANAGING THE DATABASE ENVIRONMENT (second edition)	COMPUTER NETWORKS AND DISTRIBUTED PROCESSING	DATA COMMUNICATION TECHNOLOGY	VIEWDATA AND THE INFORMATION SOCIETY
DATABASE ANALYSIS AND DESIGN	DESIGN AND STRATEGY FOR DISTRIBUTED DATA PROCESSING	DATA COMMUNICATION DESIGN TECHNIQUES	**SAA: Systems Application Architecture**
VSAM: ACCESS METHOD SERVICES AND PROGRAMMING TECHNIQUES	**Office Automation**	SNA: IBM's NETWORKING SOLUTION	SAA: COMMON USER ACCESS
DB2: CONCEPTS, DESIGN, AND PROGRAMMING	IBM OFFICE SYSTEMS: ARCHITECTURES AND IMPLEMENTATIONS	LOCAL AREA NETWORKS: ARCHITECTURES AND IMPLEMENTATIONS (second edition)	SAA: COMMON COMMUNICATIONS SUPPORT: DISTRIBUTED APPLICATIONS
IDMS/R: CONCEPTS, DESIGN, AND PROGRAMMING	OFFICE AUTOMATION STANDARDS	DATA COMMUNICATION STANDARDS	SAA: COMMON COMMUNICATIONS SUPPORT: NETWORK INFRASTRUCTURE
Security		COMPUTER NETWORKS AND DISTRIBUTED PROCESSING: SOFTWARE, TECHNIQUES, AND ARCHITECTURE	SAA: COMMON PROGRAMMING INTERFACE
SECURITY, ACCURACY, AND PRIVACY IN COMPUTER SYSTEMS		TCP/IP NETWORKING: ARCHITECTURE, ADMINISTRATION, AND PROGRAMMING	
		ASYNCHRONOUS TRANSFER MODE: ATM ARCHITECTURE AND IMPLEMENTATION	

ASYNCHRONOUS TRANSFER MODE

A  **BOOK**

THE JAMES MARTIN BOOKS
currently available from Prentice Hall

- Application Development Without Programmers
- Asynchronous Transfer Mode: ATM Architecture and Implementation
- Building Expert Systems
- Client/Server Databases: Enterprise Computing
- Communications Satellite Systems
- Computer Data-Base Organization, Second Edition
- Computer Networks and Distributed Processing: Software, Techniques, and Architecture
- Data Communication Technology
- DB2: Concepts, Design, and Programming
- Design and Strategy of Distributed Data Processing
- An End User's Guide to Data Base
- Enterprise Networking: Data Link Subnetworks
- Enterprise Networking: Strategies and Transport Protocols
- Fourth-Generation Languages, Volume I: Principles
- Fourth-Generation Languages, Volume II: Representative 4GLs
- Fourth-Generation Languages, Volume III: 4GLs from IBM
- Future Developments in Telecommunications, Second Edition
- Hyperdocuments and How to Create Them
- IBM Office Systems: Architectures and Implementations
- IDMS/R: Concepts, Design, and Programming
- Information Engineering, Book I: Introduction and Principles
- Information Engineering, Book II: Planning and Analysis
- Information Engineering, Book III: Design and Construction
- An Information Systems Manifesto
- Local Area Networks: Architectures and Implementations, Second Edition
- Managing the Data-Base Environment
- Object-Oriented Analysis and Design
- Object-Oriented Methods: A Foundation
- Object-Oriented Methods: Pragmatic Considerations
- Principles of Data-Base Management
- Principles of Data Communication
- Principles of Object-Oriented Analysis and Design
- Recommended Diagramming Standards for Analysts and Programmers
- SNA: IBM's Networking Solution
- Strategic Information Planning Methodologies, Second Edition
- System Design from Provably Correct Constructs
- Systems Analysis for Data Transmission
- Systems Application Architecture: Common User Access
- Systems Application Architecture: Common Communications Support: Distributed Applications
- Systems Application Architecture: Common Communications Support: Network Infrastructure
- Systems Application Architecture: Common Programming Interface
- TCP/IP Networking: Architecture, Administration, and Programming
- Technology's Crucible
- Telecommunications and the Computer, Third Edition
- Telematic Society: A Challenge for Tomorrow
- VSAM: Access Method Services and Programming Techniques

with Carma McClure

- Action Diagrams: Clearly Structured Specifications, Programs, and Procedures, Second Edition
- Diagramming Techniques for Analysts and Programmers
- Software Maintenance: The Problem and Its Solutions
- Structured Techniques: The Basis for CASE, Revised Edition

ASYNCHRONOUS TRANSFER MODE
ATM Architecture and Implementation

JAMES MARTIN

with

Kathleen Kavanagh Chapman / Joe Leben

PRENTICE HALL P T R
Upper Saddle River, New Jersey 07458
http://www.prenhall.com

To join a Prentice Hall PTR
mailing list, point to:
http://www.prenhall.com/register

Library of Congress Cataloging-in-Publication Data

MARTIN, JAMES (date)
   Asynchronous transfer mode : ATM architecture and implementation /
James Martin, Kathleen Kavanagh Chapman, Joe Leben.
     p.   cm.
   "James Martin books."
   Includes index.
   ISBN 0-13-567918-4
   1. Asynchronous transfer mode.   2. Computer architecture.
I. Chapman, Kathleen Kavanagh. II. Leben, Joe. III. Title.
TK5105.35.M33 1997
621.382—dc20   96-26713
                                              CIP

Editorial/production supervision: *Kathryn Gollin Marshak*
Liaison: *Beth Sturla*
Jacket design: *Design Source*
Manufacturing buyer: *Alexis R. Heydt*
Acquisitions editor: *Paul W. Becker*
Cover design director: *Jerry Votta*

Published by Prentice Hall P T R
Prentice-Hall, Inc.
A Simon & Schuster Company
Upper Saddle River, New Jersey 07458

The publisher offers discounts on this book when ordered
in bulk quantities. For more information write:
        Corporate Sales Department, Prentice Hall P T R
        One Lake Street
        Upper Saddle River, New Jersey 07458
        Phone: (800) 382-3419; Fax: (201) 236-7141
        E-mail: corpsales@prenhall.com

Printed in the United States of America

10 9 8 7 6 5 4 3 2 1

ISBN 0-13-567918-4

Prentice-Hall International (UK) Limited, *London*
Prentice-Hall of Australia Pty. Limited, *Sydney*
Prentice-Hall Canada Inc., *Toronto*
Prentice-Hall Hispanoamericana, S.A., *Mexico*
Prentice-Hall of India Private Limited, *New Delhi*
Prentice-Hall of Japan, Inc., *Tokyo*
Simon & Schuster Asia Pte. Ltd., *Singapore*
Editora Prentice-Hall do Brasil, Ltda., *Rio de Janeiro*

ASYNCHRONOUS TRANSFER MODE
ATM Architecture
and Implementation

JAMES MARTIN

with

Kathleen Kavanagh Chapman   /   Joe Leben

PRENTICE HALL P T R
Upper Saddle River, New Jersey 07458
http://www.prenhall.com

To join a Prentice Hall PTR
mailing list, point to:
http://www.prenhall.com/register

Library of Congress Cataloging-in-Publication Data

MARTIN, JAMES (date)
    Asynchronous transfer mode : ATM architecture and implementation /
James Martin, Kathleen Kavanagh Chapman, Joe Leben.
      p.   cm.
    "James Martin books."
    Includes index.
    ISBN 0-13-567918-4
    1. Asynchronous transfer mode.   2. Computer architecture.
I. Chapman, Kathleen Kavanagh. II. Leben, Joe. III. Title.
TK5105.35.M33 1997
621.382—dc20   96-26713
                                            CIP

Editorial/production supervision: *Kathryn Gollin Marshak*
Liaison: *Beth Sturla*
Jacket design: *Design Source*
Manufacturing buyer: *Alexis R. Heydt*
Acquisitions editor: *Paul W. Becker*
Cover design director: *Jerry Votta*

Copyright © 1997 by James Martin

Published by Prentice Hall P T R
Prentice-Hall, Inc.
A Simon & Schuster Company
Upper Saddle River, New Jersey 07458

The publisher offers discounts on this book when ordered
in bulk quantities. For more information write:

        Corporate Sales Department, Prentice Hall P T R
        One Lake Street
        Upper Saddle River, New Jersey 07458
        Phone: (800) 382-3419; Fax: (201) 236-7141
        E-mail: corpsales@prenhall.com

Printed in the United States of America

10 9 8 7 6 5 4 3 2 1

ISBN 0-13-567918-4

Prentice-Hall International (UK) Limited, *London*
Prentice-Hall of Australia Pty. Limited, *Sydney*
Prentice-Hall Canada Inc., *Toronto*
Prentice-Hall Hispanoamericana, S.A., *Mexico*
Prentice-Hall of India Private Limited, *New Delhi*
Prentice-Hall of Japan, Inc., *Tokyo*
Simon & Schuster Asia Pte. Ltd., *Singapore*
Editora Prentice-Hall do Brasil, Ltda., *Rio de Janeiro*

TO CORINTHIA
—*JM*

TO JOHN AND MY PARENTS
—*KKC*

TO CAROL
—*JL*

Contents

Preface   *xi*

Preface

The world of electronic communication currently has three fundamentally different information infrastructures: the telephone network for voice communication, the cable television and broadcasting system for video, and packet-switching networks for communication between computers. In addition to these three infrastructures, most organizations employ still other types of communication technologies in local area networks that operate over privately installed transmission media.

There is some overlap among the three communication infrastructures and the transmission technologies used in private local area networks. Transmission facilities intended to support voice communication are used to implement packet-switched computer networks. The high-speed, long-distance circuits of the telephone network are used to transmit video signals and also to interconnect individual local area networks for long-distance computer traffic. The cable television industry is also making some inroads in allowing computer communication to coexist on the same cable used to transmit television signals. But for the most part, the various types of communication technologies have evolved in parallel for fundamentally different purposes.

There are some common threads in the evolution of the three major communication infrastructures. All three are moving from the use of analog technology to digital technology for transmission, multiplexing, and switching. Networking and communication professionals are now beginning to agree that it is desirable for our separate information infrastructures to merge so that a single network infrastructure can be used to support the transmission of any type of information.

This merging of our three communication infrastructures is currently underway, but it will be some time before it can be completely accomplished. Many hurdles, not all of which are technical, will need to be overcome. New technologies are being developed that are a step in the direction of allowing the merging of these three information infrastructures to take place. The Asynchronous Transfer Mode (ATM) transmission, switching, and multiplexing technology described in this book is an important step in the evolution of a future integrated communication infrastructure.

PLAN OF THE BOOK

The chapters of this book are divided into five parts. Part I consists of a prologue that presents arguments for why Asynchronous Transfer Mode technology is necessary in today's networking environment and introduces the nature of ATM transmission and switching.

Part II consists of five chapters that examine how ATM technology can be integrated into the enterprise networks that organizations are building. The chapters in Part II discuss the characteristics of traffic that flows over an enterprise network, describe various architectures to which enterprise networks conform, the network and transport services provided by enterprise networks, the characteristics of data link subnetworks, and subnetwork interconnection technologies.

Part III consists of five chapters that describe the fundamental architecture on which ATM technology is built. The chapters in Part III examine the different layers into which ATM functions are divided, ways in which ATM subnetworks can be monitored and controlled, and the architectures on which various ATM switch products are based.

Part IV describes ways in which vendors and service providers are implementing the ATM standards in products and services. It also introduces ways in which ATM technology can be used in constructing or expanding an enterprise network.

Part V consists of four appendices that examine the standards organizations important in the telecommunications industry, the ubiquitous TCP/IP networking technology used in many enterprise networks, the OSI reference model, and the network addressing structure defined in standards for the OSI model.

WHO SHOULD READ THIS BOOK

This book is intended for a broad range of readers, including the following:

- Information systems and network administration managers and technical staff members who maintain and administer communication networks for data, voice, and other applications.

- Information systems and network administration technical staff members who select, install, and support networking hardware and software products and who deal with the complexities of the client/server computing environment.

- Executives and technical staff members in user departments who employ networking technology and who desire an understanding of the technology behind Asynchronous Transfer Mode networking.

- End users who will be using ATM networking products or will be helping information technology professionals determine their requirements.

- Students who are studying telecommunications or computer networking technology.

James Martin
Kathleen Kavanagh Chapman
Joe Leben

ASYNCHRONOUS TRANSFER MODE

PART ▎

PROLOGUE

Chapter 1   The Promise of ATM

*DILBERT reprinted by permission of UFS, Inc.

Chapter 1

The Promise of ATM

The design, installation, and operation of computer networks is vital to the functioning of modern computerized organizations. Over the last decade, organizations have installed complex and diverse networks, tying together mainframes, minicomputers, personal computers, workstations, terminals, and other devices. Today's enterprise networks are complex organisms in which a variety of different transmission, switching, and multiplexing mechanisms are intertwined to meet the organization's communications requirements.

Asynchronous Transfer Mode (ATM) technology is a new technology for electronic communication that has the potential for replacing the many conflicting technologies that must now be integrated into a cohesive whole. ATM represents a single communication technology that can operate both over the short distances spanned using typical local area network (LAN) technology and over the long distances spanned by wide area network (WAN) technology.

Before we begin examining the characteristics of ATM and exploring how it fits into today's computing environment, it will be useful to briefly describe the various switching and transmission technologies currently used for carrying computer data over the public telecommunications network. We will follow this introduction to current networking mechanisms by providing a high-level introduction to Asynchronous Transfer Mode (ATM) technology. Here, we will show how ATM uses a cell switching mechanism to provide significant advantages over the conventional switching and transmission technologies commonly used today.

The conventional switching and transmission technologies we examine in this chapter before looking at ATM are as follows:

- Conventional circuit-switching technology
- Local area network technology
- Computer network packet-switching technology
- ISDN services
- Frame relay technology

CONVENTIONAL CIRCUIT-SWITCHING TECHNOLOGY

A connection between two computing systems used for data transmission over long distances can be implemented in a number of different ways. It can be implemented using some form of privately owned transmission service, such as radio or microwave facilities that a company itself may operate and manage. However, it is more common to use a long-distance telecommunications data link implemented using the services offered by a telecommunications service provider, such as a telecommunications common carrier in the United States (AT&T, MCI, Sprint, etc.).

Point-to-Point Connections

Data transmission over the public telecommunications network normally takes place over point-to-point connections between pairs of computers. Figure 1.1 illustrates the general approach used to implement a long-distance data link using the facilities of a telecommunications service provider.

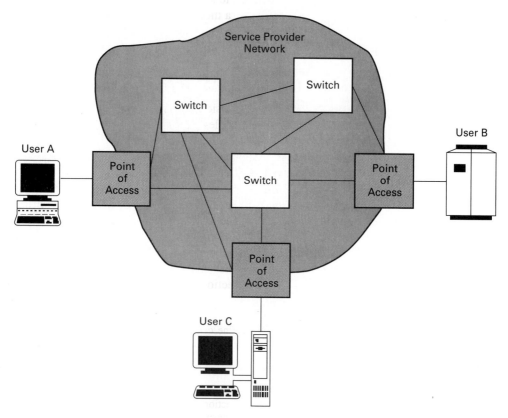

Figure 1.1 Using the services of a telecommunications common carrier to interconnect computer systems.

If we look inside the public telecommunications network, we will find physical communication circuits and various types of devices that act as switches and multiplexors to interconnect the communications circuits and allow them to be shared by many users. Two computer systems that wish to exchange data with one another over the public network each implements a connection to a point-of-access device, often by simply plugging the computer's modem into a phone jack. With some types of telecommunications circuits, the service provider may supply the user with a specialized access device tailored to the type of circuit being used. No matter how the connection is physically implemented, there appears to be a direct point-to-point circuit over which two connected users communicate.

All devices and communication circuits implemented by the telecommunications service provider are transparent to users, other than possibly a specialized access device into which the computer plugs. The service provider is responsible for transporting signals across the network between each pair of users that wish to communicate.

When, for example, user A has data to send to user B, user A transmits the data to its point of access to the network. The data then travels across the public network to the point of access for user B and from there to user B. To user A and user B, it appears as if the data travels across a direct connection, or *data link*, between them.

Plain Old Telephone Service (POTS)

A data link can be implemented using the basic transmission services offered by common carriers and other service providers that implement the global telephone network. These services are sometimes referred to as *plain old telephone service (POTS)*.

POTS uses *circuit-switching* techniques to implement *connections* between users. The global public telephone network is essentially a circuit-switching network in which a connection is established over a dedicated circuit between a pair of users for the duration of each telephone call. Each circuit provides the communicating users with a fixed bandwidth for the entire duration of the connection. Circuit switching is ideal for ordinary telephone circuits because the required bandwidth is relatively low, the full bandwidth is ordinarily required during the entire duration of a call, and calls are relatively long, (measured in minutes rather than microseconds).

There are two types of POTS connections that a service provider can supply to users:

- **Leased-line Connection.** A leased-line connection is a permanent, dedicated, point-to-point circuit that is leased from the service provider. The connection is always available to the two users connected to the ends of the circuit. It works like a permanent phone call that you never hang up. Leased-line connections can be used for ordinary telephone communication or for data transmission.

- **Dial-up Connection.** A dial-up connection requires a call to be placed to establish a circuit between two users. When data transmission is finished, the two users terminate the call, and the connection is released. Ordinary telephone calls, as well as data calls, use dial-up connections.

LOCAL AREA NETWORK (LAN) TECHNOLOGY

A local area network is a specialized form of computer network that allows a number of intelligent devices—such as personal computers, workstations, minicomputers, and mainframes—to be interconnected within a small geographic area spanning, perhaps a mile or two. A LAN implements a *multiaccess* data link that permits more than two systems to be attached to it (see Fig. 1.2). On a multiaccess data link, each system receives all transmissions from all of the other systems on the data link. All the systems on a multiaccess data link must share access to the common transmission capabilities.

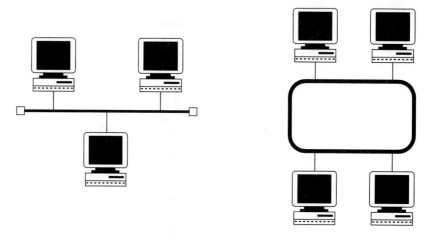

Figure 1.2 Multiaccess data links allow multiple systems to be attached to the same data link.

Multiaccess data links are most often used in subnetworks that use local area network (LAN) technology to implement short-distance communication among a collection of systems. The following is a list of the most important types of LAN data link subnetwork technologies used in building computer networks:

- Ethernet
- Token Ring
- Token Bus
- ARCnet
- Fiber Distributed Data Interface (FDDI)
- LocalTalk

LAN data link technology is used to implement a flexible, high-speed form of multiaccess data link. A LAN data link provides a simple communication path between any source system and any destination system. Each source system can generate a message and use the facilities of a LAN data link to deliver that message to any destination system on that link.

We can view a LAN data link in the same way as we view any other type of data link, such as a data link implemented using an ordinary point-to-point telecommunications facility. However, as we have already pointed out, a major difference between a LAN data link and other forms of data links used for data communication is that a LAN data link typically implements a many-to-many communication facility. A LAN data link allows any device attached to the LAN to communicate with any other attached device.

COMPUTER NETWORK PACKET-SWITCHING TECHNOLOGY

One alternative to using conventional common-carrier telecommunications circuits to span long distances is to use a specialized computer network that has been designed specifically to handle data transmission rather than voice traffic. The most widely known example of such a computer network is the Internet, which links commercial users, universities, and research organizations around the world. Telecommunications service providers also provide access to specialized computer networks that can be used to handle data transmission. These networks are often called *packet-switched data networks* (*PSDNs*). Examples of common carrier PSDNs that operate in the U.S. and Canada are SprintNet, Tymnet, and Datapac. Many such networks operate in other parts of the world as well.

The operator of a computer network provides a network of telecommunications circuits (which may be leased from a conventional telecommunications service provider), points of access to the computer network, and devices that interconnect the circuits. In many computer networks, devices called *routers* are used to interconnect the telecommunications circuits and also, sometimes, to provide users with points of access to the network (see Fig. 1.3).

To use a computer network for data transmission, a user contracts with an organization that can provide a point of access to the desired computer network. For example, a user might contract with an Internet service provider to gain access to the Internet or with a traditional telecommunications provider to gain access to that provider's own public data network. Each user machine has a single point of connection into the computer network but can exchange data with any other user machine also connected to that network. Conventional computer networks use a technique called *packet switching* rather than circuit switching to implement communication among users of the network.

Packet Switching

When user A sends a message to user B in a computer network, user A's message is broken into relatively small pieces called *packets*. Each packet from user A enters the computer network through user A's point of access. It may then flow through any number of routers before it arrives at user B's point of access and then to user B.

Each router along the path that a packet takes through the network determines the next router to which the packet is transmitted. Routers make routing decisions based on

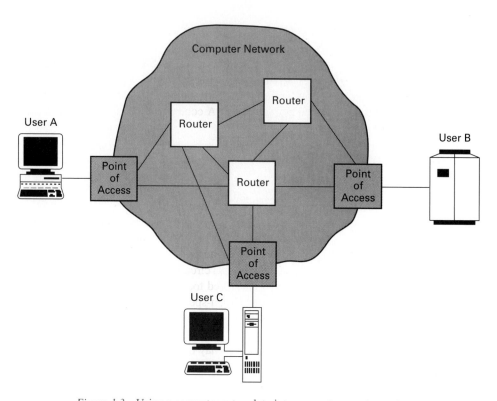

Figure 1.3 Using a computer network to interconnect computer systems.

the packet's final destination and other traffic flowing through the network. Packets may be stored in queues in the routers as they wait for transmission capacity to become available, and different packets sent between the same pair of users may end up taking different routes through the network, even though the circuits connecting routers remain fixed. This can result in variable delays in the rate at which packets are delivered and, possibly, packets being delivered out of sequence. When all the packets making up a message from user A arrive at user B, user B reassembles them to create the original message.

The data transmission service offered by a computer network can be either connection-oriented or connectionless.

Connection-Oriented Service

With a *connection-oriented* service, a logical association, called a *connection*, must be established between the source and destination systems before data can be exchanged between them. As with conventional telephone circuits, a connection in a computer network may be a permanent connection that is always available for transmission, like a conventional leased line. Alternatively, a connection can be a temporary connection that is established when there is data to be transmitted, used for transmission, and then terminated.

Connectionless Service

With a connectionless data transmission service, no connection is established between the source system and the destination system. Each packet transmitted is sent from a source system to a destination system independently of all others without requiring that a connection first be established between them. A connectionless service is sometimes called a *datagram* service.

Virtual Circuits

To support communication between pairs of users, a computer network typically establishes a *virtual circuit* between each pair of users that need to communicate. A virtual circuit makes it appear to two users as if they have an actual point-to-point link between them, just as if they were using a circuit in a telephone network for communication. Hardware and software in each user machine and in the devices that make up the network cooperate to implement the required virtual circuits.

The packet-switching techniques used today in computer networks are designed to allow a number of users to share very high-speed communication links that interconnect routers. Packet switching works well for computer data at low to moderate transmission speeds. But packet switching is not well suited for voice or video communication. The delays introduced by the packet switches may be too long and too unpredictable for these types of applications.

INTEGRATED SERVICES DIGITAL NETWORK (ISDN) TECHNOLOGY

Integrated Services Digital Network (ISDN) technology is beginning to be used in the public telecommunications network as an alternative to POTS technology. An ISDN is a public telecommunications network—typically administered by a common carrier or other telecommunications service provider—that supplies end-to-end digital telecommunications services that can be used to carry both voice and nonvoice information.

ISDN defines three general types of services:

- **Bearer Services.** Bearer services provide basic transfer of information between users. There are both packet-mode services and circuit-mode services. Packet-mode ISDN services offer services similar to those provided by a packet switched data network (PSDN). Circuit-mode services can be used as replacements for conventional telephone circuits.

- **Teleservices.** Teleservices provide both basic information transfer and higher-level functions. Examples of teleservices are facsimile, videotext, teletex, and telex.

- **Supplementary Services.** Supplementary services are additional functions that can be used with bearer services or teleservices. Examples are call waiting, conference calling, and caller ID.

ISDN Connections

To provide the foregoing types of services, ISDN uses three types of connections:

- **Circuit-switched Connection.** With a circuit-switched connection, a user places a call and the connection is established. When transmission is complete, the connection is released.

- **Packet-switched Connection.** A packet-switched connection connects a user to a packet-switching facility, which could be a separate PSDN or a facility integrated within ISDN.

- **Semipermanent Connection.** A semipermanent connection, equivalent to a leased line, is one that is established and remains available.

ISDN SONET Physical Transmission Services

Growth in transmission requirements for more complex forms of data, including images, animation, and digitized audio and video, has led to an increased need for higher data rates for data transmission. Data rates in the billions of bits per second may be required to support the combined traffic of users employing these more complex forms of data.

One of the goals in developing ISDN is to provide support for the higher data rates required for multimedia and interactive data. ISDN is built on top of Synchronous Optical NETwork (SONET) physical transmission services. SONET data rates begin at 51.84 Mbps and theoretically could reach 13,219.2 Mbps.

In order to effectively use the higher data rates provided by SONET, new forms of data transfer were developed as part of ISDN. These new data transfer techniques are Frame Relay and ATM.

FRAME RELAY TECHNOLOGY

Frame Relay technology has been developed to provide a high-speed alternative to the packet-switching techniques used in conventional computer networks. In a Frame Relay network, messages are routed from one Frame Relay node to the next based on an identifier associated with the virtual circuit being used. The major difference between Frame Relay network and a conventional computer network is in the area of error correction. In a conventional computer network, each time a packet is sent across a circuit between routers in the network, the router makes a check to ensure that the packets are not corrupted during transmission. The receiving router sends the sending router an acknowledgment for each correctly received packet. If a sending router does not receive an acknowledgment, it retransmits the packet in question.

In a Frame Relay network it is assumed that a transmission medium is being used that supports a very low error rate, and acknowledgments are not used as packets move through the network. It is assumed that error detection and retransmission will be handled by software running in the user machines that are communicating.

By eliminating much of the overhead associated with error handling, Frame Relay networks offer data rates that are often higher than those offered by conventional computer networks. Many conventional computer networks offer transmission speeds up to about 64 Kbps, while Frame Relay networks often provide transmission speeds of 2 Mbps and more.

Frame Relay networks are now available from many different providers of telecommunications services. An organization generally contracts with a Frame Relay service provider to implement point-to-point connections between pairs of user computers. As with a conventional computer network, each user computer has a single point of connection into the Frame Relay network but can make logical point-to-point connections with any other user computer also attached to the network.

ATM TECHNOLOGY

ATM is another new data transmission technology that was developed and defined as part of the work done in the Telecommunications sector of the International Telecommunications Union (ITU-T) in the creation of the ISDN standards. (Chapter 3 and Appendix A discuss standards organizations.)

ATM is designed to provide the basic transmission facility required within ISDN in order to support all the different types of services ISDN offers to its users. In order to do this, ATM provides different types of transmission services, including both connection-oriented and connectionless data transfer services. ATM networks can also provide the isochronous data delivery services. An *isochronous* service is one that is uniform with respect to time and in which the information being transmitted is guaranteed to arrive at regular intervals. Isochronous service is required for voice and video transmissions, where delays or interruptions in the transmission flow would be noticeable to the receiver.

Four classes of services are provided by ATM:

- **Class A.** Class A service is connection-oriented and isochronous. Class A service maintains a constant bit rate and timing relationship between the source and the destination. Class A service can be used to replace a conventional circuit-switched telecommunications link for voice or video transmission.

- **Class B.** Class B service is connection-oriented, has a variable bit rate, and maintains a timing relationship between the source and the destination. Class B service is intended for compressed audio and video transmission, such as that used in teleconferencing, where a variable bit rate can be tolerated as long as delays are within guaranteed boundaries.

- **Class C.** Class C service is connection-oriented with a variable bit rate and no timing relationship. This service is intended to provide data transfer similar to that provided by a virtual circuit in a conventional computer network.

- **Class D.** Class D service is connectionless with a variable bit rate and no timing relationship. This service is intended to provide the connectionless data transfer service commonly used with local area networks.

ATM NETWORK COMPONENTS

As shown in Fig. 1.4, an ATM network is made up of three major types of components: ATM switches, ATM endpoints, and transmission paths (TPs).

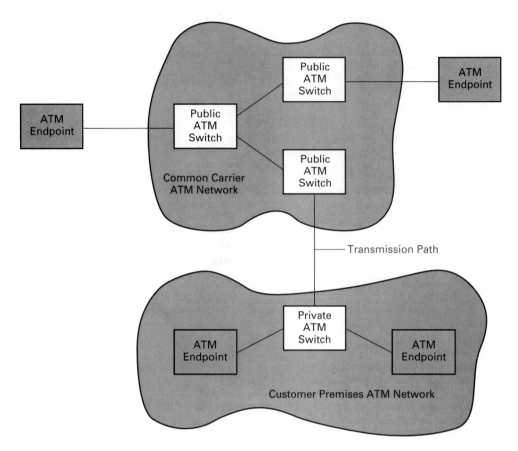

Figure 1.4   ATM network components.

ATM Switches

ATM switches perform functions related to the routing of information from the sending user to the receiving user. An ATM switch is sometimes called an *intermediate system (IS)*. ATM switches can be placed into the two major categories of public ATM switches and private ATM switches.

Public ATM Switches

A *public ATM switch* is part of a telecommunications service provider's public network and is referred to as a *network node (NN)* in the ATM standards. Public ATM switches are marketed to the telecommunications industry by many of the same vendors who provide conventional POTS switching and transmission equipment.

Private ATM Switches

A *private ATM switch* is owned and maintained by a user organization and is referred to as a *customer premises node (CPN)* in the ATM standards. Private ATM switches are marketed to user organizations by many of the same computer networking infrastructure vendors who provide user organizations with network interface cards (NICs), hubs, bridges, and routers.

Some vendors market both public ATM switches (network nodes) and private ATM switches (customer premises nodes). Some ATM switches can be used in either role in an ATM network.

ATM Endpoints

A device playing the role of an *ATM endpoint* serves as the source or destination of user data. An ATM endpoint is often called an *end system (ES)* and connects directly to a public or private ATM switch. An ATM endpoint might be implemented in an ordinary computing system by installing an ATM network interface card (NIC) in the computer and running appropriate communication software. Alternatively, an ATM endpoint might be implemented in a special-purpose network device to which one or more ordinary computing systems can be attached via conventional LAN NICs (see Fig. 1.5).

An ATM endpoint can be connected either to a public ATM switch owned by a common carrier (network node) or to a private ATM switch owned by a user organization (customer premises node) (see Fig. 1.6).

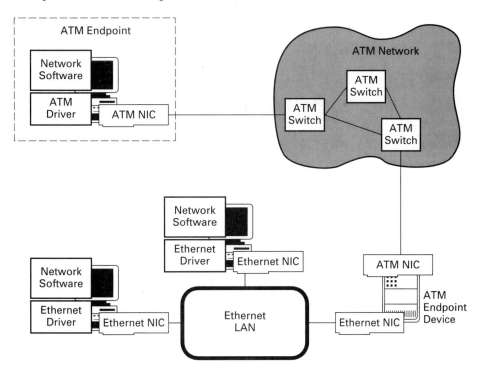

Figure 1.5 An ATM endpoint can be implemented in a user computer in which an ATM network interface card (NIC) is installed. Alternatively, an ATM endpoint can be implemented in a specialized device to which user computers are attached via some other type of data link technology.

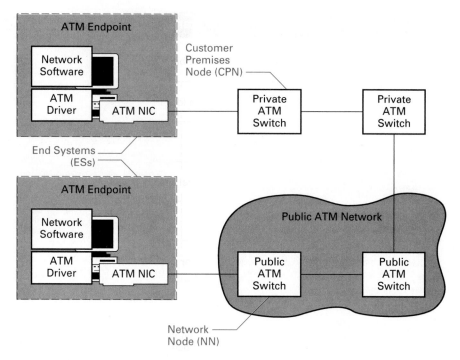

Figure 1.6　An ATM endpoint can be attached to a private ATM switch or to a public ATM switch.

Transmission Paths

ATM endpoints and ATM switches are interconnected via physical communication links called *transmission paths (TPs)*. The transmission paths interconnecting ATM switches and ATM endpoints can be implemented using different types of physical communication circuits using fiber optic or electrical transmission media.

ATM NETWORK OPERATION

Asynchronous Transfer Mode technology, also sometimes called *cell-relay* technology, is a form of packet-switched transmission that uses fixed-sized units, called *cells*, that are 53 bytes long. Box 1.1 shows the general format of the ATM cell. The cell format is discussed further in Chapter 8.

ATM assumes that the physical transmission medium being used is highly reliable. As with Frame Relay networks, ATM switches do not perform error-checking procedures or send acknowledgments in transmitting cells through the network. Eliminating error checking and using a fixed cell size minimizes the amount of overhead required by an ATM switch to process each cell. ATM networks are typically designed to support data rates of tens and hundreds of megabits per second. Also, with the small cell size, ATM is

BOX 1.1   Asynchronous Transfer Mode (ATM) cell format.

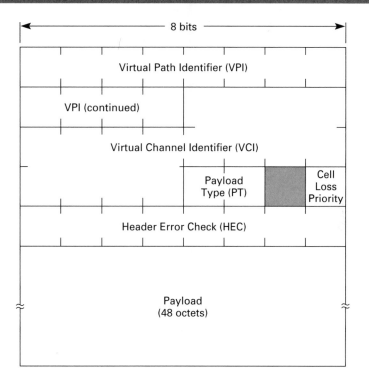

Payload
(48 octets)

- **Virtual Path Identifier (VPI).** The VPI is 12 bits in length and is used to group virtual channels into paths for routing purposes. (We will see later that in some cases, the first four bits of the VPI value are sometimes used for another purpose, but that need not concern us here.) Virtual paths and the VPI are described in Chapter 8.

- **Virtual Channel Identifier (VCI).** The VCI is a 16-bit field that identifies a particular virtual channel within a virtual path. Virtual channels and the VCI are also described in Chapter 8.

- **Payload Type (PT).** The PT field is a 2-bit field that identifies the type of information contained in the Payload field.

- **Cell Loss Priority (CLP).** The CLP field is a 1-bit field that ATM equipment uses to determine which cells to begin discarding first when congestion occurs.

- **Header Error Check (HEC).** The HEC field contains an error detection and correction code value used to detect and sometimes correct errors in the five header octets of the cell.

- **Payload.** The cell's Payload contains 48 octets (384 bits) of user data and/or additional control information. There are different formats used for the Payload field, corresponding to the different types of data delivery services that can be provided by an ATM network. ATM data delivery services, and specific Payload field formats, are described in Chapter 9.

efficient enough to provide a constant data rate for virtual circuits, so that ATM is suitable for isochronous traffic.

The result of ATM technology is to provide users with the advantages of circuit switching in that the network can guarantee a certain transmission capacity and level of service between two users. But the very high-speed transmission facilities can be shared among all users on an as-needed basis, as with packet switching.

ATM PRODUCTS

A number of different ATM products and services are available and in development. ATM switches can be used to replace many of the conventional LAN and WAN data transmission services currently used in enterprise networks.

ATM LANs

A number of network infrastructure vendors are supplying ATM NICs and ATM switches that can be used in a conventional local area network environment. A system of ATM NICs and switches might be used to interconnect end-user systems and servers to create a high-speed local area network (see Fig. 1.7).

ATM Backbone Networks

An ATM switch could also be used to implement a backbone network, interconnecting a number of LANs (see Fig. 1.8).

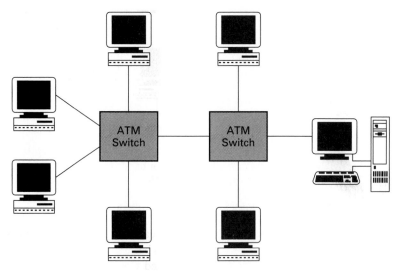

Figure 1.7 An ATM switch can be used in place of a conventional LAN transmission medium to interconnect intelligent devices.

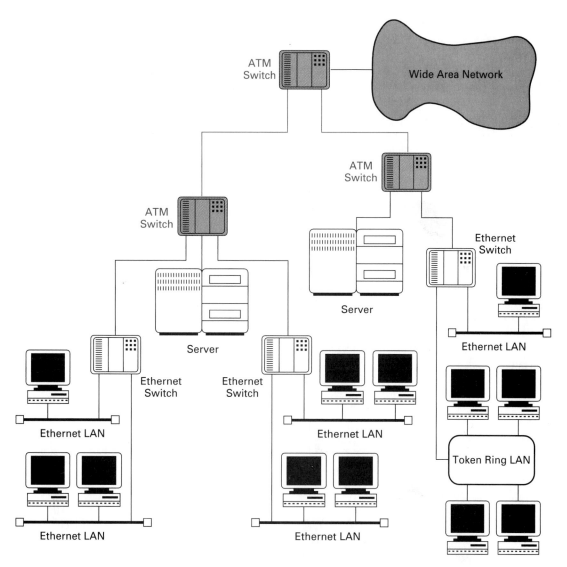

Figure 1.8   One or more ATM switches can be used to form a backbone network that can interconnect conventional LANs.

Public Network ATM Services

Public ATM services provided by a common carrier or other telecommunications services
provider can be used to implement WAN links between systems or between individual data
link subnetworks. These services can be used to interconnect ATM switches being used
locally (see Fig. 1.9). Common carrier ATM services can be used to interconnect LANs, or
they can be used to interconnect ATM switches being used locally.

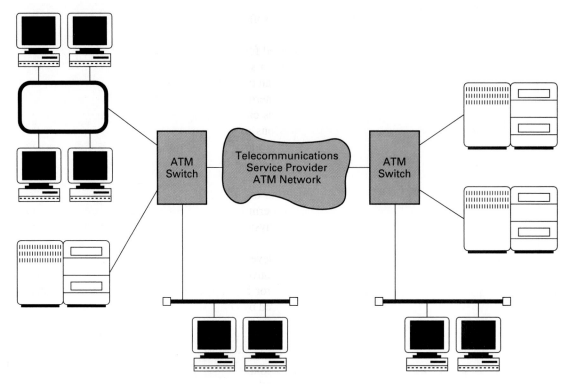

Figure 1.9 ATM services provided by a telecommunications service provider can be used to implement a wide area network data link in an enterprise network.

THE FUTURE OF ATM

The proponents of ATM claim that ATM technology will be the grand unifier of voice, video, and data transmission. For the data user, ATM has the potential of removing today's distinction between local area networking and wide area networking. ATM technology will allow the same technology to be used over short-distance, dedicated cabling as is used over long-distance common carrier circuits. With the high transmission speeds ATM technology is designed to support, it will be possible to make the distance between two communicating devices transparent to application programs. With such technology, it will be possible to build applications that work in an identical manner whether the two communicating systems are in the same room or across the globe.

SUMMARY

Conventional circuit-switching networks implement point-to-point connections between pairs of computers using technology often called plain old telephone service (POTS). The two types of POTS connections generally available are leased-line connections and dial-up connections.

A local area network is a specialized form of computer network that allows intelligent devices to be interconnected within a small geographic area. A LAN implements a multiaccess data link that permits more than two systems to be attached to it.

Computer networks, such as the Internet, provide an alternative to using conventional common carrier telecommunications circuits to span long distances. The computer networks operated by telecommunications service providers are often called packet-switched data networks (PSDNs). The data transmission service offered by a computer network can be either connection-oriented or connectionless.

Integrated Services Digital Network (ISDN) technology can be used as an alternative to POTS technology to provide three types of connections: circuit-switched connections, packet-switched connections, and semipermanent connections. ISDN is built on top of Synchronous Optical NETwork (SONET) physical transmission facilities that provide high transmission rates.

Frame Relay technology has been developed to provide a high-speed alternative to the packet-switching techniques used in conventional computer networks. By eliminating much of the overhead associated with error handling, Frame Relay networks offer data rates that are often higher than those offered by conventional computer networks.

Asynchronous Transfer Mode (ATM) is another new data transmission technology developed as part of the ISDN standards. ATM is designed to provide the basic transmission facility required within ISDN. ATM provides different types of transmission services, including both connection-oriented and connectionless data transfer services. ATM networks can also provide an isochronous service, required for voice and video transmission, that is uniform with respect to time.

ATM networks can provide four classes of service. Class A service is connection-oriented and maintains a constant bit rate and timing relationship between the source and the destination. Class B service is connection-oriented, has a variable bit rate, and maintains a fixed timing relationship between the source and the destination. Class C service is connection-oriented with a variable bit rate and no timing relationship. Class D service is connectionless with a variable bit rate and no timing relationship.

An ATM network is made up of three major types of components. ATM switches perform functions related to the routing of information from the sending user to the receiving user. ATM endpoints are devices that serve as the source or destination of user data. Transmission paths (TPs) are the physical communication circuits connecting ATM switches and ATM endpoints.

ATM technology uses a form of packet-switched transmission that uses fixed-sized units, called cells, that are 53 bytes long. ATM products and services can be used to replace many of the conventional LAN and WAN data transmission services used in enterprise networks. ATM services will make it possible to build applications that work in an identical manner whether the two communicating systems are in the same room or across the globe.

Chapter 2 begins Part II of this book in which we examine the characteristics of the conventional LAN and WAN technologies that are used in Enterprise networks. Chapter 2 examines various types of traffic that can be carried in a communication network.

PART II

THE ENTERPRISE NETWORK

Chapter 2

Integrated Network Traffic Characteristics

The world of electronic communication currently has three fundamentally different information infrastructures: the telephone network for voice communication, the cable television and broadcasting system for video, and packet-switching technologies for computer networking. There is some overlap among these infrastructures, but the three infrastructures have evolved in parallel for fundamentally different purposes. For example, transmission facilities intended to support voice communication are used to implement computer networks and are also used to transmit video signals. And the cable television industry has made some inroads in allowing computer communication to coexist on the same cable used to transmit television signals.

The three separate information infrastructures are all moving from analog technology to digital technology for transmission, switching, and multiplexing. At some point in the future, it will be desirable for these separate information infrastructures to merge so that the same network can be used to carry any type of information. This merging is currently underway, but it will be some time before it can be completely accomplished. Many hurdles, not all of which are technical, need to be overcome.

New technologies are being developed that are a step in the direction of allowing the merging of these three information infrastructures to take place. ATM technology is intended to be used in networks that transport a variety of different types of information, including integrated networks that may handle such information as:

- Voice traffic traditionally carried on telephone networks
- Data traffic typically carried on computer networks
- Multimedia traffic consisting of a mixture of image, audio, and video information

The various types of traffic that can be carried on a communications network each have different requirements and place different demands on switching and transmission facilities. In this chapter we examine the characteristics of the different types of network traffic to show the broad range of requirements that an ATM network must be designed to satisfy.

VOICE TRAFFIC

The most common form of voice traffic carried over a telecommunications network consists of telephone calls carrying conversations between people. For this type of traffic, before a particular conversation can begin one of the parties must typically make a telephone call to the other party. The calling process causes a connection to be established between the communicating parties.

ATM technology is well suited to carrying ordinary telephone traffic. An ATM network carries voice traffic in digital form using a continuous stream of bits. The bit stream required to carry a voice call might flow at either a constant or variable rate, depending on the methods of encoding used and whether or not there are relatively long periods of silence represented in the bit stream.

Bandwidth Requirements

The most commonly used encoding method used to represent a voice telephone signal with a constant bit rate is *pulse code modulation (PCM)* encoding. With PCM encoding, a constant bit rate of 64 Kbps is required to encode a single voice telephone channel.

There are various ways of compressing the full 64 Kbps PCM bit stream so it can be carried in fewer bits using a variable-rate bit stream. Using these schemes can lower the bit rate to an average of 10 Kbps and a maximum of 20 Kbps. Using such compression schemes can allow up to three voice channels to share the bandwidth typically assigned to a single voice channel.

Sensitivity to Timing

Voice traffic flowing over an ATM network is very sensitive to timing. In order to maintain an acceptable level of quality from the standpoint of the people carrying on a telephone conversation, the receiving ATM endpoint device must receive the bit stream at the same rate at which the sending ATM user sent it into the network. As we introduced in Chapter 1, ATM networks offer an *isochronous* delivery service for traffic, like telephone voice, that are sensitive to timing. Figure 2.1 illustrates a bit stream entering and leaving an ATM network.

If the rate at which the bit stream enters the network is identical to the rate at which it leaves the network, continuous transmission can be maintained without problems.

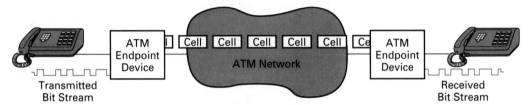

Figure 2.1 Isochronous service ensures that a bit stream is delivered at the same rate at which it enters the network.

However, if there is a difference in the rate at which the two endpoints operate—even a very small difference—problem situations of overrun or underrun can begin to occur.

Overrun

Overrun occurs if cells arrive at the destination endpoint slower than they enter the network at the source endpoint. When overrun occurs, devices in the ATM network need to discard cells to make up for the rate mismatch, and some of the information contained in the voice transmission is lost. The listening party typically notices this as words with missing syllables. In severe cases, some sentences may be missing entire words.

Underrun

Underrun occurs when the destination endpoint accepts bits faster than they are entering the network at the source endpoint. When underrun occurs, a point will eventually be reached when the source endpoint has no bits to pass on to the receiving endpoint. The listening party perceives this as empty gaps in the middle of sentences or words that contain extra periods of silence.

In order for the ATM devices processing the bit stream to maintain the proper rate and avoid overrun and underrun, they must be able to synchronize the internal clocks that control their processing. Methods typically used for synchronizing clocks across an ATM network are described in Chapter 7.

Sensitivity to Transit Delay

When a bit stream is transmitted across an ATM network, the source ATM endpoint device packages the bits into cells and transmits them over a physical transmission path. The cells are then processed by one or more ATM switches and finally arrive at the destination endpoint. The destination endpoint device then reconstructs the original bit stream from the cells it receives. Each individual cell requires a finite time to traverse the network from a source endpoint to its destination endpoint. The time required to do this in a particular network is referred to as the network's *transit delay*. Transit delay is sometimes called *latency* or *network delay*.

If the transit delay is too long in an ATM network carrying traffic for voice conversations, the delay can become noticeable to the communicating parties. Readers who have had occasion to make telephone calls using satellite circuits are familiar with this effect. The transit delay on a typical satellite circuit is about 270 milliseconds (msec.). Through experience, telecommunications service providers have found that for users to have the perception of high-quality voice transmission, the transit delay should be no longer than 50 msec. However, transit delays in the range of 100 msec. to 150 msec. may be acceptable under some circumstances. Most users are not happy with longer delays, such as those found in networks employing satellite circuits.

In a typical ATM network, the transit delay for cells transmitted over a particular connection may not always be exactly the same. The variation in transit delay that occurs in a given network is called *jitter*. Jitter is illustrated in Fig. 2.2. Buffering techniques can

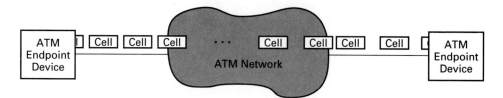

Figure 2.2 Jitter occurs in an ATM network when variations in transit delays are experienced over a particular connection.

be used to reduce the effect of jitter and to allow the receiving endpoint device to reconstruct a uniform bit stream. Buffering techniques are discussed in Chapter 7.

Sensitivity to Errors

As we have just described, voice traffic is very sensitive to timing, and the perceived quality of the voice transmission can be affected by delays or variations in synchronization. On the other hand, voice transmission is fairly tolerant of minor errors that occasionally occur in the transmitted bit stream. Even if occasional bits are lost or changed during transmission, redundancies in human language typically allow communication to be successful. Some minor errors may not even be noticed by the receiving party. For example, even if an entire cell is corrupted during transmission and is received totally in error, the information in that cell probably contains the information associated with only a very small portion of a single word. If the receiving party notices the error at all, it would probably be perceived only as a small amount of static in a single word.

The types of error detection and retransmission mechanisms used in computer networks to implement error-free links are not very useful for voice traffic, since the retransmitted portion of the bit stream would probably arrive too late to be of any use in reconstructing the bit stream. For voice transmission, it is generally better for the receiving device to simply accept the bit stream, errors and all, as long as the average error rate remains acceptably low.

As we will see, many of the mechanisms operating in ATM networks expect that highly reliable physical links are used in which the bit error rate is very low. In some ATM operational modes, ATM devices simply allow the few errors that occur to go uncorrected. Even when an ATM device detects a transmission error, its only response may be to simply discard the corrupted cell. There are, however, ATM operational modes that allow ATM endpoint devices to employ error detection and recovery mechanisms to provide an error-free transmission service. These modes are meant for the transmission of computer data and are not typically employed for ordinary voice information.

VIDEO TRAFFIC

Video information consists of a series of still images, called *frames*. Frames are typically displayed on a television set at a set rate, typically 25 or 30 frames per second. Video information is carried over an ATM network in a similar manner to voice information, although a much higher bit rate is required.

For the purposes of carrying video information in digital form, each frame may be considered to consist of some number of fixed points, often called *pixels*, each of which has certain intensity and color values associated with it.

Bandwidth Requirements

Video information has historically been transmitted using a continuous bit stream, with the bit stream containing information for every pixel in every frame and with the video bit stream transmitted at a constant rate. The bit rate required to carry a video bit stream depends on the resolution (pixels per frame), the frame rate (frames per second), and the amount of information needed to represent each pixel (bits per pixel). The total bit rate required for video transmission can vary from a few Mbps to hundreds of Mbps, depending on the video quality required.

Video information can be carried at a constant bit rate by transmitting the full information required to represent every pixel in every frame. However, video information ordinarily has a high degree of redundancy. For example, within a particular video frame, there may be areas of the picture where all the pixels have the same color and intensity. It is often also the case that one frame is not very much different from the frame that preceded it. The changes that occur from one frame to another may be in only some small percentage of the frame, generally that portion of the frame relating to the motion of a particular element within the video scene.

Various compression techniques can be used to take advantage of the high redundancy in video information. These compression schemes generally result in a video bit stream with a variable bit rate. Individual video frames are still generated at a constant rate, but the amount of data used to represent each frame varies from one frame to another.

Sensitivity to Timing

Like voice, video traffic requires an isochronous delivery service. Frames are generated at a constant rate, and the video information must be transmitted through the network and received by the destination endpoint at a rate that allows the original frames to be reconstructed and displayed at the required constant rate. As with voice traffic, overruns or underruns can occur if there is a data rate mismatch between the two endpoints. And also, as with voice, to prevent such mismatches, the endpoints must be able to synchronize their internal clocks across the ATM network.

Sensitivity to Transit Delay

Because video traffic is often transmitted in only one direction, such as in a conventional video broadcast, some video traffic is not as sensitive to delays as typical voice traffic. For example, in transmitting a video broadcast, a total network transit time measuring in seconds can be acceptable. However, it is important that *variations* in transit time (jitter) not be excessive so the received video information results in a television picture that appears continuous to the viewer.

Interactive video applications, such as video teleconferencing, are more sensitive to delay than a one-way video broadcast. As with voice, delays of up to 100-150 milliseconds are generally not noticeable to participants in the video conference.

Sensitivity to Errors

As we have already stated, video information is by its nature highly redundant. The change or loss of a few bits here and there will not ordinarily even be noticeable in the displayed television picture. Even the loss of an entire frame or two may not be readily apparent to the human eye. However, if a video stream is compressed before it is transmitted, the video information will become more sensitive to errors, since much of the redundant information has been removed by the compression process. As with voice, the time-sensitive nature of video presentation makes error detection and correction mechanisms based on retransmissions not very useful. It is generally better to present the output signal to the receiver errors and all rather than tolerate the delays inherent in error detection and retransmission mechanisms.

Audio/Video Synchronization

In some instances, the audio portion of a video signal may travel in a separate bit stream from the video portion. When audio and video information travel in separate bit streams, the receiver must be able to synchronize the two arriving bit streams so they can be appropriately synchronized before they are presented to a viewer. Any difference in time of presentation between the related audio and video information is called *skew*. In order for voice information to appear synchronized with lip movements, skew values of up to 120 milliseconds are not ordinarily apparent to the viewer.

COMPUTER DATA TRAFFIC

Traditional data traffic on a computer network consists of discrete, variable-size packets of data. Network traffic associated with computer data tends to be bursty, with entire packets of data becoming available for transmission at maximum data rates followed by periods of no activity.

Bandwidth Requirements

Bandwidth requirements for computer data traffic are much more variable than for voice or video traffic and are more difficult to predict. With interactive computer applications that are character oriented, acceptable performance can sometimes be attained using bit rates as low as 2400 bps. Many of today's computer applications are more graphics oriented. With computer applications that must transmit graphical elements across the network, the maximum data rates generally obtainable on an ordinary dial-up telephone channel using modems (14.4 Kbps to 28.8 Kbps) are not enough to achieve acceptable performance. The reader might try to access some of the home pages on the World Wide Web using an ordinary dial-up modem connection to see how bandwidth limitations can affect a computer application.

As we will see in this book, ATM technology has the potential to greatly increase the bandwidths that are available for computer data transmission.

Sensitivity to Timing

Unlike voice and video traffic, much of the traffic associated with computer data is not timing-sensitive, as long as the bit stream does not arrive at its destination faster than the receiving endpoint can accept it. The transmission of computer data does not ordinarily require an isochronous data delivery service, and ATM has operational modes in which the network does not attempt to synchronize the sending and receiving endpoints with respect to timing.

Sensitivity to Transit Delay

For interactive applications, there may be limits to acceptable transit delay based on response time requirements, but computer data can typically tolerate much higher transit delays than realtime voice or video information.

Sensitivity to Errors

With the transmission of computer data, *accuracy* is critical. If data is corrupted or lost during transmission, errors must be reliably detected and the erroneous packets retransmitted. ATM offers data delivery services that perform automatic error detection and retransmission, although, at the time of writing, some of these have not yet been fully defined (see Chapter 9). If an ATM data transmission service is used to transport computer data that does not perform automatic error detection with automatic retransmission, the higher layers of the network software must provide the required error detection and retransmission mechanisms. (Network software layers are discussed in Chapter 3.)

IMAGE TRAFFIC

Image traffic has generally the same characteristics as computer data traffic. Image data consists of a bit stream representing discrete image frames of varying size. Image data may or may not be delay sensitive depending on its application. If image data needs to be transmitted as part of an interactive application, response time requirements will determine its sensitivity to delays.

A key difference between image data and typical computer data traffic is that the bit stream required to carry a complete image is very large compared to the typical computer data packet. A single image may contain several megabytes of data. Therefore, image traffic may place higher bandwidth demands on a transmission facility.

Image information, like video information, often contains a lot of redundancy. Compression techniques can often be used to reduce the amount of information needed to accurately represent an image.

MULTIMEDIA TRAFFIC

Multimedia applications can use any combination of the different types of traffic that might be carried over a transmission facility: text, data, still images, animated graphics, audio, and video. The transmission requirements then reflect the combination of media being used. Multimedia applications are typically information-intensive and have large bandwidth requirements. When audio and video are involved, network synchronization is required. Interactive applications may also be highly sensitive to delays. Where different media are used concurrently, synchronization of the different data streams (skew) can be an issue.

SUMMARY

The world of electronic communication currently has three fundamentally different information infrastructures: the telephone network for voice communication, the cable television and broadcasting system for video, and packet-switching technologies for computer networking. The three separate information infrastructures are all moving from analog technology to digital technology for transmission, switching, and multiplexing and are merging so that the same network can be used to carry any type of information. ATM technology is intended to be used in networks that transport a variety of different types of information types.

The ATM bit stream required to carry voice information might flow at either a constant or variable rate, depending on the methods of encoding used. For voice transmission, ATM must provide an isochronous data delivery service in which the ATM endpoint device receives the bit stream at the same rate at which the sending ATM user sends it into the network. Voice transmission is fairly tolerant of minor transmission errors, and many of the mechanisms operating in ATM networks make the assumption that highly reliable physical links are used in which the bit error rate is very low. For voice transmission, an ATM network simply discards corrupted cells.

Video information consists of a series of frames that are displayed on a television set at a set rate. Video information is carried over an ATM network in a similar manner to voice information, although a much higher bit rate is required. Video information ordinarily has a high degree of redundancy, and various compression techniques can be used to create a video bit stream with a variable bit rate. Like voice, video traffic requires an isochronous delivery service that allows the original frames to be reconstructed and displayed at the required constant rate.

Traditional data traffic on a computer network consists of discrete, variable-size packets of data. Unlike voice and video traffic, much of the traffic associated with computer data is not timing-sensitive, as long as the bit stream does not arrive at its destination faster than the receiving endpoint can accept it. With the transmission of computer data, accuracy is critical. If data is corrupted or lost during transmission, errors must be reliably detected and the erroneous packets retransmitted. ATM offers data delivery services that perform automatic error detection and retransmission.

Image traffic has generally the same characteristics as computer data traffic and consists of a bit stream representing discrete image frames of varying size. Image data may or may not be delay sensitive depending on its application. Multimedia applications can use any combination of the different types of traffic that might be carried over a transmission facility: text, data, still images, animated graphics, audio, and video.

Chapter 3 examines the various network architectures that have been defined for helping to manage the complexity of electronic communication.

Chapter 3

Architectures for Enterprise Networking

In the past, mainframes and minicomputers, with their attached terminals, formed the basis of most forms of corporate network computing. Since the early 1980s, individual workgroups in organizations have begun to use local area networks (LANs) as a way of sharing resources. Workgroup LANs administered by individual departments often coexist with the corporate networks administered by the central information systems organization. The traditional large information systems vendors, such as IBM and Digital, have been changing their networking products to better serve the needs of individual desktop users. At the same time, the vendors in the workgroup computing arena, such as Microsoft and Novell, have been expanding their products to better serve the needs of enterprisewide computing.

This chapter begins by discussing how the individual communication networks an organization uses can be interlinked to form *enterprise networks*. This chapter also describes a number of network architectures, including the ATM architecture, that are used to divide hardware and network software functions into functional layers.

ENTERPRISE NETWORKS

The term *enterprise networking* refers to a form of integrated networking that attempts to integrate the large wide area networks constructed by information systems organizations with the local area networks created by users in individual workgroups. We use the term *subnetwork* in this book to refer to individual departmental networks in order to distinguish between an individual network and the enterprise network as a whole.

The goal of enterprise networking is to enable *enterprise computing*, where users throughout an organization are able to communicate with each other and to access data, processing services, applications, and other resources without regard to where they are located. The challenge for enterprise networking is to provide the organization with networking facilities that meet the needs of enterprise computing at reasonable cost.

The different individual subnetworks an organization employs are likely to use different types of networking hardware and software and might interconnect very different types of machines. A key challenge in developing an enterprise network is in finding ways of interconnecting a set of existing networks that might be quite incompatible with one another. The goal is to enable a user or an application program using a machine on one network to communicate with a user or application program using a machine on any other network in the organization. As we will see, this can be a difficult task.

We will begin our investigation of enterprise networking by looking at network technology from a very high-level perspective. Later chapters will then show how ATM technology can be used in the enterprise network environment.

NETWORKING TECHNOLOGY

As we have already mentioned, different types of networks might employ different types of networking technologies. An important way in which networking technologies can be classified is by the distances the networking technology is designed to span. With this form of classification, we can identify two major types of computer networking technology used today in enterprise networks:

- Wide area network (WAN) technology
- Local area network (LAN) technology

Wide Area Network Technology

Many of the very first networks organizations install employ public telecommunications facilities that allow machines to communicate over long distances. Such networks might be used so that users at far-flung locations all have access to the resources maintained in centrally located computer complexes. Such networks might permit fast interchange of information among users. Networks that tie together users who are widely separated geographically are called *wide area networks (WANs).*

The wide area networks organizations use have evolved over time. The first wide area networks consisted of dumb terminals communicating with large mainframes. As the cost of microelectronic devices has dropped, the intelligence in the various devices attached to a wide area network has increased. Today's wide area networks might interconnect intelligent terminals, personal computers, graphics workstations, minicomputers, and other diverse forms of programmable devices.

Local Area Network Technology

As wide area networks have expanded in scope, organizations have also expanded their use of personal computers and individual workstations to support the computer needs of users throughout the organization. Today's organizations make heavy use of small computers for word processing, financial analysis, sales reporting, engineering, order processing, and many other business functions. As the use of small computers has grown, a need also has grown for these computer systems to communicate—with each other and with the larger, centralized data processing facilities the organization maintains.

Small computers are often initially used in a stand-alone manner to support applications local in nature. But typically, additional requirements soon arise, such as:

- To access existing data that might be stored on a machine in some other department
- To allow a group of computer systems to share devices too expensive to be used by only one person
- To give users of small machines the ability to exchange electronic messages with one another, using the computers already in place

The type of networks users of small computers often begin using for such purposes are called *local area networks (LANs)*. LANs provide a means for meeting the requirements for high-speed, relatively short-distance communication among intelligent devices. The range of distances supported by typical local area networks range from a few feet to a few miles.

The majority of LANs in use today are used to interconnect personal computers and workstations. Some of the machines in a LAN are often called *servers*, to which the machines of individual computers share access.

NETWORK COMPONENTS

Computer networks are typically implemented by a combination of hardware and software components. The components used to implement networks, shown in Fig. 3.1, include computing devices, network interface cards, physical communication links, interconnection devices, and network software.

Computing Devices

A computer network is typically used to interconnect general-purpose computing devices, such as personal computers or workstations, which may be the same or different types. Ordinary peripheral devices, such as hard disks and simple line printers, are not typically attached directly to the computer network. Instead, such peripheral devices are attached to one of the networked computer systems. Peripheral devices can, however, be made accessible to other systems on the network so they can be shared by all network users.

Network Interface Cards

A *network interface card (NIC)* is typically installed in each computing device directly attached to the network. A NIC performs the hardware functions required to provide a computing device with physical communication capabilities.

Some types of computing devices designed for use on specific types of networks, such as network printers or certain types of workstations, have the functions of a NIC inte-

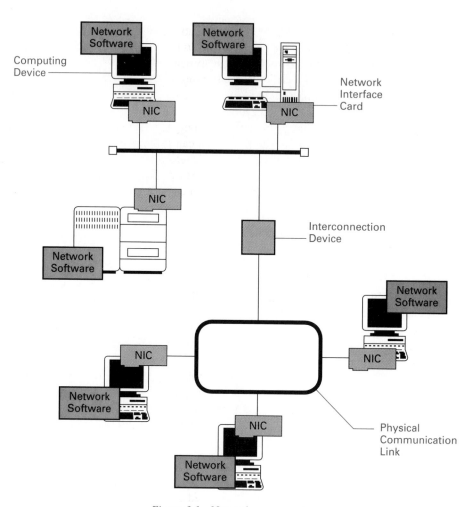

Figure 3.1　Network components.

grated directly into them. Other types of computing devices, such as general-purpose computing systems, typically allow various types of NICs to be installed in them.

In most cases, a NIC provides a computer with access to a local area network. Wide area network links are generally managed by network interconnection devices used to interconnect individual LANs. However, ATM network interface cards can often be used to connect a computer to an ATM network that uses the same technology to provide LAN-like facilities as well as long-distance data links.

Physical Communication Links

For a local area network, the physical communication link is implemented by private wire or cable used to interconnect the NICs installed in the networked computing devices. Various types of electrical cable or fiber-optic cable are used to implement LANs. The cabling system also typically includes *attachment units* that allow the devices to attach to the cable.

For a wide area network link, the physical communication link often takes the form of a circuit provided by a telecommunications provider. In some cases, the physical communication link is implemented by a wireless communication medium, such as radio, microwave, or infrared signaling.

As we introduced in Chapter 1, ATM physical communication links are called transmission paths. An ATM transmission path can be implemented over private cabling, as with a conventional LAN, or over the public telecommunication facilities administered by a telecommunications service provider. ATM transmission paths typically use fiber-optic cable for physical communication, although copper-wire cable can be used for relatively low-speed ATM links.

Interconnection Devices

Some local area network implementations use devices called repeaters, access units, concentrators, or hubs that allow multiple network devices to be connected to the LAN cabling system through a central point. Individual local area networks are often interconnected with network interconnection devices, such as bridges, routers, and gateways. Network interconnection devices might access both local area network cabling and wide area network circuits so the individual LANs in an enterprise network can be located anywhere in the world.

The main type of interconnection device used in an ATM network is the ATM switch introduced in Chapter 1. However, it is also possible to use other types of interconnection devices in conjunction with an ATM network, especially when an enterprise network uses ATM networking technology in conjunction with other types of communication links.

Network Software

Network interface cards (NICs) perform low-level functions that allow physical communication to take place between interconnected devices. High-level functions that end users employ for doing useful work are generally handled by network software that accesses a NIC on behalf of an end user. Both client systems and server systems generally must run compatible network software in order for them to communicate over the network.

The system software running on a server system is often called a *network operating system (NOS)*. Network operating systems augment a computer system's conventional system software by providing basic communication facilities and implementing various types of server functions.

NETWORK ARCHITECTURES

A key characteristic of the environment in which most enterprise networks operate is *diversity*. As we have seen, an enterprise network is ordinarily made up of a number of individual component subnetworks that may use different networking technologies. Within any of the individual subnetworks, many different types of devices may communicate. Part of the power of an enterprise network comes from its ability to allow a wide variety of different types of systems, operating in different subnetworks, to interoperate with one another.

Supporting a wide variety of systems and networking technologies can present substantial compatibility problems. For widely varying systems to be effectively linked together, the hardware and software used for communication need to be compatible, or else complex interfaces have to be built. In order to facilitate compatibility, *network architectures* have been developed to describe the various *functional layers* necessary to allow complex networks to be built using a variety of equipment.

A network architecture is a comprehensive plan and a set of rules that govern the design and operation of the hardware and software components used to create a particular type of computer network. A network architecture is a specification that defines a set of *communication protocols* that govern how communication should take place over the network. A system for communicating in a computer network generally consists of a set of compatible hardware and software components that all conform to a particular network architecture and use a particular set of communication protocols.

Layered Approach

An important characteristic common to all network architectures is the use of a *layered approach*. In modern computer networks, data transmission functions are performed by complex hardware and software in the various devices that make up the network. In order to manage this complexity, the functions performed in network devices are divided into independent *functional layers*.

The layered approach offers three key advantages:

- **Ease of Modification.** If a new technology becomes available for use in a particular layer, it can be incorporated without having a major impact on any of the other layers.

- **Diversity.** Two devices can be built using completely different hardware and software technologies. They will be able to communicate successfully as long as both devices employ the same communication protocols in each layer.

- **Transparency.** The layering concept allows the technical details of the lower layers to be hidden from the higher layers. At the top of the layering structure, the user perceives an easy-to-use interface to the network, even though the details of the layers below may be quite complex.

Services and Protocols

For each functional layer in a network architecture, the architecture defines a set of *services* the layer performs and specifies a *protocol* that governs communication in that layer:

- **Service.** A layer *service* defines *what* a layer does for the layer above it. A layer service consists of the definition of a function or set of functions a layer performs on behalf of the layer above it.

- **Protocol.** A layer *protocol* specifies *how* a layer performs its service. A layer protocol specifies the formats of messages exchanged between the layer in one machine and the same layer in another machine and rules governing the exchange of those messages.

Figure 3.2 illustrates a general model for a layered network architecture based on the idea of services and protocols.

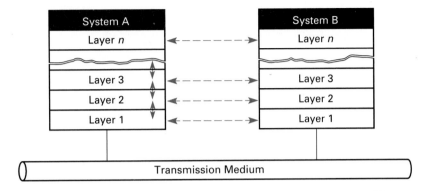

Figure 3.2　Layered model on which network architectures are based.

There is a defined *interface* between each pair of layers, and each functional layer provides a set of *services* to the layer above it. In the hypothetical layered architecture shown in Fig 3.3, the vertical arrows represent how layer 2 provides its services to layer 3.

A network architecture also defines protocols used by complementary layers in communicating systems. The horizontal arrow between complementary layer 2 entities in Fig. 3.3 represents the protocol that governs layer 2 of the hypothetical architecture. As we discussed earlier, a protocol defines the precise formats of the messages exchanged by complementary layers and the rules governing the exchange of those messages.

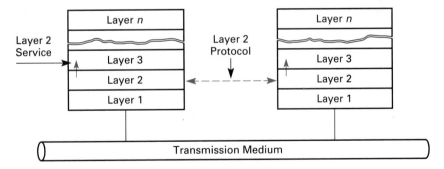

Figure 3.3　Services and protocols.

STANDARDS ORGANIZATIONS

A number of standards organizations around the world are actively involved in developing standards and architectures for telecommunications and computer and voice networking. Box 3.1 describes the key organizations that are developing standards in the area of

---

BOX 3.1 Important international standards organizations.

- **International Organization for Standardization.** A prominent standards organization is the *International Organization for Standardization (ISO)*, the largest standards organization in the world. ISO produces large numbers of standards on nearly every subject, from humane animal traps to screw threads. It is also the dominant information technology standardization organization in the world. The members of ISO are individual national standards organizations. Only national positions—positions representing an entire country—are discussed in ISO.

- **American National Standards Institute (ANSI).** Virtually every country in the world has a national standards organization responsible for publishing standards to guide that nation's industries. In the United States, this organization is ANSI. ANSI is a nonprofit organization that writes the rules for standards bodies to follow and publishes standards produced under its rules of consensus. ANSI accredits standards committees to write standards in their areas of expertise.

- **Institute of Electrical and Electronics Engineers.** The *Institute of Electrical and Electronics Engineers (IEEE)* is a professional society whose members are individual engineers. The IEEE Computer Society Local Network Committee (Project 802) has focused on standards related to local area networks, and has produced a set of LAN standards. The IEEE LAN standards have been accepted by ISO as international standards and are published by ISO as well.

- **International Telecommunication Union-Telecommunications (ITU-T).** The ITU-T is an organization that operates under the umbrella of the United Nations. Originally known as the CCITT, its members consist of organizations that provide telecommunications services within a given country. The ITU-T develops a large variety of technical recommendations related to telecommunications networks. Development of ATM standards first started in ITU-T. With respect to ATM, the focus in ITU-T is on the use of ATM technology in wide area networks.

- **ATM Forum.** The ATM Forum is a consortium of companies interested in the development of ATM network technology. The ATM Forum is not a formal standards organization, and the documents it produces are called *implementation agreements* rather than standards. Member companies agree to comply with the agreements, and in this way increase the likelihood of interoperability between their products. The focus of the ATM Forum is on the use of ATM technology in local area networks.

---

telecommunications and networking. These and several other standards organizations are described in detail in Appendix A.

THE OSI REFERENCE MODEL

During the time that today's network architectures and communication protocols were being developed, an ambitious project was underway in ISO to develop a single international standard set of communication protocols that could be used in a communication network. By 1984, ISO had defined an overall model of computer communication called the *Reference Model for Open Systems Interconnection*, or *OSI model* for short. The OSI model, described in international standard ISO 7498 and in ITU-T *Recommendation X.200*, documents a generalized model of system interconnection.

Purpose of the OSI Model

The OSI model is designed to provide a common basis for the coordination of standards development for the purpose of interconnecting *open systems*. The term *open* in this context means systems open to one another by virtue of their mutual use of applicable standards.

The OSI model describes how machines can communicate with one another in a standardized and highly flexible way by defining the functional layers that should be incorporated into each communicating machine. The OSI model does not define the networking software itself, nor does it define detailed standards for that software; it simply defines the broad categories of function each layer should perform.

The OSI Network Architecture

ISO has also developed a comprehensive set of standards for the various layers of the OSI model. These standards together make up the *OSI architecture* for computer networking.

The standards supporting the OSI architecture are not today widely implemented in commercial products for computer networking, nor does it appear that they will be widely implemented in the foreseeable future. However, the OSI model is still important. Many of the concepts and terminology associated with the OSI model have become generally accepted as a basis for discussing and describing network architectures of all types. The layering structure of the OSI model is also often used in categorizing the various communication protocols in common use today and in comparing one network architecture with another.

OSI Model Functional Layers

The OSI model defines the seven functional layers shown in Box 3.2. Each layer performs a different set of functions and should be as independent as possible from all the others. Box 3.2 also briefly describes each of the seven layers of the OSI model.

IEEE/ISO/ANSI LAN ARCHITECTURE

The IEEE has undertaken a major role in the development of local area network standards. IEEE Project 802 has defined a flexible architecture oriented specifically to the standardization of local area network data link technology. The approach the IEEE has taken in developing its LAN architecture is in conformance with the OSI model. However, IEEE Project 802 addresses only the lowest two layers of the OSI model, the Physical and Data Link layers.

The IEEE Project 802 LAN architecture has been accepted by ISO and ANSI to form the underlying basis for their own LAN standardization efforts. In this book, we refer to the architecture that began its development in IEEE Project 802 as the IEEE/ISO/ANSI LAN architecture.

BOX 3.2   OSI model functional layers.

Application Layer
Presentation Layer
Session Layer
Transport Layer
Network Layer
Data Link Layer
Physical Layer

- **Physical Layer.** The *Physical* layer is responsible for the actual transmission of a bit stream across a physical circuit. It allows signals, such as electrical signals, optical signals, or radio signals, to be exchanged among communicating machines. The Physical layer typically consists of hardware permanently installed in the communicating devices. The Physical layer also addresses the cables, connectors, modems, and other devices used to permit machines to physically communicate. Physical layer mechanisms in each of the communicating machines typically control the generation and detection of signals interpreted as 0 bits and 1 bits.

- **The Data Link Layer.** The *Data Link* layer is responsible for transmitting data over a single physical circuit from one system to another. Control mechanisms in the *Data Link* layer handle the transmission of data units, often called *frames*, over a physical circuit. Functions operating in the Data Link layer allow data to be transmitted, in a relatively error-free fashion, over a sometimes error-prone transmission medium. This layer is concerned with how bits are grouped into frames and performs synchronization functions with respect to failures occurring in the Physical layer. The Data Link layer implements error-detection mechanisms that identify transmission errors. With some types of data links, the Data Link layer may also perform procedures for flow control, frame sequencing, and recovering from transmission errors.

- **The Network Layer.** The *Network* layer is concerned with making routing decisions and with relaying data from one device to another through the network. The OSI model classifies each system in the network as one of two types: *end systems* act as the source or the final destination of data, and *intermediate systems* perform routing and relaying functions. The facilities provided by the Network layer supply a service higher layers employ for moving data units, often called *packets*, from one end system to another, where the packets may flow through any number of intermediate systems. End systems generally implement all seven layers of the OSI model, allowing application programs to exchange information with each other. It is possible for intermediate systems performing *only* routing and relaying functions to implement only the bottom three layers of the OSI model. Where the Data Link layer provides for the transmission of frames between *adjacent* systems across a single data link, the Network layer provides for the more complex task of transmitting packets between *any* two end systems in the network, regardless of how many data links may need to be traversed.

- **The Transport Layer.** The *Transport* layer builds on the services of the Network layer and the layers below it to form the uppermost layer of a reliable end-to-end *data trans-*

BOX 3.2   *(Continued)*

port service. The Transport layer hides from the higher layers all the details concerning the actual moving of packets and frames from one computer to another. The lowest three layers of the OSI model implement a common physical network many machines can use independently of one another. The functions performed in the Transport layer may include end-to-end integrity controls to recover lost, out-of-sequence, or duplicate messages. The Transport layer is the lowest layer required *only* in the computers running the programs that use the network for communication. The Transport layer need not be implemented in intermediate systems that perform only routing and relaying functions.

- **The Session Layer.** There is a fundamental difference in orientation between the bottom four layers and the top three. The bottom four layers are concerned more with the network itself and provide a general data transport service useful to any application. The top three layers are more concerned with services oriented to the application programs themselves. The *Session* layer is the lowest of the layers associated with the application programs. It is responsible for organizing the dialog between two application programs and for managing the data exchanges between them. Session layer services also include establishing synchronization points within the dialog, allowing a dialog to be interrupted, and resuming a dialog from a synchronization point.

- **The Presentation Layer.** The five layers below the *Presentation* layer are all concerned with the orderly movement of a stream of bits from one program to another. The Presentation layer is the lowest layer interested in the *meaning* of those bits. It deals with preserving the *information content* of data transmitted over the network. The Presentation layer enables two communicating systems to exchange information with one another without having to be aware of the specific data formats each system uses. The Presentation layer performs the necessary conversions that allow each system to work with data in its own preferred format without having to be aware of the data formats its partner uses.

- **The Application Layer.** The *Application* layer is the layer associated with user processes. The Application layer is concerned with high-level functions that provide support to the application programs using the network for communication. The Application layer provides a means for application programs to access the system interconnection facilities to exchange information. It provides all functions related to communication between systems not provided by the lower layers.

Box 3.3 illustrates the relationships between the OSI model and the architecture that underlies IEEE, ISO, and ANSI standards for local area networks. In the IEEE/ISO/ANSI LAN architecture, the Data Link layer is divided into two sublayers: the *Logical Link Control (LLC)* sublayer and the *Medium Access Control (MAC)* sublayer.

ATM ARCHITECTURE

The designers of the ATM technology also organized the various functions that must be performed in ATM network devices into functional layers. The three functional layers

BOX 3.3   IEEE/ISO/ANSI LAN architecture functional layers.

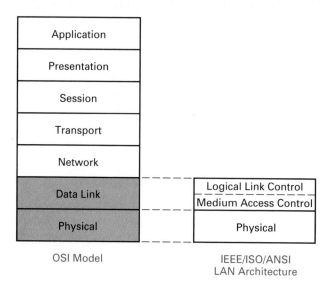

- **Physical Layer.** The Physical layer corresponds directly to the Physical layer of the OSI model. It provides services to a user of the Physical layer, which is typically the MAC sublayer. The data units exchanged by the Physical layer consist of signals that represent individual bits. This layer defines procedures for establishing physical connections to the transmission medium and for transmitting and receiving signals over it. Physical layer specifications also include descriptions of the types of cabling, plugs, and connectors to be used and the characteristics of the signals exchanged.

- **Medium Access Control Sublayer.** A local area network typically supports multiple devices that all contend for access to a shared physical transmission medium. The Medium Access Control sublayer provides services to a user of the MAC sublayer service, which is typically the LLC sublayer. The data unit MAC sublayer entities exchange is called the *medium-access-control-protocol-data-unit (MAC-PDU)*. The MAC-PDU is often called a *MAC frame*. The purpose of the MAC frame is to carry data across a physical transmission medium from one network device, often called a *station*, to another.

- **Logical Link Control Sublayer.** The Logical Link Control sublayer is responsible for medium-independent data link functions. It allows a LAN data link user to access the services of the data link without having to be concerned with the form of medium access control or physical transmission medium used. The LLC sublayer is shared by a variety of different medium access control technologies. The LLC sublayer allows different LAN technologies to present a common interface to a LAN data link user.

making up the ATM architecture are the *ATM Adaptation layer (AAL)*, the *ATM layer*, and the *Physical layer* (see Fig. 3.4).

The following sections briefly describe the major functions of the three ATM functional layers.

Physical Layer

The Physical layer sends and receives information in the form of electrical or optical signals over a physical transmission path. This physical communication function may involve converting cells to and from a continuous bit stream or transmission frame format and applying various forms of encoding and decoding to the data contained in each cell.

ATM Layer

The primary function of the ATM layer is *cell switching*. An ATM layer entity in an ATM device accepts cells received over a transmission path, determines the outbound transmission path over which each of those cells should be relayed, and formats the cell header before retransmitting each cell.

ATM Adaptation Layer (AAL)

The *ATM Adaptation layer (AAL)* provides the interface between ATM user software, typically implemented in a network software subsystem, and the ATM network. Again, notice that the ATM Adaptation layer is implemented only in ATM endpoint devices, not in ATM switches.

In a source endpoint device, an AAL entity accepts a bit stream from the ATM user software and structures it in the form of cells suitable for transport across the ATM network. In a receiving ATM endpoint device, a complementary AAL entity accepts cells from the network, reconstructs the original bit stream, and passes it to the receiving ATM user software.

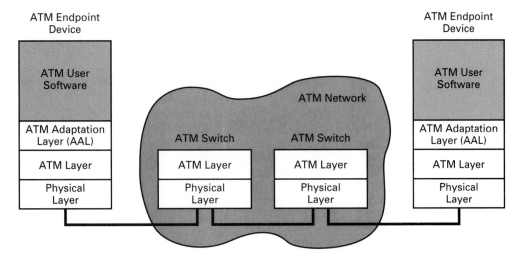

Figure 3.4   ATM architectural layers.

ATM Architecture and the OSI Model

Figure 3.5 shows the relationships among the three ATM functional layers, the functional layers of the OSI model, and the layers and sublayers of the IEEE/ISO/ANSI LAN architecture.

When an ATM data link is used in a data transmission application, much of the software characterized as ATM user software in Fig. 3.5 is implemented by a network software system implementing a particular transport protocol family—such as TCP/IP, IPX/SPX, SNA, or NetBIOS—running in an ATM endpoint device.

The sending ATM user software transmits data over a connection with the destination ATM user software. To the two ATM users, the ATM connection appears as a direct link between the ATM endpoint device used by the source user's machine and the ATM endpoint device used by the destination user's machine.

For the ATM user software, the interface to ATM services occurs at the level of the MAC sublayer in the OSI Data Link layer. Software operating in the role of an ATM user is responsible for performing any higher-layer functions associated with network processing, including performing end-to-end error checking and flow control functions.

When making a comparison with the OSI model, note that many of the functions that are ordinarily associated with the Network layer of the OSI model—such as addressing, routing, and relaying—are also performed in the ATM layer, which operates in the lower portion of the OSI Data Link layer. Also, the OSI model makes the distinction between end systems and intermediate systems in the Network layer, while ATM makes a similar distinction between endpoints and switches in the ATM Adaptation layer.

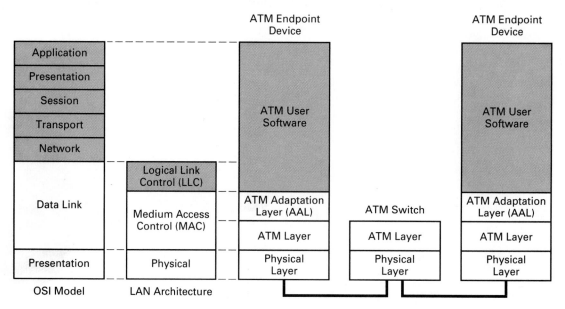

Figure 3.5   ATM architecture relationship to the OSI model and the IEEE/ISO/ANSI LAN architecture.

It is important to understand that it is possible for routing to be taking place for the enterprise network as a whole in the Network layer using conventional routers. At the same time, ATM routing can be taking place for an individual ATM subnetwork in the ATM layer. The routing function taking place in the conventional routers is not aware of the ATM routing that takes place in the ATM network. The conventional routers treat the entire ATM network as a single data link.

ATM LINKS IN ENTERPRISE NETWORKS

In an enterprise network that uses routers, only some of the data links in the network may be ATM data links. In such a network, the ATM user software is responsible for determining that a particular ATM connection is the next step in the desired path across the entire enterprise network.

ATM-Only Enterprise Network

It is possible to implement an enterprise network using only ATM data links. The enterprise network might then consist of a single, integrated ATM network. In such a case, a source computer might implement ATM user software and invoke the functions of a source ATM endpoint. The destination computer might also implement ATM user software and access the functions of a destination ATM endpoint device.

Figure 3.6 shows such a situation in which each of the communicating computers has an ATM network interface card (NIC) installed that functions as an ATM endpoint.

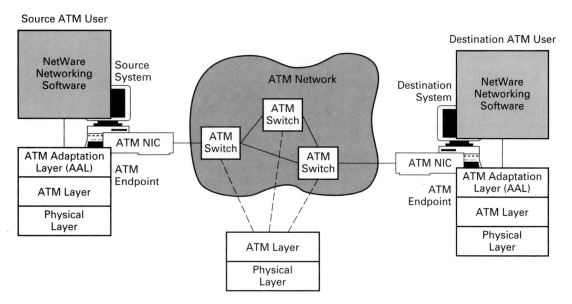

Figure 3.6   Two computers communicating across a single ATM network.

When only ATM data links are used, the computers might communicate with each other over the ATM network using a single ATM connection between the two computers. Notice that the source and destination ATM user software takes the form of NetWare network software running in the source and destination machines.

Complex Enterprise Network

In an integrated network it is more likely for ATM data links to be used in conjunction with data links of other types. Figure 3.7 shows a portion of a complex enterprise network that uses Ethernet LAN data links for local communication in each workgroup and an ATM subnetwork to implement high-speed, long-distance links between workgroups.

Notice in Fig. 3.7 that the source and destination systems are on the two Ethernet LANs but that the source and destination *ATM users* consist this time of software running in the two routers that are communicating via an ATM connection.

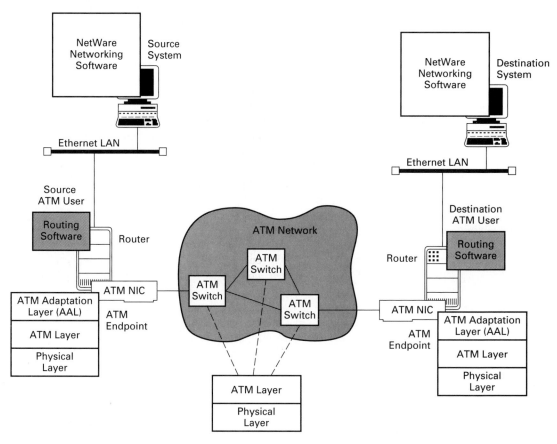

Figure 3.7 Two computers communicating across an enterprise network implemented using Ethernet subnetworks for communication within workgroups and an ATM subnetwork for long-distance communication.

Within the ATM network, ATM switching performs its own routing function. But as we pointed out earlier, the ATM routing function takes place in the OSI Data Link layer and in this case does not replace the Network layer routing functions that need to be performed by high-level network software.

Chapter 12 includes further discussion of the use of ATM equipment and services in a conventional enterprise network.

NETWORK ARCHITECTURES AND PROTOCOL FAMILIES

Today's network software and hardware is based on many different network architectures. Some networking products, such as IBM's network hardware and software for mainframes, are based on a formal network architecture, in IBM's case *Systems Network Architecture (SNA)*. SNA consists of a formal set of specifications that exists apart from any particular hardware or software implementation of the architecture. The SNA architecture was developed first, and then products were designed to conform to the architecture. Both the architecture and the products based on the architecture have evolved over time as added capabilities were required.

Some networking products are based on a more informal architecture. For example, the term *TCP/IP (Transmission Control Protocol/Internet Protocol)* refers to a *protocol family* for computer networking that has been developed one piece at a time over the years. Each protocol in the TCP/IP protocol family now has a formal specification. With TCP/IP, the network software was often developed first, and then a formal specification was written based on that working software. The complete collection of the most commonly used TCP/IP protocol standards now makes up an ad hoc network architecture for TCP/IP.

ENTERPRISE NETWORK MODEL

This book uses as an organizing tool the general architectural model for enterprise networks shown in Fig. 3.8. Our enterprise network model places the layers of the OSI model

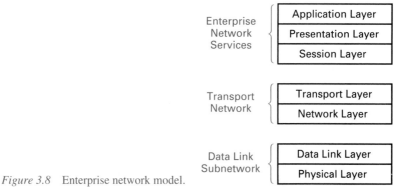

Figure 3.8   Enterprise network model.

into three groups. These groups reflect functional subsets of the various services provided by network hardware and network software subsystems.

The enterprise network model helps us to see how ATM technology relates to the various architectures, software subsystems, and technologies discussed in this book. The following sections introduce each of the three major components of the enterprise network model.

ENTERPRISE NETWORK SERVICES

The most useful kind of network software makes the network totally transparent to the user. A user should be able to access a remote file, send an electronic mail message, or print a spreadsheet on a network printer without having to know any of the details concerning the network technologies used. The software end users employ to perform such functions implements the *enterprise network services* component of the model. Some enterprise network services are required for the general operation of the network. Others consist of services application programs invoke on behalf of end users and services useful to application programs running in computers attached to the network. This component is associated with the Session, Presentation, and Application layers of the OSI model.

The enterprise network services layer of the enterprise network model is discussed further in Chapter 4.

THE TRANSPORT NETWORK

Transport network functions, running below the enterprise network services, are associated with the Transport and Network layers of the OSI model. Transport network facilities provide a basic end-to-end data delivery, or *data transport*, service. The transport network component of the enterprise network model calls on data link subnetwork services to provide the data transport service.

In the personal computer environment, the transport network is often implemented in the form of a network operating system that runs on a server systems along with client components that run on client systems. In other cases, software implementing the transport network is integrated directly into the operating system software. This has been common with TCP/IP support in the UNIX workstation environment for many years, and this trend is continuing in the personal computer environment. For example, the Windows for Workgroups, Windows 95, and Windows NT system software from Microsoft contain integrated networking support that makes it unnecessary to install separate networking software.

The following is a list of some of the most commonly used network software subsystems.

- TCP/IP
- NetWare IPX/SPX
- NetBIOS
- AppleTalk
- Systems Network Architecture (SNA)

- PATHWORKS
- VINES
- LANtastic

These network software subsystems are described further in Chapter 4. Each individual network software subsystem conforms to its own unique network architecture and implements its own family of transport protocols. A family of transport protocols is often called a *protocol family* or a *protocol suite*. Each network software subsystem and transport protocol family provides a variety of services that fall into the enterprise network services category as well.

DATA LINK SUBNETWORKS

The data link subnetwork component is the lowest level of the enterprise network model. It is associated with specific data link subnetwork transmission technologies. The data link subnetwork is responsible for managing the transmission of data over a particular physical subnetwork in the enterprise network. ATM is a data link subnetwork technology. But as we will see, it is a more powerful technology than most other data link technologies.

Most local area network data link transmission technologies are different from the technologies used to control data transmission over wide area network data links. The following are commonly used WAN subnetwork technologies:

- Analog telecommunications circuits
- Digital telecommunications circuits
- X.25 packet-switched data networks (PSDN)
- Integrated services digital network (ISDN)
- Broadband ISDN (B-ISDN)
- Frame relay
- Switched multi-megabit data service (SMDS)

The following are the most important LAN data link subnetwork technologies commonly used in enterprise networks.

- Ethernet
- Token ring
- Token bus
- ARCnet
- Fiber distributed data interface (FDDI)
- LocalTalk
- Wireless LAN technologies

We can place ATM technology into both of the above categories because it can be used to supply data transmission services over both short or long distances. ATM technology can be used to build a network that supplies LAN-like services in an enterprise network that may be global in scope.

NETWORKING PERSPECTIVES

Networking literature may refer to a particular type of computer network by using the name of a network software subsystem or transport protocol family. For example, we might refer to a *NetWare network*, an *AppleTalk network*, or an *SNA network*. When you see such a reference, it is important to realize that the literature is discussing the network from the viewpoint of the type of transport network facilities the network employs.

Some computer networking literature is not concerned with the high-level data transport software but instead focuses on the specific transmission technologies used to support communication between computers. When networking literature refers to a *Frame relay* network, an *Ethernet LAN*, or a *token ring network*, you can be sure the literature is discussing a particular type of data link subnetwork technology.

PROTOCOL STACKS

The network software systems in common use today were all originally developed to use a particular set of transport protocols. For example, NetWare software is built around the IPX/SPX protocol family, and Microsoft networking software implements NetBIOS. However, given the demands that exist for network interconnection and interoperation, the network software provided by many vendors now supports other transport protocol families in addition to their own native protocols.

When a network software subsystem supports multiple transport protocol families, the terms *transport protocol stack*, *transport stack*, or *protocol stack* are often used to refer to a software component that implements a particular transport protocol family.

SUMMARY

An enterprise network is a communication network that attempts to integrate the large wide area networks that have been constructed by information systems organizations with the local area networks that have been created by users in individual workgroups. Two major types of computer networking technology are used in enterprise networks: wide area network (WAN) technology and local area network (LAN) technology.

Computer networks are typically implemented by a combination of hardware and software components, including computing devices, network interface cards, physical communication links, interconnection devices, and network software.

A network architecture is a plan governing the design and operation of a particular type of computer network. A characteristic common to all network architectures is the use of a layered approach, in which network functions are divided into independent functional layers. For each functional layer, an architecture defines services and protocols. A service defines what a layer does for the layer above it and consists of the definition of functions a layer performs in providing its services. A layer protocol specifies how a layer performs its service by specifying the formats of messages and rules for how those messages are exchanged.

The Reference Model for Open Systems Interconnection (OSI model) is a generalized model of system interconnection described in international standard ISO 7498 and ITU Recommendation X.200. The OSI model has seven layers: Application, Presentation, Session, Transport, Network, Data Link, and Physical.

IEEE Project 802 has defined an architecture for local area networks (the IEEE/ISO/ANSI LAN architecture) that addresses the Data Link and Physical layers of the OSI model. The Data Link layer is divided into two sublayers: the Logical Link Control (LLC) sublayer and the Medium Access Control (MAC) sublayer.

The enterprise network model places the layers of the OSI model into three groups: enterprise network services, transport network, and data link subnetwork. The enterprise network services component of the enterprise network model is associated with the Session, Presentation, and Application layers of the OSI model. Enterprise network services are application-oriented services that end users use directly or that support application programs. Transport network functions run below the enterprise network services and are associated with the Transport and Network layers of the OSI model. This component provides a basic end-to-end data transmission, or data transport, service. The lowest level component of the enterprise network model is associated with the Data Link and Physical layers of the OSI model. This component is concerned with specific data link subnetwork technologies responsible for managing the transmission of data over a particular data link.

Chapter 4 introduces the high-level enterprise network services component and the transport network component of the enterprise network model.

Chapter **4**

Enterprise Network Services and Transport Protocols

Different network software subsystems vary widely in their capabilities and in the services they provide. However, certain types of functions have now become commonplace in generally available network software. This chapter introduces some of the application-oriented services that network software provides in an enterprise networking environment. Application-oriented services are among those provided in the Enterprise Network Services portion of the enterprise network model, as shown in Fig. 4.1.

CATEGORIES OF ENTERPRISE NETWORK SERVICES

Box 4.1 describes five broad categories of services network software provides to users of the network. Most of these service categories represent the types of services provided by network software in a typical PC LAN implementation, but most of them are provided by network software in the mainframe and minicomputer environments as well.

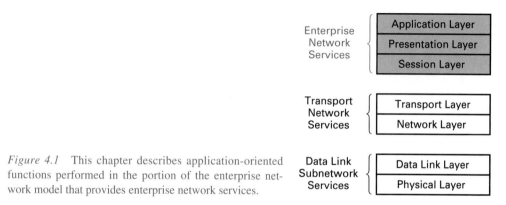

Figure 4.1 This chapter describes application-oriented functions performed in the portion of the enterprise network model that provides enterprise network services.

BOX 4.1   Enterprise network service categories.

- **Print Services.** *Print services* allow any system on the network to use a printer attached to some other system functioning in the role of a print server. With the print services implemented by most network software, an end user on one computing system in the network can direct output to a remote printer controlled by a print server exactly as if the printer were attached directly to the user's own local system. Remote printing software generally implements some form of queueing mechanism to allow end users to send printed output to the print server even when it is currently busy printing some other job. Print services might also allow users to start, end, cancel, or flush queued print jobs.

- **File Services.** *File services* allow end users to access the disk devices and files controlled by other systems in the network functioning as file servers. Network software may implement various levels of remote file access. For example, it might be possible to control sharing at the device level, where a user can access all the files on a particular hard disk drive on the file server as if the file server's hard disk were directly attached to the user's local system. Sharing might also be controlled on a directory basis, where the user is allowed to access only particular directories on a shared disk. Sharing can also be controlled at the individual file level, where users are granted the authority to access only particular files on the file server's disks.

- **Electronic Mail Services.** Network software usually provides *electronic mail services* that allow end users to compose, send, receive, and store messages and documents. Some electronic mail implementations provide messaging facilities that operate only within a particular organization's network. Other electronic mail applications provide users with access to the messaging facilities provided by other networks and with messaging facilities provided by public electronic mail services as well.

- **Directory Services.** Network users and application programs that use network software often request services based on *network names*. Network names are names used to represent network resources to which end users require access. Typical resources that might be given network names are other network users and the physical resources available in the network, such as print queues and collections of shared files. A network directory service allows end users to access network resources with easy-to-use names rather than having to know specific details concerning the network addressing scheme the network employs.

- **Network Management Services.** Network software commonly offers a variety of management and administration facilities that network administrators can use for monitoring and controlling the network. Specialized network management software is available that runs in conjunction with commonly used network software.

TCP/IP APPLICATION SERVICES

The TCP/IP architecture is the most widely used of the network architectures on which hardware and software products are based. Most network software subsystems provide support in one way or another for TCP/IP networking. The TCP/IP network architecture provides a particularly rich assortment of application services generally implemented by systems that implement the TCP/IP protocol suite. Box 4.2 describes application services commonly provided in a network that implements the TCP/IP networking protocols to form a TCP/IP internet.

BOX 4.2 TCP/IP application services.

- **FTP File Transfer.** The *File Transfer Protocol (FTP)* implements a file transfer service typically employed by TCP/IP end users. FTP allows the user to transfer data in both directions between the local system and a remote system. FTP implementations can be used to transfer files that contain either binary data or ASCII text. Certain versions of FTP also allow for the transfer of files containing EBCDIC data. Files can be transferred one at a time, or a single request can cause multiple files to be transferred. FTP also provides ancillary functions, such as listing the contents of remote directories, changing the current remote directory, and creating and removing remote directories.

- **TFTP File Transfer.** The *Trivial File Transfer Protocol (TFTP)* is a simple file transfer protocol that can be used to transfer data in both directions between the local system and a remote system. TFTP is generally used by system software that performs such functions as downline loading of program code; it is not intended to be employed directly by end users.

- **NFS Remote File Service.** The *Network File System (NFS)* implements a number of high-level services that provide users with access to files located on remote systems. System administrators generally designate one or more systems in the internet to play the role of file servers. These systems run NFS server software that makes certain designated directories on their disk storage devices available to other systems. A user accesses an NFS-mounted directory in the same manner as accessing a directory on a local disk.

- **SMTP Electronic Mail.** The *Simple Mail Transfer Protocol (SMTP)* is a protocol used for the transfer of electronic mail messages. SMTP is designed to be used by electronic mail software that provides the user with access to messaging facilities. Mail facilities allow the user to send messages and files to other network users. Many types of electronic mail systems have been implemented for the TCP/IP environment, some of which can be interconnected with the electronic messaging systems of other types of networks such as PROFS and DISOSS in the IBM environment and with public electronic mail services, such as MCI Mail, CompuServe, and the Internet.

- **DNS Directory Service.** Each system attached to a TCP/IP internet has at least one network address assigned to it. Each system also typically has a unique name to make it possible for users to refer to the system easily without knowing its network address. Since the underlying TCP/IP protocols all refer to individual systems using their network addresses, each system must implement a *name resolution* function that translates between system names and network addresses. The *Domain Name System (DNS)* is a directory service that can be used to maintain the mappings between names and network addresses.

- **SNMP Network Management.** Network management services are typically provided in a TCP/IP network through software that implements the *Simple Network Management Protocol (SNMP)*. SNMP defines a Management Information Base (MIB), which is a database that defines all the objects that can be managed in the internet. SNMP also defines the formats of a set of network management messages and the rules by which the messages are exchanged. The network management messages are used to make requests for performing network management functions and to report on events that occur in the network.

- **Kerberos Authentication and Authorization.** Kerberos is an encryption-based security system that provides mutual authentication between a client component and a server com-

(Continued)

BOX 4.2 *(Continued)*

ponent in a distributed computing environment. It also provides services that can be used to control which clients are authorized to access which servers. In the Kerberos system, each client component and each server component is called a *principal* and has a unique *principal identifier*. These principal identifiers allow clients and servers to identify themselves to each other to prevent fraudulent exchanges of information.

- **X Windows Presentation Facilities.** X Windows is a set of distributed graphical presentation services that implement a windowing system on a graphics display. It implements a client/server relationship between an application program (the client) and the windowing software in a workstation or terminal that controls a window on the graphical display (the server). The client and server can be running in different computing systems or in the same computing system. The X Window system allows a user at a graphics workstation to have multiple windows open on the screen, each of which might be controlled by a separate client application program. The X Window system defines a protocol used to transmit information between the client application program and the server windowing software.

- PING **Connectivity Testing.** *PING*, which is short for *Packet InterNet Groper*, can be used to test for connectivity between any two systems on the network. In using PING, a user typically executes a program named **ping** that sends a message to another system. When a system receives the message from PING, it sends a reply message back to the original sender. For each reply message it receives, PING calculates the amount of time elapsed since the original request message was sent. This provides the PING user with an estimate of the round-trip delay being experienced in exchanging data with the specified system.

- **Telnet Remote Login.** Telnet allows a user to log in to some other system on the network. The Telnet protocol establishes a client/server relationship between the local user (the client) and the remote Telnet application (the server). Telnet handles the data transfers required between the system implementing the client and the system implementing the server. These data transfers make it appear as if the user is logged into the remote system directly.

- **Rlogin Remote Login.** The Rlogin service is a service related to Telnet but is typically provided only by variations of the UNIX operating systems. Telnet allows a user at any type of TCP/IP system to log into any other type of TCP/IP system. The local system and remote system may be running entirely different operating systems. The Rlogin service is normally used when a user at a local UNIX system wants to login to a remote UNIX system. For the UNIX user, Rlogin is somewhat easier to use than Telnet and provides a few additional services.

- **Rsh Remote Execution.** The *Rsh* remote execution service allows the user to issue, at the local system, a command to request an operating system function or to request the execution of an application program on some other system in the internet. When using the Rsh service, the user enters a command at the local system, and the command is then sent to and executed on the remote system. The results of the command or the results of the application program execution are then returned to the user at the local system. A similar service to Rsh called *Rexec* is available on some TCP/IP systems as well.

OSF DISTRIBUTED COMPUTING ENVIRONMENT

The Open Software Foundation (OSF) has developed an important architecture for client/server, network-based computing called the *Distributed Computing Environment (DCE)*. Most of the OSF DCE services fall into the enterprise network services category.

DCE is intended to provide a set of standardized services that can be made available across a variety of different system environments so a distributed application developed using DCE services can support different operating systems, different network software subsystems, and different transport protocols. DCE services operate above the level of the network software and below the level of the application-oriented services specific application programs provide.

OSF took a unique approach to standardization when it defined DCE and DME. Instead of writing specifications from scratch for each of the services the DCE and DME define, OSF published requests for technology and invited all the members of OSF to submit working code implemented each of the services OSF was attempting to define. OSF then selected what it felt were the best technologies from among all the submissions. In this manner, each of the services DCE and DME defines is based on proven, working technology rather than being abstract sets of specifications.

DCE and DME are not just paper architectures; they also consist of working code available from OSF in source form. The source code is written in a portable fashion that can be adapted to run on a wide variety of UNIX-type operating systems. It can also be tailored to run on other operating systems, such as Windows and OS/2 in the personal computer environment. It is the responsibility of a particular vendor, not OSF, to tailor the source code for a particular platform.

Box 4.3 provides brief descriptions of the six DCE services included in DCE at the time of writing and specifies the source of the technology for each service.

THE TRANSPORT NETWORK

We next examine the *transport network* component of the enterprise network model. The transport network provides services associated with the Transport and Network layers of the OSI model. The Transport and Network layers make use of the facilities provided by one or more physical data transmission facilities. These are implemented by data link subnetworks operating below the transport network in the enterprise network model (see Fig. 4.2).

TRANSPORT NETWORK SERVICES

The exact details of the services provided by the transport network, and the protocols used to provide data transport services, vary from one network architecture to another and from one network software subsystem to another. But the primary function of the trans-

BOX 4.3   DCE services.

- **DCE Remote Procedure Call Service (DCE RPC).** This service allows an application component running in one computer system to use a simple procedure call mechanism to invoke a procedure running in some other computing system in the network. This allows procedure calls to be used to hide many of the complexities of network communication from application developers. The DCE RPC Service is based on RPC technology jointly submitted to the OSF by Digital Equipment Corporation and Hewlett-Packard.

- **DCE Threads Service.** This service provides application programmers with the ability to create independent execution threads within the same program. This gives an application the ability to carry out multiple computing tasks concurrently. The DCE Threads Service is based on the *DECthreads* implementation of the *Concert Multithread Architecture (CMA)* submitted to the OSF by Digital Equipment Corporation.

- **DCE Directory Service.** The *DCE Directory Service* implements a distributed repository that stores information about objects in the computing environment, including users, computing systems, and distributed services application programs can request. The DCE Directory Service provides facilities for submitting a name to the Directory Service and getting back a list of the attributes associated with that name. The DCE Directory Service includes the following two components available from the OSF:

  — **DCE Global Directory Service (DCE GDS).** This is designed to handle directory operations that take place between individual cells. The DCE GDS is based on the ITU X.500 standard as implemented by the DIR-X X.500 directory service submitted to the OSF by Siemens.

  — **DCE Cell Directory Service (DCE CDS).** This is designed to handle directory operations that take place within a single cell. The DCE CDS is based on the *DECdns* implementation of the Distributed Name Service architecture submitted to the OSI by Digital Equipment Corporation.

  In addition to the two OSF DCE directory technologies, the DCE Directory Service also integrates the TCP/IP Domain Name System (DNS) that can be used as an alternative to the DCE GDS for performing directory operations between cells.

- **DCE Distributed File Service (DCE DFS).** This allows users to access and share files maintained by computing systems operating in the role of *file servers* that can be located anywhere in the network. DCE DFS is based on the *Andrew File System (AFS)* technology submitted to the OSF by Transarc Corporation. It performs many of the same functions as the Network File System (NFS) widely implemented in the TCP/IP networking environment.

- **DCE Distributed Time Service.** This service allows application programs to request services that work with date and time-of-day values in a standardized manner that is the same across all computing platforms. The Distributed Time Service also implements a set of distributed algorithms that ensure the clocks in all the computing systems in the network are synchronized and contain correct values for the date and time of day. DCE DTS is based on the *Distributed Time Service (DTS)* technology submitted to the OSF by Digital Equipment Corporation. The DCE DTS interoperates with the *Network Time Protocol (NTP)* widely used in the TCP/IP environment.

- **DCE Security Service.** This provides facilities for implementing secure communications in a networked environment and for controlling access to resources in the computing environment. The DCE Security Service is based on the *Kerberos* security system submitted to the OSF by Project Athena. It is augmented by a number of additional security components submitted by Hewlett-Packard.

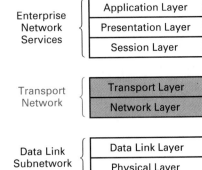

Figure 4.2   This chapter describes functions performed in the portion of the enterprise network model
that implements the Transport Network.

port network is to move data from a source end system to a destination end system. The
end-to-end communication function of the transport network is associated with the Transport layer of the OSI model.

Box 4.4 lists some of the most commonly used network software subsystems. Each
of the network software subsystems listed in Box 4.4 conforms to its own unique network
architecture and implements its own family of transport protocols. A family of transport
protocols is often called a *protocol family* or a *protocol suite*. Each software subsystem
and transport protocol family provides a variety of services that fall into the enterprise
network services category as well.

BOX 4.4   Transport network software subsystems and protocol families.

- **TCP/IP.** *TCP/IP*, which stands for *Transmission Control Protocol/Internet Protocol*, refers to
a set of communication protocols that grew out of a research project funded by the United
States Department of Defense. The TCP/IP networking scheme implements a peer-to-peer
network configuration. Any computing system in the network can run TCP/IP server software and can provide services to any other computing system that runs complementary
TCP/IP client software.

- **NetWare IPX/SPX.** *NetWare* is a family of network operating system software marketed by
Novell. The type of data transport services NetWare uses is often referred to by the names
of the two major NetWare communication protocols: the *Sequenced Packet Exchange
(SPX)* protocol and the *Internetwork Packet Exchange (IPX)* protocol. Novell software is
available for personal computers and UNIX workstations. At the time of writing, NetWare
is the most popular of all the networking software used in the personal computer environment. NetWare provides file and print sharing facilities as well as a broad range of other
networking services. Many other network software systems now implement the IPX/SPX
protocol family for compatibility with NetWare products.

- **NetBIOS.** Early IBM and Microsoft network software introduced an interface and protocol
called NetBIOS for communication over a local area network. NetBIOS network software is
part of the *LAN Manager* and *LAN Server* network operating systems codeveloped by

(Continued)

BOX 4.4 *(Continued)*

Microsoft and IBM. NetBIOS has become a de facto standard for communication over LANS and is implemented by Microsoft operating systems, such as Windows for Workgroups, Windows 95, and Windows NT. NetBIOS capabilities are provided by a number of other network software subsystems as well, including the Novell networking products.

- **AppleTalk.** *AppleTalk* is Apple Computer's networking scheme used for many years to network Apple Macintosh equipment and its successors. Apple system software contains integrated AppleTalk networking support that allows Apple computing systems to participate in peer-to-peer networks and to also access the services of dedicated AppleShare file and print servers. NICs and network software are available for a variety of other types of computing systems, including IBM-compatible personal computers and Unix workstations, that allow them to participate in AppleTalk networks.

- **Systems Network Architecture.** *Systems Network Architecture (SNA)* is IBM's proprietary networking scheme widely used in the mainframe environment. A form of SNA called *Advanced Peer-to-Peer Networking (APPN)* provides SNA communication support for smaller systems.

- **DECnet.** *DECnet* is a term Digital Equipment Corporation uses to refer to its proprietary networking software. DECnet networking facilities are typically used in the DEC minicomputer and workstation environments.

- **PATHWORKS.** *PATHWORKS* is a family of personal computer network operating system software marketed by Digital Equipment Corporation. The original goal of PATHWORKS was to provide personal computers with access to DECnet networking capabilities. However, PATHWORKS now supports access to other forms of networking as well.

- **VINES.** *VINES* is a family of network operating system software marketed by Banyan Systems. VINES supports a client/server network configuration and provides many facilities especially well suited for large networks.

- **LANtastic.** *LANtastic* is a family of network operating systems for the personal computer environment marketed by Artisoft. LANtastic network software implements a peer-to-peer network configuration.

The end-to-end data transport function of the transport network may involve the use of intermediate systems, as shown in Fig 4.3. Therefore, the transport network may include a *routing* function to determine the path each message should take through the network and a *relaying* function that moves each message through intermediate systems on its way to the destination end system. The routing and relaying functions of the transport network are generally associated with the Network layer of the OSI model. The routing and relaying functions are further discussed later in this chapter.

Chapter 1 introduced the ATM switches in an ATM network that also perform routing and relaying functions. However, the routing and relaying functions that an ATM network performs take place in the Data Link layer of the OSI model. ATM routing often does not replace the Network layer routing function that must often also be performed in an enterprise network.

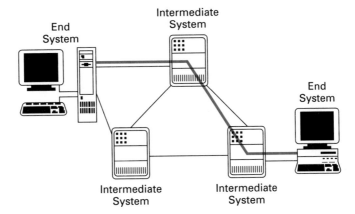

Figure 4.3   Data transport between end systems can involve intermediate systems.

ADDRESSING MECHANISMS

The network architectures and protocol families discussed in this book all provide *addressing mechanisms* in many of their layers. With most network architectures, addressing is important in the Transport, Network, and Data Link layers.

- **Transport Layer Addressing.** Addressing in the Transport layer is intended to uniquely identify a program using data transport services within a particular computer system. Addressing in the Transport layer generally consists of a simple identifier assigned to each executing program. The identifier assigned to a program need be unique only among the programs concurrently running within a particular computer system.

- **Network Layer Addressing.** Addressing in the Network layer is intended to uniquely identify a particular computing system attached to the network. Addressing in the Network layer consists of a *network address* value assigned to each point of attachment to the network. Network address values must be unique within the entire enterprise network.

- **Data Link Layer.** Addressing in the Data Link layer is intended to uniquely identify a network interface card (NIC) installed in a particular computing system and is attached to a particular data link subnetwork. Addressing in this layer consists of a *station address* value assigned to a NIC that must be unique only among the systems attached to a given data link. (In many cases, a NIC address is also *globally* unique, but this is not a requirement for operation in many networks.)

The following sections further discuss the addressing requirements for the Transport, Network, and Data Link layers.

Transport Layer Addressing Mechanisms

Most modern computing systems allow more than one program or process at a time to be active and executing in a given computing system. Therefore, it is possible for multiple processes to be managing network communication activities at the same time in the same computing system. The addressing mechanisms associated with the OSI Transport layer are designed to differentiate between multiple concurrent users of the data transport service active in the same machine.

Transport layer addressing mechanisms are generally simple and straightforward and often involve an identifier called a *port* used to control communication activities within a computing system. Each active process uses a different port, and each active port generally has a different port identifier associated with it.

In many network architectures, certain port identifiers may be reserved and associated with particular types of data transport services. For example, a file transfer service might be assigned one port identifier, an electronic mail message service might be assigned another, a remote procedure call service another, and so on. Generally, some port assignments are available for use by end user processes, and mechanisms may be available for automatically assigning user processes to unused transport ports.

Network Layer Addressing Mechanisms

In order to be able to route and relay data to a particular destination computing system, there must be a mechanism that uniquely identifies each system in the enterprise network. This is normally done by assigning a unique *network address* to each point at which a network device is physically attached to the enterprise network. This level of addressing is normally handled by mechanisms associated with the OSI Network layer.

Network Address Assignment

A device attached to a network, such as an end user system with a single point of attachment to the network, is generally assigned a single network address. A device, such as a network interconnection device, with multiple points of attachment to the network, is assigned multiple network addresses, one for each point of attachment.

Depending on the particular network architecture and network software subsystem in use, the network software may create network addresses automatically or it may be necessary for a network administrator to assign them manually.

Network Address Formats

Each network architecture and protocol family uses a different Network layer addressing mechanism, and each uses a different data structure for network address values. For example, each system in an enterprise network that implements TCP/IP networking software must have a unique network address that conforms to the TCP/IP network address structure. In the same manner, each system in a network that uses Novell NetWare software has a unique network address that conforms to the NetWare network address structure.

In most instances, a network address consists of two parts: a *network identifier* that identifies some subset of the entire enterprise network, and a *node identifier* that identifies a specific system within the subset defined by the network identifier. Each full network address, made up of a combination of a network identifier value and node identifier value, must be unique throughout the entire enterprise network.

Data Link Layer Addressing Mechanisms

A computing system is generally attached to a transmission medium segment through a *network interface card (NIC)*. Each NIC may be assigned a *station address*. Data link station addresses are typically processed in the Data Link layer and are used to control the transmission of a frame from a sending device to a receiving device in a given data link subnetwork.

WAN Data Link Station Addressing

On a point-to-point WAN data link, station addresses are not typically used, since each frame sent has only one destination: the NIC at the other end of the data link. WAN data links often use a protocol in which an address field is part of the transmission frame used. The address field is often simply set to zeros on a simple point-to-point data link in which data link addressing is not important.

LAN Data Link Station Addressing

On a local area network data link it is necessary to assign a unique *station address* to each of the NICs on that data link. Station addresses are used to identify the source and destination of each frame transmitted over the LAN. A local area network NIC's station address is often called its *MAC address* because it is typically the Medium Access Control (MAC) sublayer of the Data Link layer that processes station addresses. Each particular form of data link subnetwork technology uses its own data link addressing scheme and defines its own specific station address format.

A Data Link layer station address identifies a particular NIC attached to a data link. A computing system that has multiple NICs installed can be connected to more than one data link. Each of the system's NICs has its own station address.

On local area network data links that conform to the IEEE/ISO/ANSI LAN architecture, each network interface card used to attach a system to the data link ordinarily has a 48-bit physical hardware address associated with it. This hardware address is usually permanently set at the time the network interface card is manufactured and is never changed. The NIC's physical hardware address is most often used as its station address.

Data Link layer station addresses may be globally unique. For example, the global address administration scheme defined by the IEEE/ISO/ANSI LAN architecture guarantees that no two NICs, manufactured anywhere in the world, will ever have the same station address. However, some types of LAN data links allow a network administrator to manually assign station addresses to NICs. With such types of LAN data links, it is not necessary for Data Link station addresses to be globally unique. Station addresses need only be unique within a particular data link subnetwork.

ATM Data Link Endpoint Addressing

As we have seen, ATM technology can be applied to either short-distance LAN-like communication or to long-distance WAN data links. ATM technology defines a data link addressing scheme used to give a unique identifier to each ATM endpoint in an ATM subnetwork. The addressing scheme recommended by the ATM Forum used is the international standard Network Service Access Point (NSAP) addressing system defined for use in the Network layer of the OSI model. This addressing scheme defines a 20-octet address administered such that no two ATM endpoint devices anywhere in the world have the same endpoint address.

Note that although an ATM network may use the OSI NSAP address format that was defined for the OSI Network layer, ATM endpoint addressing is a function that takes place in the Data Link layer of the OSI model. The 20-octet address assigned to an endpoint is a data link address. In many networks, a Network layer addressing scheme will also be implemented in higher layers of the network software.

Network Address and NIC Station Address Mapping

In a particular network, there must be a one-to-one mapping between each NIC's *station* address and the *network* address assigned to that point of network attachment.

With some networks, a NIC's station address is used directly to form the node identifier portion of a system's network address. The Novell NetWare architecture uses such a scheme. The node identifier portion of a device's NetWare network address consists of the 48-bit NIC station address associated with the NIC installed in that device. Therefore, in a NetWare network that uses conventional LAN data links, there is a simple one-to-one mapping between a NIC station address and the Network address associated with that station.

With other networks, the node address portion of a network address does not correspond directly to NIC addresses but conforms to some other data format. With a network architecture in which node identifier values do not consist of NIC station addresses, there must be some mechanism provided to map between a station address and the node identifier portion of a network address.

For example, when conventional LAN data link subnetwork technology is used in a TCP/IP network, each network address is 32 bits in length, and some subset of those 32 bits is used as a node identifier.* The TCP/IP *Address Resolution Protocol (ARP)* and *Reverse Address Resolution Protocol (RARP)* are used to translate between NIC station addresses and their corresponding TCP/IP network addresses.

When ATM data link subnetwork technology is used in a TCP/IP network, the same 32-bit network addresses are used to identify systems, and 20-octet NSAP addresses may be used to identify ATM endpoint devices in the Network Interface layer. An adaptation of ARP called ATMARP is used to translate a TCP/IP network address to the NSAP address used to uniquely identify an ATM endpoint.

DATA TRANSMISSION THROUGH THE TRANSPORT NETWORK

Figure 4.4 illustrates the general procedure the transport network uses to transmit user data from a source system to a destination system. The following steps make up the data transmission procedure:

*At the time of writing, an addressing architecture for TCP/IP that allows for larger network addresses is under development. It is likely that these larger TCP/IP network addresses will become widely used in the years ahead.

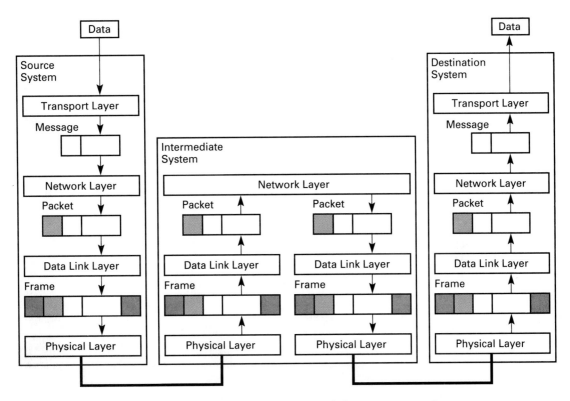

Figure 4.4   Message transmission through the transport network.

1. A transport network user sends data to a distant transport network user by passing the data down to a process running in the Transport layer of the communication system. The user also supplies information about the user to which the data should be sent, such as the network address of the destination user's system. The Transport layer process adds any necessary control information, such as a sequence number, checksum, and the destination network address, to the user data to create a Transport layer *message*. The Transport layer then passes the message down to a Network layer process.

2. Based on the destination network address of the system to which the message is being sent, the Network layer in the source system determines the next system to which the message should be transmitted and the particular data link to be used to reach that system. The Network layer adds additional control information to the transport message, creating a *packet*. The Network layer then passes the packet down to the Data Link layer in the source system.

3. The Data Link layer adds additional control information to the packet in the form of a header and a trailer, creating a *frame*. It then uses the services of the Physical layer to send the frame across the specified data link. The Data Link layer in the system that receives the frame removes the Data Link control information and passes the resulting packet up to the Network layer.

4. Only one intermediate system is shown in the diagram, but a packet can flow through any number of intermediate systems in reaching the destination system. The Network layer in

each system that receives a packet determines a destination for the next hop, makes any modifications to the packet's control information necessary, and passes it to the Data Link layer. The Data Link layer encloses the packet in a new frame for each data link the packet traverses in reaching the final destination system. The Data Link layer in the final destination system eventually receives the final frame and passes the enclosed packet to the Network layer.

5. The Network layer in the final destination system removes the Network control information and passes the original packet up to the Transport layer there. The Transport layer process in the destination system then removes the remaining control information from the message and passes a copy of the original data to the destination transport network user.

As we will see in Chapter 8, there are more steps and additional data units defined for the Data Link layer when ATM subnetwork technology is used. These details need not concern us at this time.

ROUTING AND RELAYING FUNCTIONS

As we introduced early in this chapter, an important function of the transport network component of the enterprise network model is to determine the route each message should take through the network and to relay each message from system to system on its way to the destination end system. The routing and relaying functions we are discussing here takes place in the OSI Network layer. Systems capable of playing the role of intermediate systems and performing the routing function are typically called *routers*.

A router must have sufficient routing information available so it can examine the destination network address associated with a message and determine the address of a system that will bring the message closer to its final destination. A router must also have a way of updating the routing information to reflect changes that occur in the topology of the enterprise network.

Each of the major transport protocol families has its own unique routing protocols that routers use for exchanging routing information with other systems in order to update their stored routing information.

As we have already discussed, the routing and relaying functions that take place in the transport network component are separate from and independent of the Data Link layer routing and relaying that takes place in an ATM subnetwork.

TRANSPORT INTERFACES

Application programming interfaces (APIS) that network software implement allow application programs to request basic network data transport services. Each of these APIS define services at roughly the level of the OSI Transport layer. They have each been developed for use with a particular network architecture and communication protocol family. However, some data transport APIS are being used to provide access to the Transport layer protocols in networks that implement different network architectures. Box 4.5 introduces some of the Transport APIS that modern network software systems provide.

BOX 4.5   Transport layer APIs.

- **Remote Procedure Call.** A *Remote Procedure Call (RPC)* facility can make it possible for programmers to implement a client/server application without needing to explicitly issue requests for communication services. The idea behind a remote procedure call facility is that procedure calls are a well-understood mechanism for transferring control and data from one procedure to another in a computing application. It is of great utility to extend the procedure call mechanism from a set of procedures in a single-computer environment to a set of procedures in a distributed, client/server environment.

- **Named Pipes.** The *Named Pipes* facility is a system for interprocess communication codeveloped by IBM and Microsoft for their respective network operating system products. The Named Pipes mechanism has become a de facto standard that has been implemented in other network operating systems, including Novell NetWare software. The Named Pipes application programming interface allows a program to send data to or receive data from another program in a way similar to issuing ordinary file management commands.

- **Sockets.** The *Sockets* application programming interface was initially developed for use with TCP/IP networking software in the BSD UNIX operating system environment. By using the Sockets API, two application programs, one running in the local system and another running in the remote system, can communicate with one another in a standardized manner. The Sockets API is typically used to implement a client/server relationship between two application programs running in different computing systems. The client and server programs each invoke functions that set up an association between them. The client and server applications then invoke functions to send and receive information over the network in a similar manner to the Named Pipes API described previously.

- **Windows Sockets.** A variation of the Sockets application programming interface is now being widely used in networks of systems using Microsoft operating system software, such as Windows. The *Windows Sockets*, or WinSock, API has been developed in an effort to provide a standardized API for network communication in the Microsoft operating system environment. The WinSock API is based on the BSD UNIX Sockets API and supports both a connectionless data transport service and a connection-oriented data transport service.

- **Common Programming Interface for Communications (CPI-C).** CPI-C is an application programming interface developed by IBM as a standard method of accessing SNA LU 6.2 communication services. CPI was developed as part of IBM's Systems Application Architecture (SAA). IBM has now reduced its commitment to the SAA effort, but CPI-C has become a widely used data transport API in the IBM computing environment. CPI-C defines a set of callable services that a program, written in any of several supported programming languages, can issue via a standard subroutine call mechanism.

- **IPX/SPX Services.** The IPX/SPX Services application programming interface is used by application programmers in the Novell NetWare networking environment to implement communication using the IPX or SPX communication protocols. The IPX/SPX Services API consists of a set of function calls. To send data using the IPX or SPX communication protocol, the application must provide a properly formatted IPX or SPX Data packet. IPX/SPX Services API calls use a data structure called an *Event Control Block (ECB)* to control data transmission.

- **NetBIOS Network Control Blocks (NCBS).** The NetBIOS API is based on the use of control blocks called *Network Control Blocks (NCBs)* for requesting the NetBIOS data transport services provided by a network software subsystem. A program using the NetBIOS interface constructs an NCB data structure that specifies information about the desired data transport service. The program requests a transport service by invoking a NetBIOS communication function that references a formatted NCB.

SUMMARY

General categories of application services provided in most networking environments include print services, file services, electronic mail services, directory services, and network management services. TCP/IPO networks provide a broad range of application services that fall into the enterprise network services category. The Distributed Computing Environment (DCE), developed by the Open Software Foundation (OSF), defines application services useful in a heterogeneous, distributed computing environment.

The transport network provides services associated with the Transport and Network layers of the OSI model. These layers make use of the facilities provided by one or more data link subnetworks operating below the level of the transport network. The primary function of the transport network is to move data from a source end system to a destination end system. The transport network provides an end-to-end communication function associated with the Transport layer. It also provides Network layer routing and relaying functions that may involve intermediate systems in addition to the two end systems.

Network architectures and protocol families provide three types of addressing mechanisms. Transport layer addressing uniquely identifies programs using data transport services within a particular computer system and generally consists of identifiers assigned to each executing program. Transport layer addresses need to be unique only among the programs concurrently running within a particular computer system. Network layer addressing uniquely identifies each computing system attached to the network and consists of a unique network address value assigned to each point of attachment to the network. Data Link layer addressing consists of station address values assigned to network interface cards that uniquely identify the stations attached to a particular data link. The addresses used to address endpoints in an ATM network are data link addresses.

The various application programming interfaces that network software provides for accessing data transport services include remote procedure calls, named pipes, sockets, Common Programming Interface for Communications (CPI-C), IPX/SPX Services, and network control block (NCBs).

Chapter 5 introduces technologies associated with the Data Link Subnetwork component of the enterprise network model.

Chapter **5**

Data Link Subnetwork Technologies

This chapter introduces the functions performed by the *data link subnetwork* portion of the enterprise network model. Figure 5.1 reviews the enterprise network model and shows that the data link subnetwork component is associated with the Data Link and Physical layers of the OSI model. Most modern network architectures have layers that correspond very closely with the OSI model Data Link and Physical layers.

The exact details of how data link services are provided vary from one type of data link subnetwork to another. However, certain elements are common to most types of data link subnetworks. This chapter examines the common elements that many data link subnetworks have in common. For more information on specific data link technologies other than ATM, see *Enterprise Networking: Data Link Subnetworks,* in this series (Martin, Chapman, Leben, 1996).

DATA LINK TYPES

The primary function of a data link subnetwork is to transfer data between two systems attached to the same data link. An important way of categorizing conventional data link subnetworks is according to how many different devices can be accommodated on the

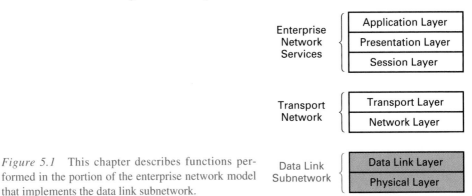

Figure 5.1   This chapter describes functions performed in the portion of the enterprise network model that implements the data link subnetwork.

link. A *point-to-point* data link subnetwork connects exactly two devices, while a *multi-access* data link subnetwork can connect two or more devices.

Point-to-Point Data Links

The simplest type of data link is a *point-to-point* data link implemented through a direct connection between exactly two systems. For example, a point-to-point data link can be implemented through a physical connection between two systems via a wire or cable (see Fig. 5.2).

Figure 5.2   Point-to-point data link.

A point-to-point connection can alternatively consist of a *logical* connection, where two systems are connected using facilities that a service provider implements using a complex network to provide the connection (see Fig. 5.3).

A logical point-to-point link is often referred to as a *virtual circuit* or *virtual channel*. Systems connected using a virtual circuit implemented by a service provider perceive a simple direct link between them.

Conventional WAN Data Links

Point-to-point data links are most often used to implement conventional wide area network (WAN) data links that span long distances. Box 5.1 describes the most important types of WAN data link technology used in constructing enterprise networks.

Multiaccess Data Links

A *multiaccess* data link is a subnetwork that permits more than two systems to be attached to it (see Fig. 5.4). On a multiaccess data link subnetwork, each system receives all transmissions from all of the other systems on the data link. All the systems on a multiaccess data link must share access to the data link's transmission capabilities.

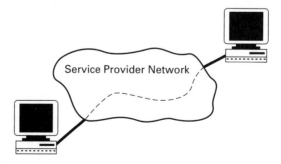

Figure 5.3   Virtual point-to-point data link implemented by a service provider.

BOX 5.1   WAN data link subnetwork technologies.

- **Analog Telecommunications Circuits.** Analog telecommunications circuits are often used for data transmission by employing devices called *modems* (short for modulator/demodulator) on each end of the circuit. A number of protocols for the data link subnetwork have been developed to control transmission over long-distance telecommunications circuits.

- **Digital Telecommunications Circuits.** In addition to analog circuits, telecommunications providers offer digital transmission facilities in which computer data can be carried directly in digital form.

- **X.25 Packet-Switched Data Networks (PSDN).** *X.25* is the name of an ITU-T Recommendation that describes standards for *packet-switched data networks (PSDN)*. A PSDN carries data in data units called *packets* that can be routed individually through the PSDN. An X.25 PSDN implements *virtual circuits* that appear to end users as simple point-to-point data links.

- **Integrated Services Digital Network (ISDN).** An *Integrated Services Digital Network (ISDN)* is a public telecommunications network—typically administered by a telecommunications provider—that supplies digital end-to-end data transmission services that can be used for any purpose, including voice, data, graphics, image, and facsimile.

- **Broadband ISDN (B-ISDN).** *Broadband ISDN (B-ISDN)* represents a probable future direction of the telephone industry based on fiber-optic communication. B-ISDN is designed to provide much higher data rates in addition to those supplied by ISDN. B-ISDN defines *interactive* services, which involve two-way transmission, and *distribution* services, where transmission occurs primarily in one direction. B-ISDN is intended for the transmission of all types of information, including text, documents, graphics, sound, and full-motion video.

- **Frame Relay.** *Frame Relay* is a data transmission technology based on international standards for the Data Link and Physical layers of the OSI model that were originally defined as part of ISDN. Telecommunications providers now offer data transmission facilities based on the Frame Relay standards that provide data rates higher than can ordinarily be achieved over conventional telecommunications circuits.

- **Switched Multi-megabit Data Service (SMDS).** *Switched Multi-megabit Data Service (SMDS)* is a high-speed data transmission technology that can be used to implement high-speed WAN data links that can carry data at LAN speeds. SMDS technology is based on a standard for *metropolitan area networks (MANs)* called *Distributed Queue Dual Bus (DQDB)*.

- **Wireless WAN Technologies.** Telecommunications providers and other organizations have developed various technologies for implementing data transmission over relatively long distances using wireless transmission media, such as radio signals.

Conventional LAN Data Links

Multiaccess data links are most often used in subnetworks that use local area network (LAN) technology to implement short-distance communication among a collection of systems. Box 5.2 briefly describes some important types of multiaccess LAN data link subnetwork technologies used in building an enterprise network.

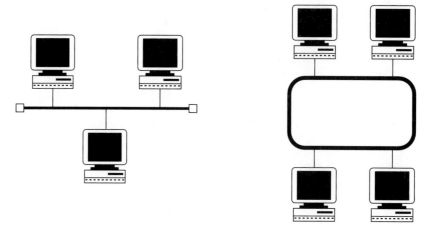

Figure 5.4 Multiaccess data links allow multiple systems to be attached to the same data link.

BOX 5.2   LAN data link subnetwork technologies.

- **Ethernet.** *Ethernet* is a LAN data link technology in which systems are attached to a common transmission facility, such as a coaxial cable or twisted-pair cable, to form a bus- or tree-structured configuration. A system typically attempts to transmit whenever it has data to send. Ethernet is the most widely used form of LAN data link technology.

- **Token Ring.** *Token ring* is a LAN data link technology in which systems are connected to one another using point-to-point twisted-pair cable segments to form a ring structure. A system is allowed to transmit only when it has the token, which is passed from one system to another around the ring.

- **Token Bus.** *Token bus* is a LAN data link technology in which systems are connected to a common transmission medium in a similar manner as an Ethernet LAN. A system is allowed to transmit only when it has a special data unit, called the *token*, passed from one system to another. Token Bus LANs are sometimes used in factory automation environments.

- **ARCnet.** *ARCnet* is the name of a family of LAN products that implement a relatively low-speed form of LAN data link technology in which all systems are attached to a common coaxial cable. Like the Token Bus form of LAN, a system transmits when it has the token.

- **Fiber Distributed Data Interface (FDDI).** *FDDI* is a high-speed LAN data link technology in which systems are connected to one another using point-to-point fiber-optic cable segments to form a ring structure. A system is allowed to transmit only when it has the token.

- **LocalTalk.** *LocalTalk* is a low-speed LAN data link technology—part of Apple Computer's AppleTalk networking scheme—in which systems are attached to a common cable. LocalTalk technology has been built into most of the computing devices that Apple Computer has manufactured for many years, although Apple has been building Ethernet technology as well into much of its more recent equipment.

- **Wireless LAN Technologies.** Local area network infrastructure vendors have developed various technologies for implementing LAN communication over wireless transmission media, such as radio and infrared signals.

ATM Data Links

Notice that we have not included ATM in either the point-to-point or multiaccess categories. An ATM network is a collection of ATM endpoints and ATM switches that are interconnected by point-to-point data links. An ATM network can be used to implement point-to-point WAN data link facilities, but an ATM network can also be used to provide many of the functions generally associated with multiaccess LAN data links. ATM networks can be used to provide LAN-like services over either short or long distances.

DATA LINK SUBNETWORK SERVICES

The primary service provided by a data link subnetwork is a data delivery service. Three basic types of data delivery services can be provided by a data link subnetwork.

Connectionless Service

With a *connectionless* data delivery service, one message at a time is exchanged between a source and destination system. A connectionless service provides a best-efforts delivery service in which a message might be lost, duplicated, or delivered out of sequence with respect to other messages. With a connectionless Data Link layer service, no two messages are related in any way, no sequence checking is performed, and no acknowledgments are sent. Any mechanisms for error handling must be implemented in the higher layers. A connectionless data delivery service is sometimes referred to as a *datagram* service.

A typical LAN data link provides a datagram delivery service. Some types of ATM data links also provide a connectionless data delivery service.

Connection-Oriented Service

With a *connection-oriented* data delivery service, the service begins by establishing a logical association, called a *connection*, between the source and destination systems. The service then transmits one or more messages over the connection, in sequence, between the two communicating systems. A connection may be a permanent connection always available for transmission. The connection may alternatively be a temporary connection, where the connection is established when there is data to be transmitted, used for transmission, and then terminated. A connection-oriented data link service provides a reliable data delivery service using sequence checking, acknowledgments, error correction, and flow control procedures.

A conventional WAN data link typically implements a connection-oriented data link in which error detection and retransmission services are provided. Some types of ATM data links also provide connection-oriented data delivery services.

Isochronous Service

An *isochronous* data delivery service is uniform with respect to time. This type of data delivery service guarantees that the data being transmitted will arrive at regular, predefined intervals. Isochronous service is often required for the transmission of voice and video information, where delays or interruptions in the flow of data would be noticeable to the receiver. Most conventional WAN and LAN data links are oriented toward transporting computer data that does not have precise timing requirements. Some forms of ATM service are able to provide the isochronous data delivery service required for transporting voice and video information.

DATA LINK PROTOCOLS

A data link subnetwork uses a *data link protocol* to provide one, two, or all three of the types of data delivery services described above. Data link protocols implement various functions in the Data Link layer and in the underlying Physical layer of the OSI model. Box 5.3 lists the general functions for these OSI model layers. Note that not all the functions listed in Box 5.3 are performed by all data link protocols for all data link subnetworks. The exact functions performed by the data link protocol for a particular data link subnetwork depend on a number of factors, such as the physical transmission medium used and the type of data delivery service offered.

BOX 5.3   Data link protocol functions.

Data Link Layer Functions

- **Data Link Connection Establishment and Release.** Dynamically establishes, for a *connection-mode* service, a logical data link connection between two users of the data link service and releases the connection when it is no longer required. These functions are not provided for a *connectionless* service, in which connections are not established or released.

- **Framing.** Creates a single Data Link protocol-data-unit (DLPDU) from the data unit passed from a user of the Data Link layer service, marks the beginning and the end of the DLPDU when sending, and determines the beginning and ending of the DLPDU when receiving. The informal name most often used for the DLPDU exchanged between peer Data Link layer entities is *frame*.

- **Data Transfer.** Transfers frames over a physical circuit, extracts the data unit from each frame and passes it up to the user of the Data Link layer service in the receiving device.

- **Frame Synchronization.** Establishes and maintains synchronization between the sending device and the receiving device. This means the receiving device must be capable of determining where each frame begins and ends.

- **Frame Sequencing.** Uses sequence numbers to ensure that frames are delivered in the same order in which they were transmitted (does not apply to a connectionless service).

- **Error Detection.** Detects transmission errors, frame format errors, and procedural errors on the data link connection using a value carried in the frame control information.

BOX 5.3   *(Continued)*

- **Error Recovery.** Recovers from errors detected on data links using frame sequencing and acknowledgments (does not apply to a connectionless service).

- **Flow Control.** Controls the rate at which a user of a connection-mode Data Link layer service receives frames to prevent a user of the Data Link layer service from being overloaded (does not apply to a connectionless service).

- **Physical Layer Services.** Uses the services of the Physical layer to transmit and receive data and to control the operation of the physical communication link.

Physical Layer Functions

- **Circuit Establishment and Release.** Allows a physical circuit to be dynamically established when it is required and released when the circuit is no longer needed. This function is provided for a circuit implemented by a temporary facility, such as a dial-up line in the telephone network.

- **Bit synchronization.** Establishes synchronization in a receiving device with a stream of bits coming in and clocks data in from the communication circuit at the correct rate.

- **Data Transfer and Sequencing.** Allows electrical or optical signals to be exchanged over the circuit connecting two communicating devices and allows bits to be accepted by the receiving device in the same order in which they are delivered by the sending device.

- **Fault Condition Notification.** Notifies the Physical layer user when fault conditions occur.

- **Medium Specific Control Functions.** Provides control functions for specific forms of transmission medium, such as encoding/decoding, carrier sensing, collision detection and collision announcement functions, and detection of illegal cabling topologies.

SUMMARY

An important way of categorizing data link subnetworks is according to how many different devices can be accommodated on the link. A point-to-point data link subnetwork connects exactly two devices, and a multiaccess data link subnetwork can connect two or more devices. Point-to-point data links are most often used to implement wide area network (WAN) data links that span long distances.

A multiaccess data link is a data link that permits more than two systems to be attached to it. Multiaccess data links are most often used in subnetworks that use local area network (LAN) technology to implement short-distance communication among a collection of systems.

An ATM data link cannot be placed into either the point-to-point or multiaccess categories. An ATM network is a collection of ATM endpoints and ATM switches that are interconnected by point-to-point data links. An ATM network can be used to provide many of the functions generally associated with multiaccess LAN data links over either short or long distances.

Three types of data delivery services can be provided by a data link subnetwork: connectionless service, connection-oriented data delivery service, and isochronous data service. A data link subnetwork uses a data link protocol to provide one, two, or all three types of data delivery service. Most conventional WAN and LAN data links provide connectionless or connection-oriented delivery services but are not capable of proving the isochronous data delivery required for audio and video. ATM data links can provide all three types of data delivery service.

Some of the functions provided by a data link protocol include data link connection establishment and release, framing, data transfer, frame synchronization, frame sequencing, error detection, error recovery, and flow control.

Chapter 6 looks at some of the strategies and technologies available for interconnecting individual subnetworks to form larger enterprise networks.

Chapter **6**

Subnetwork Interconnection

To create flexible enterprise internets, it is often necessary to interconnect individual LAN data links, both locally and using WAN data links to span long distances. A number of different types of devices can be used to accomplish the required interconnection. Each has its own unique uses and is appropriate for different forms of network interconnection. ATM technology is designed to eliminate the need for complex interconnection strategies by relying on a single technology for both short- and long-distance data links. However, until entire enterprise networks can take advantage of ATM technology, the types of interconnection devices described in this chapter will most likely continue to be important.

The four major types of interconnection devices that are important in today's enterprise networks are:

- Repeaters
- Hubs
- Bridges
- Routers

The following sections describe each of these four types of subnetwork interconnection devices.

REPEATERS

A specific type of conventional LAN technology may place a limit on the physical length of any single LAN cable segment. This limit is determined by the particular LAN technology and is based on the type of physical medium and the transmission technique used. A *repeater* allows a LAN data link to be constructed that exceeds the length limit of a single physical cable segment. A repeater receives a signal from one cable segment and retransmits it, at its original strength, over one or more other cable segments. The number of repeaters that can be used in tandem is generally limited by a particular LAN technology.

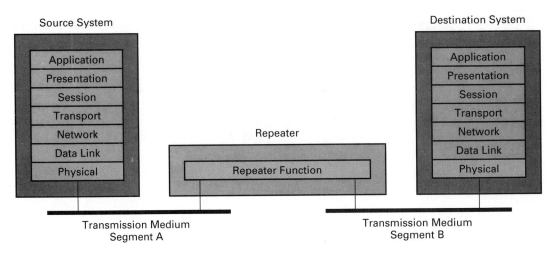

Figure 6.1   A repeater performs its function in the Physical layer.

A device implementing a repeater function operates in the OSI model Physical layer and is transparent to all the protocols operating in the layers above the Physical layer (see Fig. 6.1).

Using a repeater between two or more LAN cable segments requires that the same Physical layer protocols be used to send signals over all the cable segments. Repeaters are typically used to interconnect cable segments located relatively close together. Repeaters cannot be used to interconnect a LAN data link and a wide area network data link.

Figure 6.2 shows some possible repeater configurations on an Ethernet LAN. Note that a repeater may be designed to support different types of LAN cabling in the same local area network, as long as the Physical layer protocols are compatible on all the cable segments.

Simple repeaters are not often used in private ATM networks, since the interconnections between ATM switches can generally be made using single cable segments. If a particularly long cable span is required, then one or more repeaters might be used to span the long distance using multiple cable segments. The use of repeaters is more common in public ATM networks in which long distances must be spanned between ATM switches. The use of simple repeaters in an ATM network is a purely Physical layer function and is transparent to ATM endpoint devices and ATM switches.

HUBS

The multipoint repeater depicted in Fig. 6.2 is an example of a hub. A hub can be used in a conventional LAN to create a star structure in which the hub is at the center of the star. Devices classified as hubs are also often used in ATM networks as well as in networks that use conventional LAN technology.

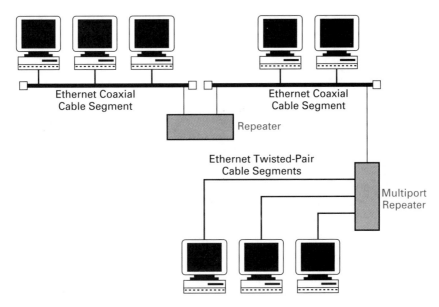

Figure 6.2 Using repeaters to interconnect LAN cable segments.

A simple hub provides a single connection to a primary transmission medium segment and a number of *ports*, each of which can be attached to a single station using a point-to-point connection. A simple hub allows a number of devices to be attached at a single point, such as in a wiring closet, as shown in Fig. 6.3.

In an ATM network, a hub function can be performed by an ATM switch that simply allows a number of endpoints to be connected to the switch, which resides in a central location. An ATM endpoint might also implement a hub function in which individual stations are connected to the ATM endpoint using some other form of data link technology, such as Ethernet or FDDI.

Configurable Hubs

A configurable hub is a hub that allows the cable segments that terminate at the ports of the hub to be interconnected in different ways depending on the type of configuration desired. Configurable hubs are often used with conventional LAN technology to allow groups of devices to be configured in different workgroups. A variety of configurable hubs are available, and these devices vary in the capabilities they provide.

There are three primary purposes for using configurable hubs:

- To make it easier to change LAN configurations
- To increase the bandwidth available to individual devices on the LAN
- To allow the traffic flowing between workgroups to be controlled

A configurable hub generally allows the hub to be connected to two or more primary LAN transmission medium segments through a component called a *backplane*. The backplane

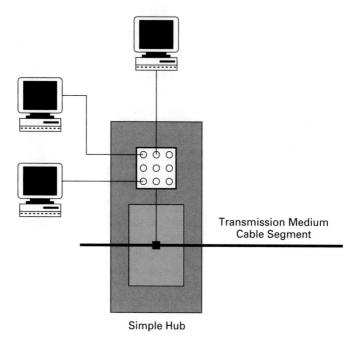

Transmission Medium
Cable Segment

Simple Hub

Figure 6.3   Simple hub.

is used to control the way in which the systems connected to the ports of the hub are connect-ed to the cable segments attached to the backplane. There are three primary types of config-urable hubs: module assignment hubs, bank assignment hubs, and port assignment hubs.

Module Assignment Hubs

With *module assignment* hubs, shown in Fig. 6.4, each hub connects its entire set of ports to one of the LAN transmission medium segments in its backplane. When a signal is received over one port, it is retransmitted over all other ports in the module and over the primary transmission medium segment to which the ports are connected.

All the devices attached to the hub, and all the devices connected to the selected primary transmission medium segment, form a workgroup. With a system of module assignment hubs, the traffic generated by devices in one workgroup can be isolated from devices in other workgroups. The stations attached to a given hub can be connected to a different workgroup by changing the connection within the hub to one of the other prima-ry transmission medium segments.

A disadvantage of the module assignment hub is that all the devices attached to the hub's ports must be in the same workgroup, and all must be attached to the same primary transmission medium segment.

As we introduced earlier, one use for hubs is to increase the transmission capacity available within each workgroup. When the number of devices attached to the same LAN segment gets too large, the transmission capacity can be exceeded, especially when systems

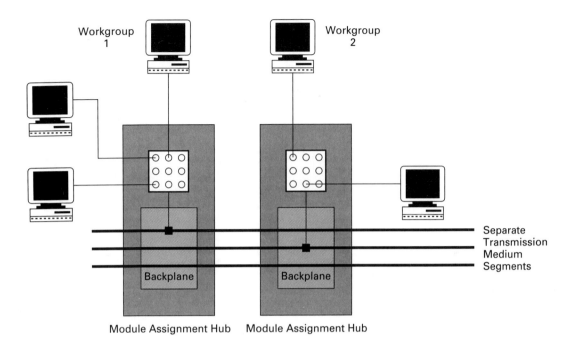

Figure 6.4   Module assignment hubs.

are exchanging large quantities of data. Hubs make it easy to establish multiple parallel transmission medium segments to which different groups of systems can be attached. With fewer systems attached to each segment, there should be less total traffic on each segment.

Other network interconnection devices, such as routers or bridges (discussed later in this chapter), can be used to interconnect the individual cable segments and thus allow some traffic to flow from one segment to another, as shown in Fig. 6.5. As we will see, a router provides more traffic isolation between workgroups than a bridge.

Bank Assignment Hubs

Bank assignment hubs offer more flexibility for workgroup configuration. With this type of hub, the ports in a single hub are divided into subsets called *banks*. The hub allows each bank of ports to be connected to a different primary transmission medium segment (see Fig. 6.6). When a signal is received over a port, it is retransmitted only over all other ports in the same bank and over that bank's primary transmission medium segment. Therefore, all the devices attached to a single bank, and all the systems connected to the selected transmission medium segment, form an individual workgroup.

Port Assignment Hubs

With a *port assignment* hub, sometimes called a port-switching or configuration-switching hub, a more sophisticated backplane allows ports to be assigned to transmission medium segments on an individual basis (see Fig. 6.7). When a signal is received

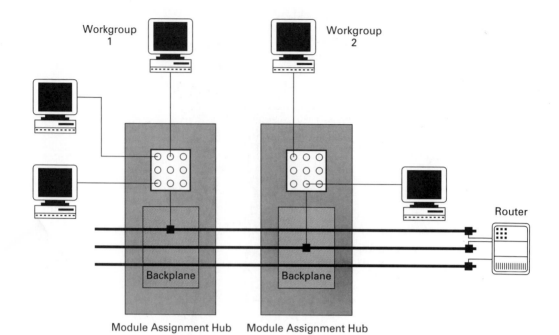

Figure 6.5   Module assignment hubs with a router.

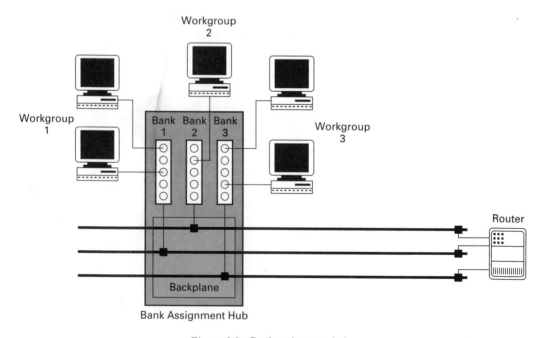

Figure 6.6   Bank assignment hub.

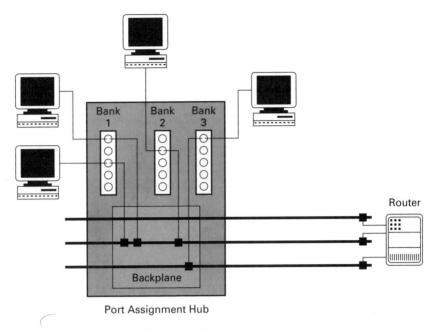

Figure 6.7   Port assignment hub.

over a port, it is retransmitted to all other ports assigned to the selected transmission medium segment. Such hubs allow for great flexibility in workgroup assignment and for making changes in the way devices are assigned to workgroups.

Static Versus Dynamic Hubs

The hubs described in the previous section are all examples of devices classified as *static hubs*. With static hubs, the assignment of ports to LAN segments is controlled by explicitly configuring the hub. With some hubs, hub configuration is controlled physically by setting DIP switches or jumpers in the hub. With other static hubs, the configuration can be controlled through network management software.

All such hubs are considered static hubs because an explicit network management action is required to reconfigure the hub. However, the ability to change assignments through software, particularly with port assignment hubs, makes it considerably easier for the network administrator to add and remove systems and to control the way in which workgroups are configured.

Switching Hubs

The last category of hubs we discuss are *dynamic hubs,* which are able to change configuration automatically on the fly. Dynamic hubs are generally referred to as *LAN switches* or *switching hubs.* Dynamic hubs are designed to provide the switching flexibility generally associated with ATM networks using conventional LAN transmission technology.

A switching hub employing conventional LAN technology might use two methods to establish connections and to direct frames to the appropriate destination ports:

- **Cross-Point Operation.** With *cross-point connection,* or *switching,* operation the switching hub analyzes each frame as it is received, establishes the connection as soon as it has analyzed the destination address, and immediately begins transmitting the frame while the rest of the frame is still being received.
- **Bridging Store-and-Forward Operation.** With *bridging store-and-forward* operation, the switching hub receives an entire frame and temporarily stores it. The hub then analyzes the frame's destination address, establishes the required connection, and forwards the frame to its destination.

A cross-point switch typically offers lower latency, or lag time, between receiving a frame and sending it to its destination. A bridging store-and-forward switching hub may have greater reliability than a cross-point hub, since error checking can be performed on the frame before it is forwarded. Some switching hubs support both methods of operation and allow the network administrator to choose one or the other form of operation, depending on network requirements.

A switching hub implements more intelligence than a static hub and generally performs some of its functions in the Data Link layer rather than in the Physical layer. A switching hub examines the destination address of each frame it receives. When the hub receives a frame over a port, it dynamically establishes a connection with the port associated with the frame's destination and directs the frame to the appropriate destination port.

With switching hubs, connections are established across the backplane of the switch. Simultaneous connections share the backplane's total bandwidth. Switching hubs may incorporate high-bandwidth backplanes, so that each connection can be given dedicated bandwidth comparable to the full bandwidth associated with a LAN segment. For example, Ethernet LANs commonly operate at a total bandwidth of 10 Mbps. Many Ethernet switches will support multiple connections, with each connection supporting a full 10 Mbps data rate.

The following sections describe some different forms of switching hubs that network infrastructure vendors have developed.

Station Switching Hubs

A *station switching hub* allows only a single system to be attached to each of the hub's ports. Therefore, each port can have only one station address associated with it. A station switching hub can be used to replace a shared LAN transmission medium segment, creating what is commonly referred to as a switched LAN.

Figure 6.8 shows an example of a simple switched LAN using a station switching hub. Such a hub might allow any of the stations attached to the hub's ports (the stations on the right) to communicate with one another. At the same time, any single station on either of the two LANs attached to the backplane can communicate at full bandwidth with any of the stations attached to the hub's ports.

A switching hub has the ability to dynamically establish connections between any pair of stations on the fly and to support multiple simultaneous connections. The number of simultaneous connections the hub supports depends on the capabilities of the hub.

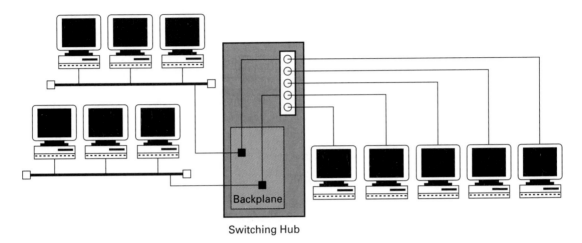

Switching Hub

Figure 6.8   Switching hub.

Segment Switching Hubs

A more complex switching hub is a *segment switching hub*. A segment switching hub allows the attachment of LAN segments, as well as individual systems, to its ports. The backplane then allows any port to communicate with any other port. This type of hub allows multiple station addresses to be associated with each port. A segment switching hub can be used to form a collapsed backbone network, as shown in Fig. 6.9.

The backplane in such a hub is generally engineered to provide a maximum total bandwidth that can be used to support some maximum number of concurrent connections among the stations or LANs attached to its ports.

High-Performance Switching Hubs

Some hubs are marketed as high-performance hubs, possibly supporting a backplane with a total bandwidth of 10 Gbps or so. A high-performance switching hub is sometimes called a *super hub*, an *enterprise hub*, or a *hub-of-hubs*. Such switching hubs may offer additional capabilities, such as support for multiple architectures in the attached LAN segments (e.g., Ethernet and Token Ring) and hierarchical connections of hubs.

Figure 6.10 illustrates how segment switching hubs can be connected in a hierarchical arrangement. The lowest level of the hierarchy consists of switched Ethernet LANs. Switched FDDI networks provide backbone capability in the middle of the hierarchy, and an ATM switch provides high-bandwidth connectivity between the backbones as well as wide area network connectivity.

Virtual Networks

A capability often associated with switching hubs is *virtual networking*. Virtual networking refers to an ability to logically assign systems to two or more logical LAN subnetworks, each having full bandwidth, without physically changing the physical attachments

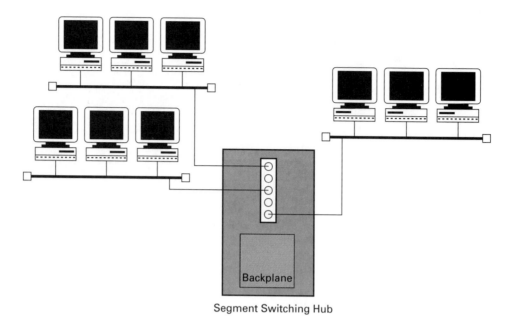

Figure 6.9   Segment switching hub.

of the systems. This is illustrated in Fig. 6.11. Some switching hubs allow logical LANs to be created and reconfigured on the fly using network management software. The concept of virtual LANs is discussed further in Chapter 12.

BRIDGES

Bridges are typically used in the conventional LAN environment to interconnect two or more separate LAN subnetworks. A bridge essentially forwards frames from one LAN sub-network to another. Some bridges learn the addresses of the stations that can be reached over each data link subnetwork they bridge so they can selectively relay only traffic that needs to flow across each bridge.

The bridge function operates in the Medium Access Control sublayer of the Data Link layer and is transparent to software operating in the layers above the MAC sublayer (see Fig. 6.12). A bridge can interconnect networks that use different transmission techniques and/or different medium access control methods. For example, a bridge might be used to interconnect an Ethernet LAN using coaxial cabling with an Ethernet LAN using twisted-pair cabling. A bridge might also be used to interconnect an Ethernet LAN with a Token Ring or FDDI LAN.

Bridges can be used to directly interconnect LANs, or a pair of bridges with a WAN data link between them can be used to interconnect two or more LANs in different geographical locations, using a conventional WAN data link or an ATM data link to implement the long-distance link. Figure 6.13 shows two examples of networks implementing inter-

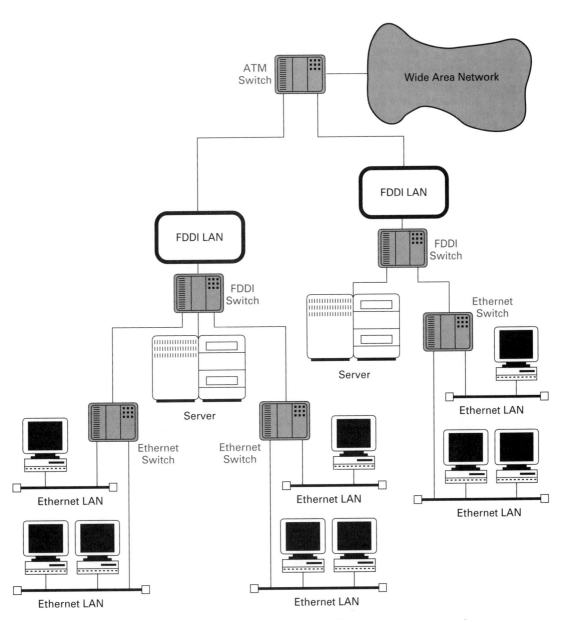

Figure 6.10   LANs implemented using switching hubs can be interconnected in a hierarchical configuration.

connected LANs using bridges. The mechanism implemented by a bridge is often called a *store-and-forward* facility, since frames are usually temporarily *stored* in the bridge and then *forwarded* to a station on some other LAN.

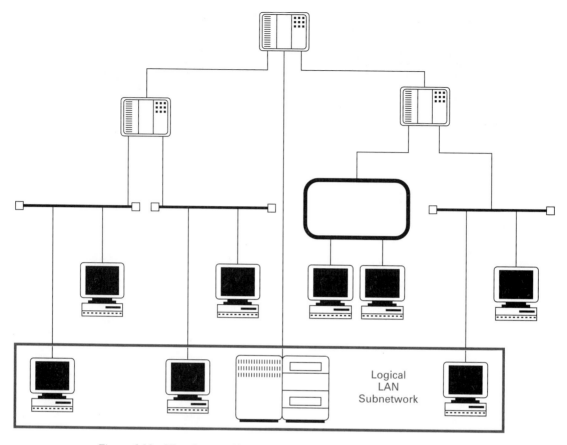

Figure 6.11 Virtual networking refers to the capability of assigning systems to different logical LAN subnetworks without respect to their physical attachment points.

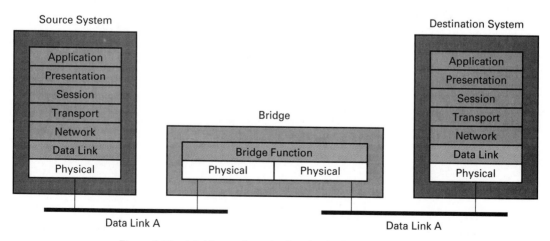

Figure 6.12 A bridge performs its function in the Data Link layer.

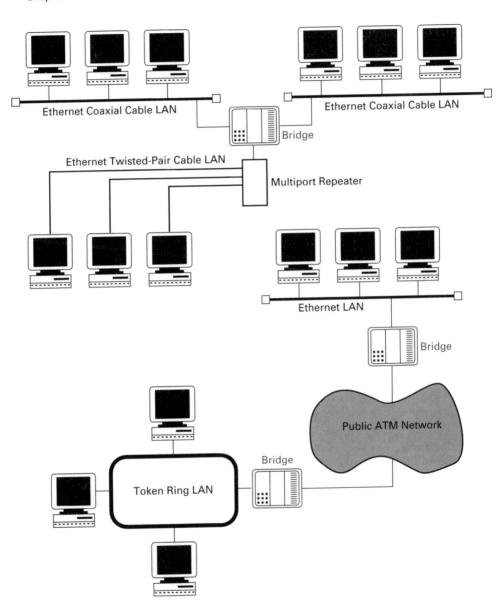

Figure 6.13   Two examples of using bridges to interconnect LANs.

Extended LANs

A collection of individual LAN data links interconnected by bridges are considered to be a single subnetwork. Each of the station addresses throughout the subnetwork must be unique and must use the same station address format. A LAN subnetwork constructed using bridges is sometimes called an *extended LAN* to differentiate it from a single physical LAN. Software operating in the layers above the MAC sublayer view the extended LAN as if it were a single LAN data link.

Frame Filtering

A bridge can implement a *frame filtering* mechanism. Such a bridge, often called a *filtering bridge*, receives all frames transmitted over each data link to which it is attached. The bridge then determines, based on each frame's destination address, whether or not the frame should be transmitted across the bridge to any of the other data links to which it is also attached. Thus, a bridge can isolate some of the network traffic generated on one LAN data link from the other LAN data links in the extended LAN.

Broadcast traffic generated on one LAN, however, is typically always transmitted across a bridge to all the other data links to which it is attached. Therefore, broadcast traffic generated by any station is received by all the stations on the extended LAN.

Bridge Types

Two types of bridges are in common use in enterprise networks: *spanning tree* bridges and *source routing* bridges:

- **Spanning Tree Bridges.** A spanning tree bridge learns appropriate routes for frames by observing transmissions that take place on the data links to which the bridge is connected. It then forwards frames over the appropriate data links when required. Spanning tree bridges determine a tree structure to be used for an extended LAN in which only one active path connects any two stations in the extended LAN. If there is more than one physical path between two stations, only the path reflected in the tree structure is used.

- **Source Routing Bridges.** With source routing bridges, each station is expected to know the route over which to send each frame, and to include routing information as part of the frame. Source routing bridges then use the routing information in the frame to determine whether or not to forward the frame. If a station does not know the route, or if a previously known route is no longer active, the station broadcasts Route Discovery frames over the extended LAN and then uses the responses that come back to determine the appropriate route to use. With source routing bridges more than one path can interconnect any two LAN stations. Source routing bridges are typically used only with token ring LANs.

Source routing bridges are typically used when bridging individual token ring LANs to create a larger token ring extended LAN. An advantage to using source routing bridges is that multiple bridges can be installed to create parallel, active paths between individual rings. Multiple active paths allow for higher throughput and load balancing through the various bridges.

A disadvantage of the source routing technique is that source routing bridges often cannot be used to interconnect token ring LANs with other types of LANs. Problems can sometimes occur in extended LANs that include both source routing bridges and spanning tree bridges.

ROUTERS

Routers provide the ability to route packets from one system to another where there may be multiple paths between them. Routers typically have more intelligence than bridges and can be used to construct enterprise networks of almost arbitrary complexity. A router performs its function in the OSI model Network layer, as shown in Fig. 6.14.

A system of interconnected routers in an enterprise network all participate in a distributed algorithm to decide on the optimal path over which each packet should travel from a source system to a destination system. The algorithm used varies from one family of transport protocols to another. Routers must be aware of the protocols associated with the Network and Transport levels, and can be used only with the specific transport stack or stacks for which they are designed. Unlike bridges and hubs, routers are *not* transparent to the Transport network protocols.

Keep in mind that the routing function performed by a conventional router takes place in the Network layer of the OSI model and is separate from the routing function that takes place in the Data Link layer of the OSI model in an ATM subnetwork. The scope of ATM routing is within a particular ATM subnetwork. The scope of Network layer routing is the enterprise network as a whole.

The Routing Function

In general, a router performs the routing function by determining the next system to which a packet should be sent. It then transmits the packet to the next system over the appropriate data link to bring the packet closer to its final destination. In an enterprise network implemented using routers, a packet may pass through a series of routers in

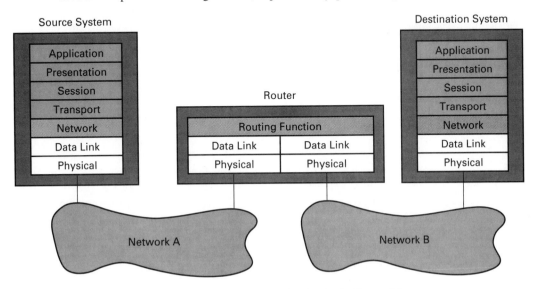

Figure 6.14 A router performs its function in the Network layer.

arriving at its final destination. And there may be more than one possible sequence of systems through which a packet might pass in traveling from the source system to the destination system.

A system of routers can implement multiple active paths between any two systems. In some network implementations, it is possible for different packets traveling from a source system to a destination system to take different routes, and a series of packets may arrive at the destination system out of sequence. Protocols operating in the layers above the Network layer in such networks must have the capability for resequencing received packets.

A router is sometimes called an *intermediate system*. By contrast, systems that originate data traffic and that serve as the source or final destination for that traffic are called *end systems* (see Fig. 6.15).

LAN Traffic Isolation

On an individual LAN subnetwork, each station on the LAN typically receives all packets transmitted. With an extended LAN implemented using bridges, the bridges can filter some of the frames, but broadcast traffic generated on one LAN is generally propagated to all the stations on the extended LAN.

Routers can be used to interconnect a number of individual LANs or extended LANs in such a way that the traffic generated on one LAN is better isolated from the traffic generated on other LANs in the network. A frame is forwarded only as required as part of its

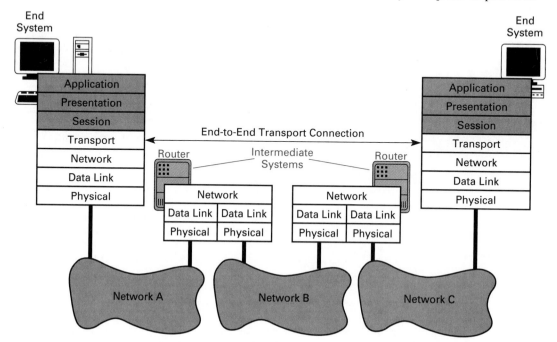

Figure 6.15   Routers act as intermediate systems between end systems.

route to its destination. By using routers instead of bridges to interconnect subnetworks, broadcast traffic can be restricted to each individual LAN subnetwork.

Network Addresses

Routing is typically performed based on the values of the destination network address fields in packets flowing through the network. As we introduced in Chapter 5, a network address typically consists of two parts: a *network* identifier and a *node* identifier. The network identifier typically identifies a particular network, and the node identifier identifies a particular system within that network. The structure and format of the network address varies from one family of transport protocols to another.

Based on the destination network address, the router determines the next system along the route to the destination system and the data link to be used to bring the packet closer to that system.

If two or more LANs are interconnected by routers, each of the individual LANs is considered to be a separate subnetwork. Although station addresses may be unique across the entire enterprise network, this is not a requirement. Station addresses need only be unique within each subnetwork.

Routing Algorithms

A variety of different mechanisms can be used by routers in performing routing and relaying functions. The routing function is generally performed using a routing algorithm. A routing algorithm is a distributed algorithm in which all the routers in the enterprise network participate. Routers use the routing algorithm to build logical maps of the network topology. These logical maps help the routers calculate optimal routes for the packets that move through the network.

The routing algorithms routers typically employ in an enterprise network are *distributed adaptive* algorithms that allow routers to update their routing information on the fly as the network topology changes. There are two major types of distributed adaptive routing algorithms: distance-vector algorithms and link-state algorithms. The following sections introduce the operation of each of these major types of distributed adaptive routing algorithms.

- **Distance-Vector Routing.** With a *distance-vector* routing algorithm, also sometimes called a *Bellman-Ford* algorithm, each router in the network learns about the network topology by exchanging routing information packets with its neighbors. In effect, each router learns what its neighbors think the enterprise network looks like. Each router then constructs a new description of the network topology and communicates this new picture to its neighbors. The process is repeated as many times as necessary and eventually stabilizes when all the routers learn they have the same description of the network topology.

- **Link-State Routing.** With a *link-state routing algorithm* routers also exchange routing information with one another. However, unlike with a distance-vector algorithm, each router determines only what its individual area of the enterprise network looks like and then broadcasts that information to all the other routers in the network. Each router sends out routing packets called *link-state vectors* that describe the systems it can reach on its directly attached links. The link-state vectors also contain metrics that represent weighted values representing the relative cost for using each data link.

A distance-vector routing algorithm is a simple algorithm that is relatively easy to design and implement. A link-state algorithm is more complex than a distance-vector algorithm and may require more router processing power. But a link-state algorithm typically scales better than a distance-vector algorithm and can support much larger networks.

Using Backbone Networks

Network interconnection devices can be used to connect two or more physical LAN data links to a *backbone LAN*. A backbone LAN often consists of a LAN to which only network interconnection devices leading to other LANs, and to possible servers, are attached. Individual end users systems are not attached directly to the backbone but to the attached LANs, as shown in Figure 6.16. Note that for simplicity, the network interconnection devices are not shown.

In many cases, the backbone LAN may support a higher transmission speed than the individual LANs attached to it. Optical fiber links are particularly well suited for use in a backbone LAN because of their ability to provide high bandwidth over relatively long distances. Chapter 12 shows how ATM subnetworks can also serve as backbones in an enterprise network.

SUMMARY

Repeaters are used to interconnect individual cable segments within the same LAN data link. A repeater receives a signal from one cable segment and retransmits it, at its original strength, over one or more other cable segments.

A simple hub is a multipoint repeater that can be used to create a star-structured network segment in which the hub is at the center of the star. A configurable hub is a hub that allows the cable segments that terminate at the ports of the hub to be interconnected in different ways depending on the type of configuration desired. With module assignment hubs each hub connects its entire set of ports to one of the LAN transmission medium segments in its backplane. With a bank assignment hub, the ports in a single hub are divided into subsets called banks. The hub allows each bank of ports to be connected to a different primary transmission medium segment. With a port assignment hub, a more sophisticated backplane allows ports to be assigned to transmission medium segments on an individual basis.

Switching hubs, or dynamic hubs, implement intelligence that allows them to act as switches to provide full network bandwidth to multiple pairs of devices. Switches attempt to implement the type of flexibility associated with ATM networks. A switching hub examines the destination address of each frame it receives and dynamically establishes a connection with the port associated with the frame's destination. A station switching hub allows only a single system to be attached to each of the hub's ports. A segment switching hub allows the attachment of LAN segments, as well as individual systems, to its ports. The backplane then allows any port to communicate with any other port. A high-performance switching hub is sometimes called a super hub, an enterprise hub, or a hub-of-hubs.

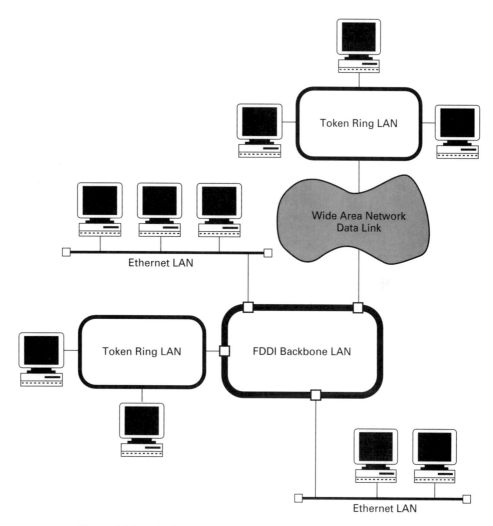

Figure 6.16   A backbone LAN can be used to interconnect other LANs.

A bridge interconnects separate LAN data links and typically learns the addresses of stations that can be reached over each data link connected to the bridge. A bridge operates in the Medium Access Control sublayer and is transparent to software operating in the Network layer and above. A bridge can interconnect networks that use different transmission techniques and/or different medium access control methods. Two types of bridges in common use in enterprise networks are spanning tree bridges and source routing bridges.

Routers provide the ability to route packets from one system to another where there may be multiple paths between them. A router performs its function in the OSI model Network layer. A router runs a routing algorithm that determines the next system to which each packet should be sent. The major types of distributed adaptive routing algorithms used by routers are distance-vector algorithms and link-state algorithms.

Chapter 7 begins Part III of this book in which we examine in detail the architecture on which ATM network technology is based. Chapter 7 examines the Physical layer of the ATM architecture.

PART **III**

ATM ARCHITECTURE

Chapter 7

The Physical Layer

In this part of the book we take a detailed look at the ATM architecture by working from the bottom up. This chapter describes the bottom-most ATM functional layer—the Physical layer—and describes the services and protocols that apply to it (see Fig 7.1). Before we examine the Physical layer of the ATM architecture, it will be helpful to further discuss the physical nature of an ATM network and describe the physical components used to actually construct one.

ATM NETWORK COMPONENTS

As we briefly introduced in Chapter 1, an ATM network is made up of three types of components: ATM switches, ATM endpoints, and transmission paths (TPs). These three major categories of physical components are shown in Fig. 7.2.

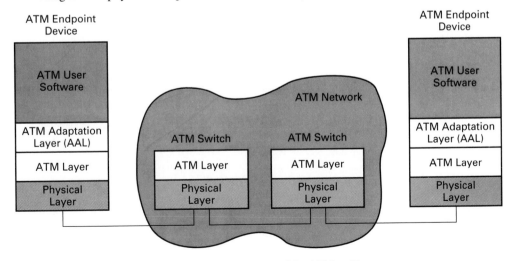

Figure 7.1   The Physical layer of the ATM architecture.

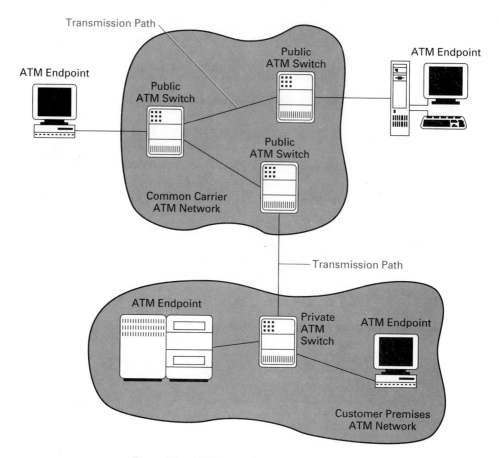

Figure 7.2   ATM network physical components.

ATM Switches

ATM switches perform functions related to routing and relaying information from the sending user to the receiving user. An ATM switch is sometimes called an *intermediate system (IS)*.

ATM switches can be placed into the two major categories of public ATM switches and private ATM switches.

Public ATM Switches

A *public ATM switch* is part of a telecommunications service provider's public network and is referred to in the ATM standards as a *network node (NN)*. Public ATM switches are marketed to the telecommunications industry by many of the same vendors who provide conventional POTS switching and transmission equipment.

Private ATM Switches

A *private ATM switch* is owned and maintained by a user organization and is referred to in the ATM standards as a *customer premises node (CPN)*. Private ATM switches are marketed to user organizations by many of the same network infrastructure vendors who provide user organizations with network interface cards (NICs), hubs, bridges, and routers. Some vendors market both public ATM switches (network nodes) and private ATM switches (customer premises nodes), and some ATM switches can be used in either role in an ATM network.

ATM Endpoints

A device playing the role of an *ATM endpoint* connects directly to a public or private ATM switch and serves as the source or destination of user data. An ATM endpoint is often called an *end system (ES)*. An ATM endpoint might be implemented in an ordinary computing system by installing an ATM network interface card in the computer and running appropriate communication software. Alternatively, an ATM endpoint might be implemented in a special-purpose network device to which one or more ordinary computing systems can be attached (see Fig. 7.3). Different ways in which ATM network components can be interconnected in an enterprise network are explored further in Chapter 12.

Notice in Fig. 7.3 that the ATM endpoint device connecting the Token Ring LAN subnetwork to the ATM subnetwork is not an end-user computer that is the source or destination of user data. Instead, the device functions as a router that relays data between the ATM subnet-

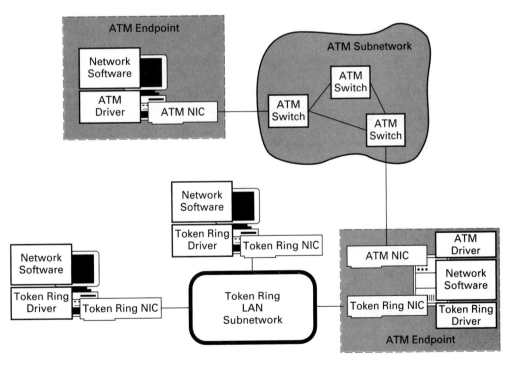

Figure 7.3 An ATM endpoint can be implemented in a user computer in which an ATM network interface card (NIC) is installed. Alternatively, an ATM endpoint can be implemented in a specialized device to which user computers are attached via some other type of data link subnetwork technology.

work and the Token Ring subnetwork. The router is an ATM endpoint device because it lies on the boundary of the ATM subnetwork and acts as the source or destination of ATM traffic.

An ATM endpoint can be connected either to a public ATM switch owned by a common carrier (network node) or to a private ATM switch owned by a user organization (customer premises node) (see Fig. 7.4).

Transmission Paths

The Physical layer of the ATM architecture, which operates in both end nodes and ATM switches, handles the transmission of data across a physical link. ATM endpoints and ATM switches are interconnected via physical communication links called *transmission paths (TPs)*. Different types of signaling techniques are used to transmit a bit stream over a physical transmission path, depending on the bit rate required and the type of transmission medium used. Various signaling techniques described in the ATM standards are discussed later in this chapter.

PHYSICAL LAYER SUBLAYER STRUCTURE

The ATM Physical layer is made up of two sublayers: the *Transmission Convergence (TC)* sublayer and the *Physical Medium (PM)* sublayer. The structure of the Physical layer is shown in Fig. 7.5.

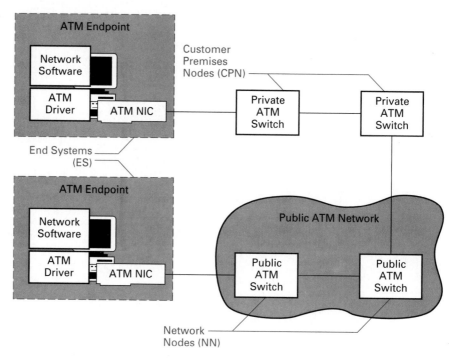

Figure 7.4 An ATM endpoint can be attached to a private or a public ATM switch.

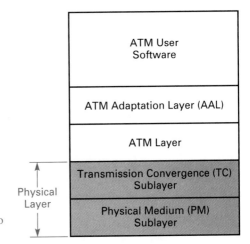

Figure 7.5 The Physical layer is divided into two sublayers.

Transmission Convergence Sublayer

For outgoing transmissions, the Transmission Convergence sublayer accepts cells from the ATM layer, combines cells to form a data stream, and passes the data stream to the Physical Medium sublayer. For incoming transmissions, the PM sublayer passes a data stream to the TC sublayer, which extracts cells and passes them to the ATM layer.

Transmission Convergence Sublayer Functions

The Transmission Convergence sublayer is responsible for performing the following functions:

- **HEC Generation and Checking.** As TC accepts cells from the ATM layer, it generates an appropriate value for the Header Error Check (HEC) field in the cell header. As cells are received, TC checks the HEC value to be sure the cells were transmitted correctly. (The ATM cell format was introduced in Chapter 1 and is described further in Chapter 8.)

- **Cell Delineation.** The PM sublayer processes data as a continuous stream of bits. TC is responsible for accepting the received data stream from the PM sublayer and then identifying cell boundaries within it.

- **Transmission Frame Structuring and Delineation.** Some Physical layer interface protocols transmit data on the link in the form of structured transmission frames. For these protocols, TC structures outgoing cells into an appropriate frame format and extracts cells from incoming frames.

- **Cell Rate Decoupling.** For most Physical layer protocols, the PM sublayer requires a continuous stream of data, without gaps. If there are no cells to send, TC inserts empty, or idle, cells in the outgoing transmission stream. The TC layer in the receiving device discards the idle cells from the incoming stream. An idle cell is one having the following field setting in the cell header: VCI = 0, VPI = 0 and CLP = 1.

Cell Delineation

The cell delineation function of the Transmission Convergence sublayer deserves additional comment. This function involves determining where within a data stream each cell starts. There are several ways this can be done:

- **Delimiters.** A character with a unique bit sequence can be used to mark the beginning, and if need be, the end of a unit of data. Delimiter values must be values that do not occur within the data stream.

- **Framing.** With some transmission systems, cells are incorporated within a frame structure for transmission. The frame may contain a pointer that identifies the location of cell boundaries, or cells may be placed at fixed locations within the frame.

- **HEC Calculation.** Cell boundaries can be located based on the HEC field in the cell header. As the data stream is received, each group of 5 octets is checked to see if the fifth octet is a valid HEC value for the previous four octets. If so, this is assumed to be a cell header. This same check is repeated on what is presumed to be the next cell header, 53 octets later in the data stream. After a sequence of some number of correct HEC values has been detected, the cell boundaries are assumed to have been located.

The method used for performing cell delineation depends on the particular Physical layer interface used.

Physical Medium (PM) Sublayer

For outgoing transmission, the Physical Medium (PM) sublayer accepts a data stream from the TC sublayer and transmits it in the form of an electrical or optical signal on a physical link (transmission path). For incoming transmission, the PM sublayer receives the physical signal and converts to a data stream that it passes up to TC. This involves the following functions:

- **Encoding.** Transmission across a physical transmission path takes the form of an electrical or optical signal. When the signal is received, the receiver must be able to identify the portion of the signal that corresponds to each bit value. To interpret the signal properly, the receiver's processing rate must by synchronized with the sender's processing rate. In order to keep signal processing synchronized, the signal must be structured in a way that allows sender and receiver to resynchronize periodically. Generally, when there is a transition, or state change, in the signal, this represents a boundary between bits and can be used to resynchronize sender and receiver. When the data stream contains a continuous sequence of the same bit value, this can result in a portion of the signal having no transitions, which can allow sender and receiver to lose synchronization. The bit stream is encoded to ensure that the signal used to represent the data stream contains enough transitions so that the sender and receiver stay synchronized. There are a number of different methods of encoding, and different ones are used with different Physical layer interfaces.

- **Bit Timing.** When a signal is transmitted, it must be sent at the appropriate bit rate. When the signal is received, the correct timing must be used to interpret and process it. A clock function is generally used to control this timing.

- **Transmission.** The PM sublayer is responsible for placing an electrical or optical signal on the transmission medium and for receiving a signal from the medium.

The following sections further describe a number of noteworthy characteristics and functions of the ATM Physical layer.

DATA ENCODING

As we discussed above, one of the reasons the Physical layer encodes data for transmission is to ensure that the signal transmitted on the link contains sufficiently frequent transitions, or state changes. Transitions in the signal permit the receiver to interpret the signal properly and to extract the bit values represented in it. In the Transmission Convergence sublayer, a process called *scrambling* can be applied to the cell. Scrambling uses pseudo-random numbers to transform the bit patterns of the data in the cell. This randomization process helps avoid a sequence of nonvarying bits that could affect synchronization. It also provides a more even distribution of bit patterns, which can lead to more efficient use of the transmission frequency spectrum and reduces the probability of getting an erroneous HEC value match when determining cell boundaries within the data stream.

In the PM sublayer, block coding can be used to translate a group of bits into another bit pattern. Typically, a group of 4 bits is translated into a 5-bit pattern. The values used for the 5-bit or 10-bit pattern are chosen so there will be frequent transitions when the group is transmitted. Since the larger number of bits has a larger number of possible values, some bit combinations are not needed to represent data values. These nondata values can be used for control purposes, such as acting as delimiters that identify the beginning or end of a unit of data in the data stream.

Line Coding

Line coding is an important function of the PM sublayer that determines how different bit combinations in the data stream are represented as electrical or optical signals. Various forms of encoding are used with the different Physical layer interfaces. Box 7.1 shows some of the line coding methods used to transmit computer data. The sections that follow describe characteristics of the Physical layer interfaces used with ATM technology.

FRAMED TRANSMISSION AND CLOCK SYNCHRONIZATION

Physical transmission over many types of ATM transmission media use a form of framed transmission based on the time division multiplexing (TDM) approach often used for the transmission of digitally encoded voice information. With TDM and framed transmission, a frame with a predetermined format is transmitted across the link every 125 microseconds. Framed transmission is used with a number of different bit rates, with the frame size varying according to the bit rate.

One possible use of a uniform frame rate is to allow nodes across the network to synchronize their clocks. Although ATM uses an asynchronous transmission technique, some types of ATM services require the sending and receiving endpoints to process the data stream at the same rate. Box 7.2 shows the process typically used to synchronize sender and receiver clocks. Once the clocks are synchronized, the two endpoints can use the clocks to control the timing of data stream processing.

PHYSICAL LAYER SIGNALING

As we pointed out earlier in this chapter, the ATM standards specify a number of different signaling techniques and Physical layer interface standards that can be employed for car-

BOX 7.1 Commonly used signal encoding schemes.

RS-232-D Encoding

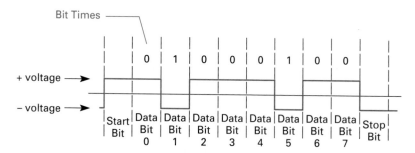

A technique often used for low-speed data communication is defined in a standard called RS-232-D, which is published by the Electronics Industry Association (EIA). With RS-232-D transmission, a negative voltage on the line for a bit time represents the value 1 and a positive voltage the value 0.

Nonreturn-to-Zero-Inverted

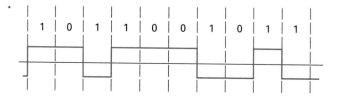

With nonreturn-to-zero-inverted (NRZI) coding, the presence or absence of a transition at the beginning of a bit time represents the bit value. The signal level then stays constant through the bit interval. With this technique, a transition on the line from negative to positive or from positive to negative at the beginning of a bit time indicates the value 1; the lack of a transition at the beginning of a bit time represents the value 0.

Manchester Encoding

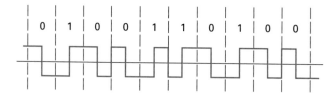

For electrical purposes, it is desirable in many data link implementations that transitions from positive to negative and from negative to positive occur often with pre-

BOX 7.1   *(Continued)*

dictable regularity. A form of encoding, called Manchester encoding, produces the desired number of transitions and is used on many types of LAN data links. With a typical implementation of Manchester encoding, a negative voltage for the first half of the bit time followed by a positive voltage for the second half of the bit time represents the value 1; a positive voltage followed by a transition to a negative voltage represents the value 0. Thus, with Manchester encoding, a transition from negative to positive or from positive to negative occurs every bit time.

With Manchester encoding, bit times in which the signal is held either positive or negative for the entire bit time are used to represent something other than a bit value, for example the beginning or ending of a transmission block.

Differential Manchester Encoding

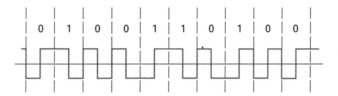

A form of Manchester encoding, called differential Manchester encoding, is used with some forms of LAN technology. With this technique, illustrated above, a transition occurs during each bit time, as with conventional Manchester encoding. However, the interpretation of the transition from positive to negative or from negative to positive depends on whether the previous bit time represented a 0 or a 1. To represent the value 1, the polarity remains the same as it was at the end of the previous bit time and then changes in polarity at the midpoint of the bit time only. To represent the value 0, the polarity changes at the beginning of the bit time and also at the midpoint of the bit time. With this form of encoding, a change from positive to negative can represent either a 0 or a 1, depending on the state of the line at the end of the previous bit time. It is the transition that occurs, or does not occur, at the beginning of the bit time that indicates the value. No transition at the beginning of the bit time indicates the value 1; a transition at the beginning of the bit time indicates the value 0.

As with conventional Manchester encoding, bit times in which no transition occurs at the midpoint of the bit time are often used for control purposes.

rying a bit stream over various types of physical transmission media. The following sections describe some of these standards.

Plesiochronous Digital Hierarchy

One set of interface standards used with ATM is the *Plesiochronous Digital Hierarchy (PDH),* developed by the telecommunications industry to provide a standard way of carry-

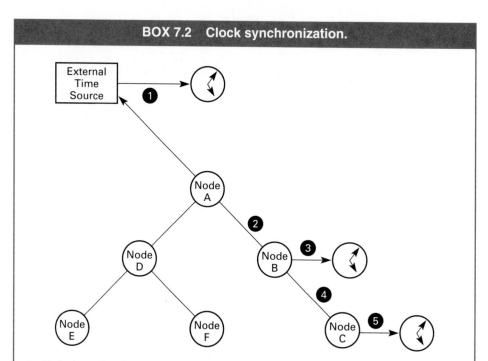

BOX 7.2   Clock synchronization.

1. Node A synchronizes its clock to an accurate external time source.
2. Node A uses its synchronized clock to control the frame rate for transmission to node B.
3. Node B derives timing from the frames it receives from node A and uses that to synchronize its clock.
4. Node B uses its synchronized clock to control the frame rate for transmission to node C.
5. Node C derives timing from the frames it receives from node B and uses that to synchronize its clock.

A similar process is used to synchronize nodes D, E, and F.

ing multiple voice channels on a single high-speed circuit. One hierarchy is defined for multiplexing the U.S. "T" system, and another for multiplexing the European "E" system. The PDH hierarchies are shown in Fig. 7.6.

Figure 7.7 shows the frame format used with the DS3 (T3) interface. A PDH transmission frame contains 12 ATM cells, with each cell preceded by 4 octets of protocol control information (PCI). Each complete frame ends with a 7-octet trailer. The synchronization bits contain delimiters that identify the beginning of the frame. The delimiters, combined with the constant rate (one frame every 125 microseconds) at which frames are sent, allow the sender and receiver on each side of the transmission path to stay synchronized. Within the frame, cells are located at defined positions, and cells can be located directly without needing to perform time-consuming cell delineation calculations.

United States

Level	Speed in Mbps	Voice Channels
DS0	64 Kbps	1
T1, DS1	1.544	24
T2, DS2	6.312	96
T3, DS3	44.736	672
T4, DS4	274.176	4032

Europe

Level	Speed in Mbps	Voice Channels
E1	2.048	30
E2	8.448	120
E3	34.368	480
E4	139.264	1920
E5	564.992	7680

Figure 7.6   Plesiochronous Digital Hierarchy (PDH) speeds in the United States and Europe.

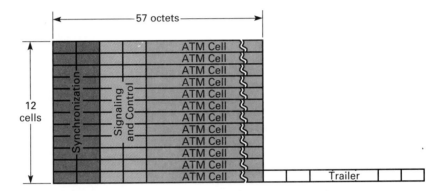

Figure 7.7   Physical Layer Convergence Protocol (PLCP) frame format for a T3 (DS3) transmission facility.

Synchronous Optical Network

The Synchronous Optical Network (SONET) standards define a transmission technique used by telecommunications providers in the U.S. for transmission across optical fiber telecommunications links. As with PDH, one frame is sent every 125 microseconds. At the lowest level, called Synchronous Transport Signal level 1 (STS-1), an 810-octet frame is sent, which corresponds to a bit rate of 51.84 Mbps. The frame consists of 9 rows of 90 octets, as shown in Fig. 7.8. The first three octets of each row are for overhead octets used to carry administrative and control information.

Multiple STS-1 frames can be combined together to provide higher bit rates. For example, three STS-1 frames can be combined to provide an STS-3 frame with a bit rate of 155.52 Mbps.

Octet Multiplexing

There are two ways in which the frames can be combined. *Octet multiplexing*, illustrated in Fig. 7.9, interleaves octets from each STS-1 frame to create the STS-3 frame.

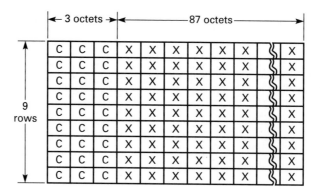

Figure 7.8   A SONET Synchronous Transport Signal level 1 (STS-1) frame consisting of 9 rows of 90 octets each. Each row contains 3 octets of control information and 87 octets of information.

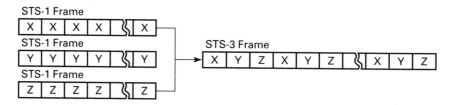

Figure 7.9   Octet multiplexing interleaves octets from multiple frames to create a new frame.

Concatenation

With *concatenation*, the STS-1 frames are aligned and then combined so that each row contains 9 octets of overhead and 261 octets of payload. The resulting STS-3 frame is illustrated in Fig. 7.10.

Synchronous Digital Hierarchy

The *Synchronous Digital Hierarchy (SDH)* physical transmission standards, defined by the ITU-T, accommodate both the U.S. SONET line speeds and European line speeds. The basic SDH frame, called *Synchronous Transport Module level 1 (STM-1)*, has the same format as the STS-3 frame. Within the STM-1 frame, slower speed channels are carried by using consecutive columns within the payload. A T1 channel (1.544 Mbps) uses 3 columns, and an E1 channel (2.048 Mbps) uses 4 columns. This gives a T-1 channel 27 octets, of which it actually uses 24. The E-1 channel is given 36 octets and uses 32. This results in some wasted payload, but this is minimal compared to the benefits gained from being able to multiplex the channels in such a simple manner. STM-1 frames can be combined to support higher bit rates. This can be done using either octet multiplexing or concatenation, as with the SONET standards. Interfaces have been specified for STM-1, at 155.52 Mbps, and STM-4c, at 622.08 Mbps.

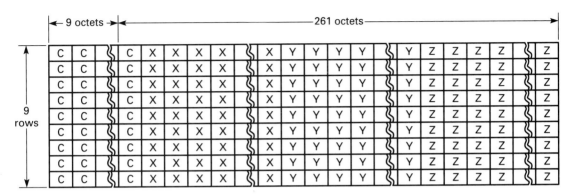

Figure 7.10 STS-3 frame consisting of a concatenation of three STS-1 frames.

Figure 7.11 shows how ATM cells are carried within an SDH frame. Cells are stored sequentially in a synchronous payload envelope, or virtual container, and may cross row and envelope boundaries. The cells are not in fixed locations within the frame, so the standards define a method for locating cell boundaries. The overhead octets in the virtual container include pointers to cell boundaries. However, the HEC calculation method described earlier in this chapter has become the preferred method for cell delineation.

A virtual container can be located anywhere within the physical frame payload area and can span two physical frames, as shown in Fig. 7.12. Pointers in the frame overhead information point to the start of virtual containers.

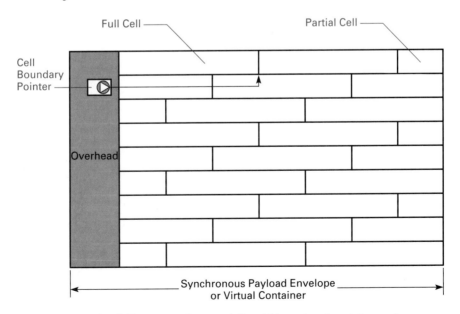

Figure 7.11 Cells are stored sequentially within a virtual container and can cross rows.

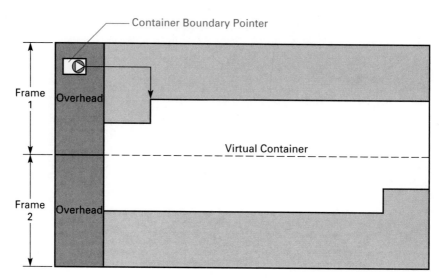

Figure 7.12   A virtual container can start anywhere within a physical frame and can span two or more physical frames.

Cell scrambling is used to randomize frame contents and to avoid a continuous nonvarying bit pattern. It also reduces the probability of a false match in the HEC calculation. Non-return to Zero (NRZ) line coding is used for signaling over an optical fiber transmission medium.

100-Mbps Multimode Fiber Interface

The *100-Mbps Multimode Fiber Interface* is the Physical layer protocol defined for FDDI LAN equipment. Use of this protocol allows existing FDDI components to be used in building ATM equipment, thus permitting more rapid and cost-effective product development. Framing is not used with the FDDI Physical interface. Cells can be transmitted whenever the line is idle. When no cell is available to send, idle codes are transmitted. When idle codes are sent, they must be sent at least once every 0.5 second. A start-of-cell delimiter is used to identify the beginning of a cell.

The form of physical signaling used with FDDI employs 4b/5b code conversion. With 4b/5b encoding, data is divided into 4-bit segments, and each 4-bit value is converted to a 5-bit value before being encoded for transmission using the NRZI encoding scheme. After transmission, the 5-bit values are converted back to the original 4-bit values. Figure 7.13 shows the corresponding 4-bit and 5-bit values. The 5-bit values used were chosen so there are never more than three consecutive 0 bits in any transmission.

Midrange User Network Interface

Midrange User Network Interface (MUNI) transmission, also called the *25.6-Mbps interface*, is based on the form of physical signaling used on a token ring LAN. As with FDDI,

Code Group	Symbol	Interpretation
Data		
11110	0	hex 0
01001	1	hex 1
10100	2	hex 2
10101	3	hex 3
01010	4	hex 4
01011	5	hex 5
01110	6	hex 6
01111	7	hex 7
10010	8	hex 8
10011	9	hex 9
10110	A	hex A
10111	B	hex B
11010	C	hex C
11011	D	hex D
11100	E	hex E
11101	F	hex F
Control		
00000	Q	Quiet
11111	I	Idle
00100	H	Halt
11000	J	Start Delimiter (1st symbol)
10001	K	Start Delimiter (2nd symbol)
01101	T	Ending Delimiter
00111	R	Reset
11001	S	Set

Figure 7.13   FDDI 4b/5b code.

framing is not used, and cells can be transmitted whenever the link is free. The beginning of each cell is marked by a starting delimiter. When there are no cells to send, random data patterns are sent to maintain signal synchronization.

A special 8-bit strobe signal is sent every 125 microseconds. The strobe signal is inserted between two octets in the data stream whenever required to maintain exact 125 microsecond timing. The strobe signal serves the same purpose as the uniform frame rate in framed transmission.

Cell data is scrambled and a form of 4b/5b block coding is used. The 4b/5b coding used is similar to that used on an FDDI LAN but uses a different set of 5-bit values. Differential Manchester encoding is used for data representation.

SUMMARY

An ATM network is made up of three types of components: ATM switches, ATM endpoints, and transmission paths (TPs). ATM switches, sometimes called intermediate systems, perform functions related to routing and relaying information from a sending user to a receiving user. There are two major categories of ATM switches: public ATM switches and private ATM switches. An ATM endpoint, often called an end system (ES), connects directly to a public or private ATM switch. An ATM endpoint can be implemented in an ordinary computing system or in a special-purpose network device to which computing systems are attached. Transmission paths are physical links that interconnect ATM endpoints and ATM switches.

The ATM Physical layer is made up of two sublayers: the Transmission Convergence (TC) sublayer and the Physical Medium (PM) sublayer. For outgoing information, the TC sublayer accepts cells from the ATM layer and structures them into a data stream for transmission by the PM sublayer. For incoming information, the PM sublayer passes a data stream to the TC sublayer, which extracts cells and passes them to the ATM layer. The TC sublayer is responsible for HEC generation and checking, cell delineation, transmission frame structuring and delineation, and cell rate decoupling.

For outgoing transmission, the Physical Medium (PM) sublayer accepts a data stream from the TC sublayer and transmits it in the form of an electrical or optical signal on the link. For incoming transmission, the PM sublayer receives the physical signal, converts it to a data stream, and passes it up to TC. This involves encoding, bit timing, and physical transmission. Various forms of encoding can be used to ensure that the signal transmitted on the link contains sufficiently frequent transitions to permit the receiver to interpret the signal properly and extract the bit values represented in the signal.

Physical transmission over many types of ATM transmission media use a form of framed transmission based on the time division multiplexing (TDM) approach often used for the transmission of digitally encoded voice information. The ATM standards specify a number of different signaling techniques and Physical layer interface standards that can be employed for carrying a bit stream over various types of physical transmission media. These include the Plesiochronous Digital Hierarchy (PDH) interface standards for multiplexing the U.S. "T" system and European "E" system, the Synchronous Optical Network (SONET) standards for transmission across optical fiber telecommunications links, the Synchronous Digital Hierarchy (SDH) physical transmission standards that accommodate both the U.S. SONET line speeds and European line speeds, the 100-Mbps Multimode Fiber Interface defined for FDDI LAN equipment, and the Midrange User Network Interface (MUNI) 25.6-Mbps interface based on the form of physical signaling used on a Token Ring LAN.

Chapter 8 describes the ATM Layer that operates above the Physical layer in ATM equipment and software.

Chapter **8**

The ATM Layer

The ATM layer is where the real work of moving information through the network is done. Like the Physical layer, the ATM layer is implemented in ATM endpoint devices and in ATM switches (see Fig. 8.1).

As we introduced in Chapter 1, an ATM network *operates* in essentially a *connection-oriented* manner. However, as we also saw, an ATM network can be used to supply three types of transmission services:

- *Connection-oriented* data transmission services similar to those provided by a WAN data link.

- *Connectionless* data transmission services similar to those supplied by a conventional LAN data link.

- *Isochronous* delivery services suited to the transmission of voice and video information.

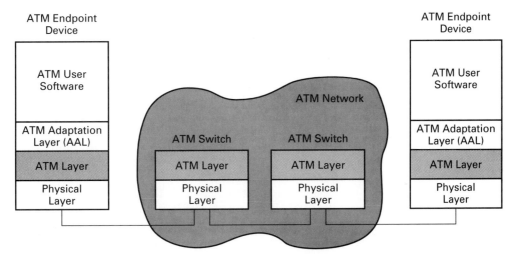

Figure 8.1 The Physical layer of the ATM architecture.

In this chapter we see how the ATM layer makes it possible for ATM devices to supply all three types of transmission services.

ATM PHYSICAL INTERFACES

There are two key physical interfaces that are important to functions operating in the ATM layer. These are the *user-network interface (UNI)* and the *network-network interface (NNI)*. Each of these interfaces is specified in the standards primarily by defining the format of the ATM cells passed between network devices by functions operating in the ATM layer.

The interpretation of the ATM standards adopted by the ATM Forum with respect to the UNI and NNI is illustrated in Fig. 8.2.

User-Network Interface (UNI)

The *user-network interface (UNI)* is the interface that exists between an ATM endpoint (end system) and an ATM switch (intermediate system). The ATM Forum differentiates between a public UNI and a private UNI, but, as of the time of writing, both define the same cell format.

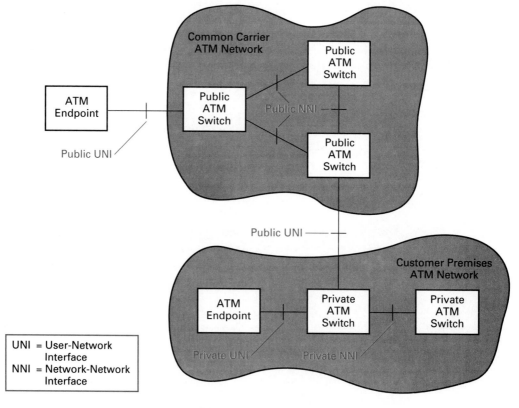

Figure 8.2   ATM network interfaces.

Public UNI

The public UNI defines the format of the cells passed between a telecommunications service provider's public ATM switch (network node) and an ATM device in some organization's private network. This interface can exist between a public ATM switch and an ATM endpoint device or between a public ATM switch and an organization's private ATM switch (customer premises node).

Private UNI

The private UNI defines the format of the cells passed between a private ATM switch (customer premises node) and an ATM endpoint device (end system).

Network-Network Interface (NNI)

The *network-network interface (NNI)* is the interface that exists between two ATM switches. As with the UNI, the ATM Forum differentiates between a public NNI and a private NNI. As with the UNI, at the time of writing both NNIs define the same cell format.

Public NNI

The public NNI defines the format of the cells passed between one public ATM switch (network node) and another public ATM switch. The interface can exist between two ATM switches in the same ATM public network or between an ATM switch in one public network and an ATM switch in another public network.

Private NNI

The private NNI defines the format of the cells passed between two private ATM switches (customer premises nodes). The private NNI can exist between two private ATM switches in the same organization's ATM network or between a private ATM switch in one organization's network and a private ATM switch in some other organization's network.

ATM CELL FORMATS

Both the UNI and the NNI are defined in terms of the formats of the 53-octet cells that are passed across the interface. Box 8.1 describes the ATM cell formats used to define both the user-network interface (UNI) and the network-network interface (NNI). The cell formats for the UNI and NNI are similar and differ only in the interpretation of the first four bits of the cell header.

VIRTUAL PATHS AND VIRTUAL CHANNELS

One of the key functions of an ATM switch is to relay data from a source endpoint to a destination endpoint. This function, often called *cell switching*, is done based on values contained in the Virtual Path Identifier (VPI) and Virtual Channel Identifier (VCI) fields in the cell headers.

BOX 8.1   Asynchronous Transfer Mode (ATM) UNI and NNI cell formats.

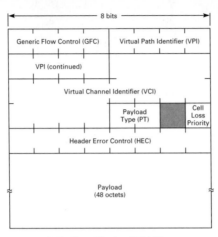

ATM User/Network Interface (UNI) Cell Format

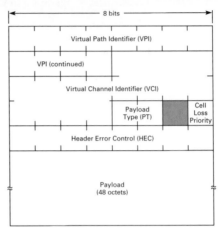

ATM Network/Network Interface (NNI) Cell Format

- **Generic Flow Control (GFC).** The GFC field is a 4-bit field used only in the cell defining the user-network interface (UNI). The GFC field is intended to be used in defining a simple multiplexing scheme. At the time of writing, the ATM standards define only a single *uncontrolled mode*, in which this field contains all 0 bits.

- **Virtual Path Identifier (VPI).** The VPI is 8 bits in length in the cell format that defines the user-network interface (UNI) and 12 bits in length in the cell that defines the network-network interface (NNI). The VPI is used to group virtual channels into paths for routing purposes. Virtual paths and the VPI are described later in this chapter.

- **Virtual Channel Identifier (VCI).** The VCI is a 16-bit field that identifies a particular virtual channel within a virtual path. Virtual channels and the VCI are described later in this chapter.

- **Payload Type (PT).** The PT field is a 2-bit field that identifies the type of information contained in the Payload field.

- **Cell Loss Priority (CLP).** The CLP field is a 1-bit field that ATM equipment uses to determine which cells to begin discarding first when congestion occurs.

- **Header Error Check (HEC).** The HEC field contains an error detection and correction code value used to detect and sometimes correct errors in the header octets of the cell.

- **Payload.** The cell's Payload contains 48 octets (384 bits) of user data and/or additional control information. There are different formats used for the Payload field, corresponding to the different types of data delivery services that can be provided by an ATM network. ATM data delivery services, and specific Payload field formats, are described in Chapter 9.

Some terminology is important in understanding how the cell switching function is associated with the concepts of virtual paths and virtual channels. As we have already seen, data is carried between one ATM device and another over physical links called *transmission paths (TPs)*. The cells flowing across a particular transmission path between one device and another can be grouped into virtual paths (VPs) and virtual channels (VCs) based on the values contained in the VPI and VCI fields of the cells flowing across that transmission path.

The following sections describe transmission paths and the concepts of virtual paths and virtual channels.

Transmission Paths

A transmission path is a physical circuit connecting two ATM devices (ATM endpoints or ATM switches). Figure 8.3 presents a conceptual view of a transmission path and possible virtual paths and virtual channels associated with it.

We might compare cells flowing through an ATM network to vehicles traveling over a system of roadways. In this analogy, a transmission path can be compared to a physical roadway between two cities over which vehicles travel. ATM cells flow over the system of transmission paths making up an ATM network much as vehicles travel over a system of roads.

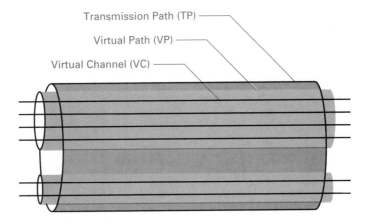

Transmission Path (TP)

Virtual Path (VP)

Virtual Channel (VC)

Figure 8.3   A transmission path implements virtual paths and virtual channels.

Virtual Paths

A virtual path is a route through some portion of an ATM network that begins at one ATM device and ends at another. A typical ATM network may implement a great many virtual paths. A particular virtual path is implemented by the set of transmission paths that connects the two ends of the virtual path. Since a virtual path may involve only a small portion of an ATM network, it is possible that a cell traveling from one ATM *endpoint* device to another may have to flow over multiple virtual paths.

A given transmission path may carry traffic associated with multiple virtual paths. Each virtual path within a transmission path has a VPI value associated with it that is unique within that transmission path. Cells associated with different virtual paths carry in their headers the VPI values of their respective virtual paths. Figure 8.4 shows a transmission path implementing two virtual paths, one with VPI value 1 and another with VPI value 2.

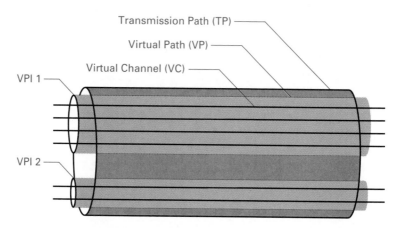

Figure 8.4 Each virtual path within a transmission path has a different VPI value associated with it.

An ATM network is generally constructed using a number of ATM endpoints and ATM switches, all connected by point-to-point transmission paths. Figure 8.5 illustrates a set of transmission paths and virtual paths implementing a simple ATM network.

Now we can show that a complete virtual path is defined by the set of transmission paths over which cells associated with that virtual path must flow. For example, the virtual path between ATM switch 3 and ATM endpoint 5 is implemented by the two transmission paths in Fig. 8.5 labeled TP G and TP I.

Virtual paths define the first level in a hierarchy specifying how transmission paths can be shared among multiple communicating users. Note that the devices at the ends of a virtual path can be either ATM endpoints or ATM switches.

To continue our roadway analogy, we might compare a virtual path to a particular numbered route over a system of roads. In a highway system, a particular numbered route begins at one point, ends at another, and it may switch from one physical roadway to another at various points. In the same manner, a virtual path begins at one ATM device, ends at another, and may switch from one physical transmission path to another.

Just as a particular physical roadway segment in a highway system may be shared by a number of different numbered routes, a particular transmission path may carry traffic associated with more than one virtual path. A virtual path tells a cell when to switch from one physical transmission path to another in making its way from the beginning of the virtual path to its end.

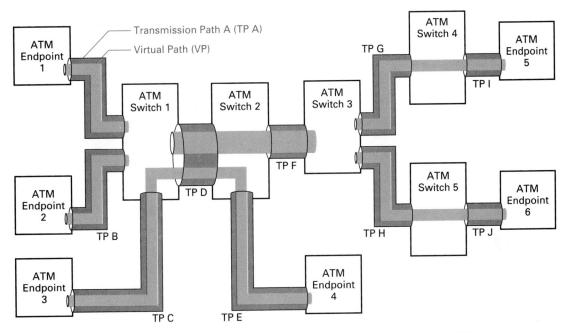

Figure 8.5 A virtual path (VP) is a route through some portion of an ATM network.

Virtual Path Connections (VPCs)

A *virtual path connection (VPC)* is a logical association between communicating entities in the devices at the ends of a virtual path. For example, we might establish a VPC over the virtual path between a user in ATM endpoint 3 and a user in ATM endpoint 4. The two users could use the VPC to exchange cells with one another.

Cells associated with a particular VPC flow over the transmission paths associated with that virtual path. For example, cells associated with a VPC between ATM endpoint 3 and ATM endpoint 4 flow over the transmission paths labeled TP C and TP E in Fig. 8.5.

Note that a virtual path connection can be established only over a single virtual path. In Fig. 8.5, a virtual path connection cannot be established between ATM endpoint 1 and ATM switch 2 because more than one virtual path would need to be traversed.

It is important to understand that a virtual path is not associated with a single VPI value. A particular virtual path or VPC is identified by a *series* of VPI values. A different VPI value can be used for each transmission path over which a particular cell must travel as it flows over that VPC. This is important because it is possible that many more virtual paths are active in an ATM network than might be indicated by the addressing capacity of eight or twelve bits occupied by the VPI field in the cell header. The VPI value need only be unique within each individual transmission path that connects a pair of ATM devices. We will look further into how this works when we examine virtual path switching later in this chapter.

Virtual Channels

Virtual channels make up a second level in the hierarchy that defines how transmission paths are shared among multiple users. Like virtual paths, virtual channels have two ends. Each virtual channel in an ATM network is associated with all the virtual paths that must be crossed in traveling from a source device at the beginning of a virtual channel to the destination device at the end. A virtual channel (VC) defines a route between two communicating entities over which cells can be transported from one ATM device to another.

As with virtual paths, the devices at each end of a virtual channel can be either ATM endpoints or ATM switches. However, the virtual paths of interest to us are those that carry user data traffic instead of only control information. The virtual channels carrying user data always have ATM endpoint devices at each end.

Each virtual path can implement one or more virtual channels. Each virtual channel has a VCI value associated with it that is unique within that virtual path. Figure 8.6 shows a portion of a transmission path implementing virtual paths and virtual channels. VPI 1 implements four virtual channels (VCI values 1 through 4); virtual path VPI 2 has two virtual channels (VCI values 1 and 2).

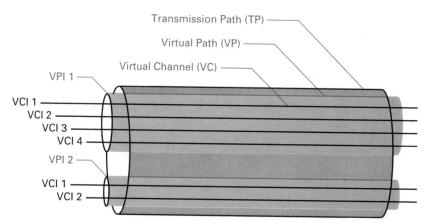

Figure 8.6 Relationships among a particular transmission path (TP) and the virtual paths (VPs) and virtual channels (VCs) implemented within it.

The solid lines between ATM endpoints in Fig. 8.7 show possible virtual channels that might be established over the virtual paths from Fig. 8.6.

Completing the roadway analogy, we might compare a virtual channel to a set of driving directions a vehicle might follow in traveling from one city to another. To make a particular trip, a vehicle may have to switch from one roadway to another in following a particular numbered route for each segment of its trip. It may also have to change from one numbered route to another at various points along the way. Any number of vehicles traveling according to different sets of driving instructions may travel over the same numbered routes and the same system of roadways. In a similar manner, cells associated with different virtual channels may travel over the same virtual paths and the same trans-

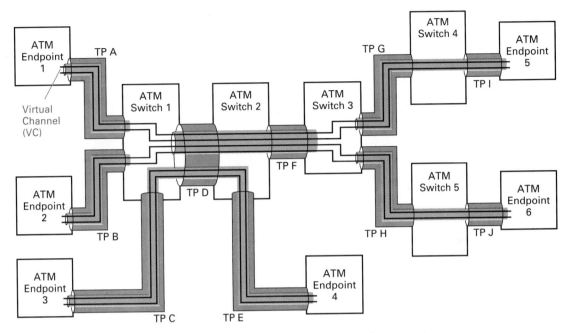

Figure 8.7 A virtual channel (VC) is a particular route between a data source
and its destination. A virtual path (VP) is a portion of a route shared by a group
of virtual channels.

mission paths in reaching their destinations. A virtual channel tells a cell when to make
the change from one virtual path to another and from one transmission path to another in
making its complete trip from a source endpoint to a destination endpoint.

Virtual Channel Connections (VCCs)

A *virtual channel connection (VCC)* is a logical association between communicating entities running in two endpoints of a virtual channel. For example, we might establish a VCC
over the virtual paths that lie between a user in ATM endpoint 3 and a user in ATM endpoint 4 (see Fig. 8.7). Cells flowing over that VCC would flow over the single logical path
between ATM endpoint 3 and ATM endpoint 4 and would cross the two transmission paths
labeled TP C and TP E.

If we establish a VCC between ATM endpoint 1 and ATM endpoint 5, cells associated
with that VCC would flow over the four virtual paths that lie between those two endpoints
and would flow over the five transmission paths labeled TP A, TP D, TP F, TP G, and TP I.

A virtual channel connection is typically unidirectional. So VCCs are normally used
in pairs, with each connection carrying data in the opposite direction from the other.

Like virtual path connections, no single identifier is associated with a VCC. A VCC is
defined by the *complete set* of VPI and VCI values that a cell must have as it flows over
that connection. As with virtual paths, this is important because it means there can be a
great many more virtual channel connections active in an ATM network than might be

indicated by the 16-bit addressing capacity of the VCI field in the cell header. A VCI value need only be unique within a particular segment of a virtual path that flows over a given transmission path.

In the next sections, we will see how switches set VPI and VCI values as cells flow through them.

ATM PROTOCOL FUNCTIONS

The ATM layer provides a set of *services* that the ATM Adaptation layer above it can request. The ATM layer provides these services to AAL through a set of protocols operating in the ATM layer. The protocol functions the ATM layer performs can be divided into the following five categories:

- **Connection Establishment.** When an ATM user requests that a switched connection be established, that user's ATM endpoint determines whether the network has sufficient capacity available to support the requested connection. The network then determines the route to be used for the connection and updates routing tables in the ATM switches along the route to reflect the chosen path through the network.

- **Cell Switching.** One aspect of cell switching concerns the *relaying* function performed by each ATM switch in the network. An ATM switch accepts each cell arriving on an input transmission path and transmits it over an output transmission path that will bring the cell closer to its final destination endpoint. Cell switching also involves a *routing* function in which ATM switches continually update the routing tables they use to determine appropriate output transmission paths.

- **Error Detection.** The ATM layer assumes that highly reliable transmission links are used to handle communication in the ATM network. Therefore, no mechanism is provided in the ATM layer for detecting errors in the Payload fields of cells. Error detection mechanisms must be provided in a layer above the ATM layer if an error-free transmission service is required. The ATM layer does, however, include an error detection mechanism for detecting corrupted cell headers.

- **Flow Control.** The congestion and flow control functions attempt to prevent the network from becoming overloaded. The primary method used for flow control is input rate control, in which a limit is placed on the rate at which each switch accepts cells arriving over input transmission paths.

- **Congestion Control.** Congestion control mechanisms come into play if the network, or some portion of it, becomes overloaded in spite of the flow control mechanisms. The principal technique used to control congestion in an ATM network is to discard cells.

The following sections further describe each of these categories of protocol functions.

CONNECTION ESTABLISHMENT

In order to transfer data between two ATM endpoints, the two endpoints must establish a logical association, called a *connection*, between them. The primary function performed during connection establishment is a routing function that determines an appropriate route through the network for cells that will flow over the connection.

Connection Types

The two types of connections an ATM network can implement are switched connections and semipermanent connections.

Switched Connections

A *switched connection* is established at the request of the user of an ATM endpoint at the time a "call" is made and data is ready to be transmitted. After a connection has been established, either of the two connected endpoints can release the connection when it is no longer needed for data transmission.

Semipermanent Connections

A *semipermanent connection* is established using administrative procedures. The connection may then remain in continuous operation for a long period of time, whether or not the connection is actually used for data transmission.

Connections for Control Information

User data is transferred over a connection between the ATM endpoints two users are employing for data transmission. Connections can also be established between an ATM endpoint and an ATM switch and between one ATM switch and another. These types of connections are used primarily for the flow of control information to monitor and control the operation of the ATM network itself. Users of the network are not aware of the flow of control information through the network.

Endpoint Addresses

As we learned in Chapter 4, an addressing scheme is used to assign a unique identifier to each endpoint to be used as a data link address. The endpoint addressing scheme the ATM Forum recommends for use in ATM networks is based on the international standard *Network Service Access Point (NSAP)* addressing scheme defined for the OSI architecture. An NSAP address is typically called a *network* address, since it is the address typically processed in the Network layer of the OSI model. However, the NSAP addressing scheme is used with ATM technology for assigning *data link* addresses.

This chapter describes only those aspects of the NSAP address used in ATM networks. The OSI NSAP addressing scheme is described in detail in Appendix C for those who are not familiar with it.

Figure 8.8 summarizes three OSI NSAP address formats the ATM Forum recommends for use in ATM networks as endpoint identifiers. Keep in mind that some public ATM networks do not follow the ATM Forum recommendations. For example, a number of operating public ATM networks use only the 8-octet E.164 address as an endpoint identifier.

ITU-T E.164 Numbering Scheme

The primary ATM NSAP address format is the one at the top of Fig. 8.8. It uses the numbering scheme described in ITU-T Recommendation E.164 to assign unique data link address-

E.164 ATM NSAP Address Format

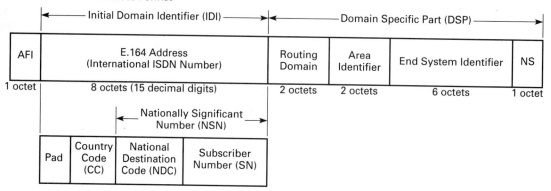

Data Country Code (DCC) NSAP Address Format

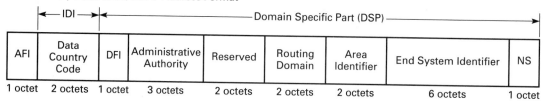

International Code Designator (ICD) NSAP Address Format

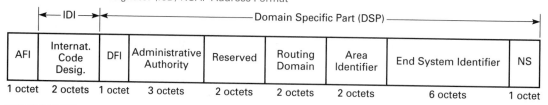

AFI = Authority and Format Identifier
DFI = Domain Specific Part (DSP) Format Identifier
NS = Network Service Access Point (NASP) Selector

Figure 8.8   ATM endpoint address formats.

es to ATM network users. The E.164 standard describes an addressing scheme that uses addresses with a hierarchical structure, in a similar manner to today's telephone numbers. The other two NSAP address formats shown in Fig. 8.8 were chosen for compatibility with computer networks that use conventional Network layer routing facilities.

Quality of Service

During connection establishment, the ATM network may use *Quality of Service (QoS)* information provided when a connection is requested to determine if the network has sufficient capacity available to support the requested connection. The way in which the network determines whether sufficient bandwidth is available is not directly addressed in the ATM specifications.

Generally, connections requiring a high level of service and availability will have the required bandwidth reserved at each point along the connection's route. But not all types of connections require bandwidth to be reserved in advance. For connections with bursty bit rates, reserving bandwidth to guarantee support for peak rates could lead to lower levels of network utilization, since it is not likely that all connections will be in use at peak bit rates all the time. Most ATM networks implement functions that attempt to increase network utilization at the risk of some congestion occurring.

CELL SWITCHING

As we pointed out earlier, ATM switches must perform a *cell switching* function to determine how to relay cells from one transmission path to another as the cells make their way through the network. Switches relay each cell through the network by choosing an appropriate output transmission path for the cell and placing appropriate values in the VPI and VCI fields in that cell's header.

ATM switches, in essence, perform a *routing* function, and switches use *routing tables* or *routing databases* to choose transmission paths and to determine how to set the VPI and VCI values. When a virtual channel connection is established, appropriate switches in the network place into their routing tables identifiers of output transmission paths and VPI/VCI values to handle the cells that will travel over the new connection. The switches in an ATM network all run a distributed routing algorithm to create the routing tables that each switch uses to assign VPI and VCI values.

Switching by each particular switch in an ATM network can be performed by setting only VPI values (virtual path switching) or by setting both VPI values and VCI values (virtual channel switching). We will first look at how virtual path switching works and then see how a virtual channel switch works.

Virtual Path Switching

ATM switches 2, 4, and 5 in Fig. 8.7 set only VPI values and are called *virtual path switches*. A virtual path switch assigns a unique number to each physical transmission path attached to the switch. Figure 8.9 shows that ATM switch 2 from Fig. 8.7 has assigned the identifiers 1, 2, and 3 to the transmission paths labeled TP D, TP E, and TP F.

An ATM switch exchanges routing information with other switches based on information gathered when connections are established. A switch uses this routing information to maintain a separate virtual path routing table for each physical transmission path over which it expects to receive cells. The routing table associated with a particular input transmission path contains an entry for each VPI value the switch expects to see in the headers of cells it receives over that transmission path. Figure 8.10 shows the virtual path routing table that ATM switch 2 is using for TP 1.

In this example, there are two virtual paths associated with TP 1, identified in this switch by VPI value 1 and VPI value 2. Figure 8.11 shows how ATM switch 2 uses its virtu-

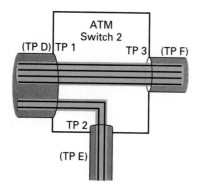

Figure 8.9 ATM switch 2 assigns a unique numeric identifier to each physical transmission path.

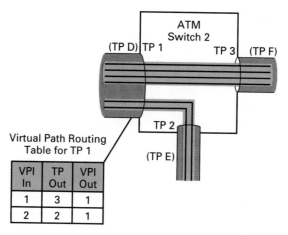

Figure 8.10 Each ATM switch has a separate virtual path routing table for each transmission path over which it expects to receive cells.

al path routing table entries for TP 1 to choose an output transmission path and virtual path for each cell it receives over TP 1.

When a cell arrives at the ATM switch over TP 1, the switch uses the VPI value in that cell to select the routing table entry to use for that cell. In the example shown in Fig. 8.11, if a cell arriving over TP 1 has VPI value 1, the switch places VPI value 1 into the cell, leaving that cell's VPI value unchanged, and sends it out over TP 3. If a cell arriving over TP 1 has VPI value 2, the switch places VPI value 1 into the cell header, thus changing that cell's VPI value, and transmits it over TP 2.

The example in Fig. 8.11 is deliberately simplified. In an actual virtual path switch, there may be many more physical transmission paths and many virtual paths associated with each transmission path.

ATM switches need not store routing information in the form of tables, nor do they necessarily use the structure and formats shown here. However, any virtual path switch must be able to switch cells based on incoming VPI values and transmit cells over the correct output transmission path with appropriate outgoing VPI values.

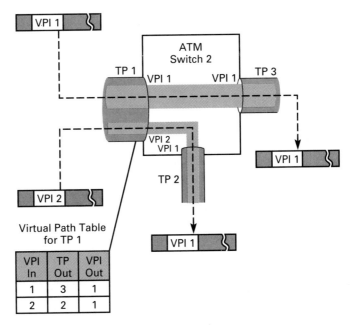

Figure 8.11 ATM switch 2 uses the virtual path routing table for TP 1 to choose an output transmission path and VPI value for each cell it receives over TP 1.

With virtual path switching, the VP table directly specifies the particular link on which the cell should be transmitted and the outgoing VPI value to use. A virtual path switch does not use or modify VCI values in the cells that pass through it. The VCI value contained in the header for a cell that passes through a virtual path switch remains unchanged when the cell goes out on an output transmission path.

We next see how a virtual channel switch uses both VPI values and VCI values in choosing an output transmission path and setting both VPI and VCI values in outgoing cells.

Virtual Channel Switching

Like a virtual path switch, a *virtual channel switch* exchanges routing information with other switches to maintain routing tables. These routing tables contain information the switch uses to choose an output transmission path for each cell it receives and to set both the VPI value and VCI value in each output cell's header. Switches place appropriate entries into their routing tables at the time that VPCs and VCCs are established. ATM switches 1 and 3 in Fig. 8.8 are examples of virtual channel switches.

Like a virtual path switch, a virtual channel switch maintains a virtual path routing table for each of its transmission paths. Each entry in the virtual path routing table in a virtual channel switch may be associated with a separate virtual channel routing table. Figure 8.12 shows selected virtual path routing tables and a virtual channel routing table for ATM switch 1 from Fig. 8.7.

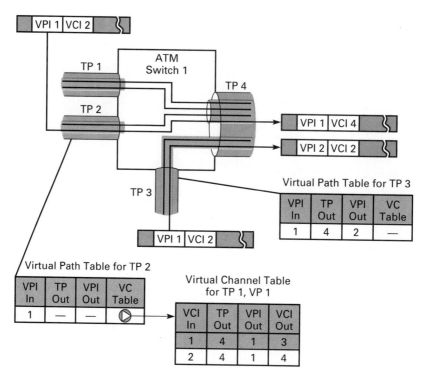

Figure 8.12　A virtual channel switch contains a virtual path routing table for each transmission path. It may also contain a separate virtual channel routing table for each of the virtual paths associated with a transmission path.

A virtual channel switch may switch cells based on VPI values alone, like a virtual path switch, or it may switch cells based on both VPI values and VCI values. For example, in Fig. 8.12 cells coming into TP 3 can be switched on VPI values alone. VCI values in cells arriving on TP 3 remain unchanged as they are sent out on TP 4. Figure 8.12 shows how a cell arriving on TP 3 that has a VPI value of 1 has its VPI value set to 1, its VCI value remains unchanged, and the cell is sent out on TP 4.

Cells arriving on TP 2, on the other hand, must have both their VPI values and VCI values set. The example in Fig. 8.12 is simple, and the virtual path routing table contains only one entry, which corresponds with the only VPI value expected in cells that arrive over TP 2. Each virtual path routing table entry points to a virtual channel routing table. In this case, it contains an entry for each VCI value expected in cells that arrive over TP 2 in the virtual path associated with VPI 1 (the only virtual path).

The example shown in Fig. 8.12 shows that when a cell arrives over TP 2 with a VPI value of 1 and a VCI value of 2, its VPI value is set to 1, its VCI value is set to 4, and the cell is sent out over TP 4. In an actual switch, of course, there are likely to be many more transmission paths, many more virtual paths per transmission paths, and many more virtual channels for each virtual path.

Multipoint Connections

In some cases, an ATM network may implement *multipoint* connections in addition to the ordinary point-to-point connections discussed thus far. Multipoint connections are used to implement multicast and broadcast functions that permit a user to send a message to multiple destinations in the same operation. Multipoint connections are especially important in ATM networks that are designed to provide LAN-like services.

To implement multipoint connections, an ATM switch may need to send multiple copies of an incoming cell out over multiple output transmission paths. To handle this type of situation, virtual path and virtual channel routing tables may need to contain the information required to implement multipoint connections. Multipoint connections are discussed further in Chapter 9, but the routing complexities associated with them are beyond the scope of this book.

ERROR DETECTION   *not on payload but on header*

The protocols operating in the ATM layer, used to control cell transmission and cell switching, make the following two assumptions:

- The physical links being used to implement the network are highly reliable, and transmission errors will occur only rarely.

- Any error detection and correction functions the end user may require will be performed in a layer above the ATM layer.

Any error checking needed to guarantee reliable data delivery must be done either in the ATM Adaptation layer or in the network software operating in the role of the ATM user. Therefore, while the ATM layer has a connection-oriented form of operation, the protocol operating in the ATM layer does not check for transmission errors that may result in a corrupted cell payload field. This is a departure from most other connection-oriented protocols, most of which perform error detection and recovery using CRC checks and a system of message numbers and acknowledgments.

Although the ATM layer protocols perform no error detection on the payload field of an ATM cell, it is important to the correct operation of the ATM layer that no errors occur in the 5-octet header of a cell. This is because the cell header tells the network equipment how to handle that cell, and an undetected error may cause the network equipment to deliver the cell to the wrong destination or to perform an undesired function. To protect against invalid headers, one of the five header octets is used to detect, and often correct, errors in the header itself.

Each time a cell is ready for transmission across a physical transmission path, the transmitting device calculates a value for the Header Error Check (HEC) field based on the value in the four other octets of the cell header. A device that receives the cell performs the same HEC value calculation. If the calculated HEC value does match the received HEC field value, the device tries to correct the error. The error detection code used in calculating the HEC value can correct all single-bit errors that can occur in the cell header. The code can also *detect* many multiple-bit errors. If an erroneous cell header cannot be corrected, the entire cell is discarded. ATM users are not notified when cells are discarded; the discarded cells simply fail to reach their destinations.

Because VCI and VPI values may change for each physical transmission path over which the cell travels, a new Header Error Check field value must be calculated and placed in the header before each cell is sent out over each new transmission path.

FLOW CONTROL

Flow control is important in an ATM to ensure that ATM user software does not send data into the network at rates that exceed the limit associated with each connection and, thus, overload the network. ATM networks implement a flow control mechanism to help prevent congestion from occurring. The flow control mechanism typically used is based on limiting the rate at which data enters the network. When a connection is established, the connection establishment request contains Quality of Service (QoS) parameters that indicate the type and level of service the connection requires, including:

- Average and peak cell rates
- Allowable end-to-end transit delay
- Performance requirements, specified in terms of the ATM service class required.

Leaky Bucket Input Rate Control

The ATM standards do not specify the method to be used for handling flow control. However, they suggest that a "leaky bucket" approach to input rate control be used. With the "leaky bucket" approach, each ATM device (ATM endpoint or ATM switch) typically implements one or more flow control counters to which it adds 1 a specified number of times per second. Whenever a device receives a cell, it subtracts 1 from a flow control counter. If a device's flow control counter reaches 0, cells are arriving too fast, and the device stops accepting cells until its counter again contains a value greater than 0. Depending on how the flow control function is implemented, cells that arrive after cells have stopped being accepted may be held temporarily in a buffer queue and then accepted later on, or cells might simply be discarded.

A "leaky bucket" rate control mechanism might use a separate counter for each virtual channel connection, a separate counter for each virtual path connection, or a separate counter for each active transmission path. Combinations of counters might also be used.

Generic Flow Control

A proposed addition to the ATM standards specifies details concerning how a "leaky bucket" approach to input rate control might be implemented based on setting different values in the Generic Flow Control (GFC) field in cell headers. The proposed mechanism operates at the level of a particular transmission path and applies to traffic flowing into an ATM switch from an ATM endpoint.

For traffic flowing into the network, the GFC field is used to identify each cell as being associated with either controlled or uncontrolled traffic. *Uncontrolled* traffic consists of cells traveling on connections that have reserved bandwidth; *controlled* traffic consist of cells traveling over connections that do not have reserved bandwidth.

Cells traveling into the network over a particular transmission path are placed into queues associated with that transmission path. For a given transmission path, there is one queue for uncontrolled traffic and one or two queues for controlled traffic. When the endpoint determines that a transmission path can accept a cell for transmission, if there is a cell in the uncontrolled queue for that transmission path, the endpoint transmits that cell over the transmission path. If there are no cells waiting in the uncontrolled queue, a cell from a controlled queue is transmitted. If there are two queues for controlled traffic, cells are sent alternately from the two queues.

For controlled queues, counters are used to control the rate at which cells are sent. An ATM switch requests a Reset function by setting the GFC value to a particular value in a cell traveling out of the network from the ATM switch to the endpoint in question. Bits in the GFC field are also used to specify to which queue the Reset function applies. The network periodically sends a Reset request to an endpoint for each controlled queue. When an endpoint receives a Reset, it sets the counter for that queue to a specified value. Each time the endpoint transmits a cell from a control queue, it decrements the counter for that queue by one. If a controlled queue counter reaches zero, the endpoint does not transmit cells from that queue until it receives a Reset request.

Another GFC-field value is used to specify a Halt request. When an ATM switch sends a Halt request to an endpoint, the endpoint stops transmission of all traffic, controlled or uncontrolled, until it receives a Restart request.

CONGESTION CONTROL

Even with an effective input rate control mechanism, problems and unexpected conditions may cause overloads to occur in portions of the network. If congestion does occur at some point, and there are more cells waiting to be transmitted than there is buffer space to hold them, cells are discarded. An ATM device uses the Cell Loss Priority (CLP) field to identify cells that have a lower priority than other cells. Lower priority cells are discarded first when congestion begins to occur.

There are competing ideas on how the CLP field should be used. In one view, only ATM switches should be allowed to set the CLP field. One way it might be used is to mark cells that are transmitted on a connection at a rate that exceeds the specified maximum cell rate. A second view suggests letting the endpoint set the CLP field. This might be done for some types of video transmission where some cells are less critical in preserving content, and it is important to maintain a uniform transmission rate for synchronization.

As with cells discarded based on header errors, no notification is sent to the ATM user software when cells are discarded due to congestion. The detection and retransmission of lost cells is left to the layers above the ATM layer. However, one bit within the Payload Type field has been defined for use in congestion notification. If a user receives a cell with this bit sent to 1, the user knows that congestion was encountered at some point along the connection. How the user should respond to this notification has not yet been specified.

One potential problem with the approach ATM networks use with respect to congestion is that typically an entire frame of data, parts of which may be contained in many other cells in addition to the discarded cell, may need to be retransmitted. The retransmissions that result from discarding cells because of congestion can have the effect of increasing traffic on the network at a time when the network is already overloaded.

SUMMARY

The ATM layer is where the real work of moving information through the network is done and is implemented in both ATM switches and ATM endpoint devices. Two key physical interfaces are important to functions operating in the ATM layer. These are the user-network interface (UNI) and the network-network interface (NNI). Each of these interfaces is specified by defining the format of ATM cells that pass across these interfaces.

Data is carried between one ATM device and another over physical links called transmission paths (TPs). A transmission path is a physical circuit connecting two ATM devices. A virtual path is a route through some portion of an ATM network that begins at one ATM device and ends at another. A virtual path connection (VPC) is a logical association between communicating entities in the devices at the ends of a virtual path. Virtual channels make up a second level in the hierarchy that defines how transmission paths are shared among multiple users. Each virtual channel in an ATM network is associated with all the virtual paths that must be crossed in traveling from a source device at the beginning of a virtual channel to the destination device at the end. Each virtual path can implement one or more virtual channels. Each virtual channel within a virtual path has a VCI value associated with it that is unique within that virtual path. A virtual channel connection (VCC) is a logical association between communicating entities running in two endpoints of a virtual channel. A virtual channel connection is typically unidirectional, carrying cells in only one direction, and VCCs are normally used in pairs with each connection carrying data in the opposite direction from the other.

The ATM layer provides a set of services the ATM Adaptation layer above it can request. The ATM layer provides these services to AAL through a set of protocols operating in the ATM layer. The major protocol functions the ATM layer performs are connection establishment, cell switching, error detection, flow control, and congestion control.

When an ATM user requests that a switched connection be established, that user's ATM endpoint determines whether the network has sufficient capacity available to support the requested connection. The network then determines the route to be used for the connection and appropriately updates routing tables in the ATM switches along the route.

Cell switching is the relaying function performed by each ATM switch in the network. An ATM switch accepts each cell arriving on an input transmission path and transmits it on an output transmission path that will bring the cell closer to its final destination. Cell switching also involves a routing function in which ATM switches update the routing tables they use to determine appropriate output transmission paths.

With respect to error detection, the ATM layer assumes that highly reliable transmission links are used to handle communication in the ATM network. Therefore, no mechanism is provided in the ATM layer for detecting errors in the Payload fields of cells. Error detection mechanisms must be provided in a layer above the ATM layer if an error-free transmission service is required. The ATM layer does specify error detection mechanisms for detecting corrupted cell headers.

The flow control function attempts to prevent the network from becoming overloaded. The primary method used for flow control is input rate control, in which a limit is placed on the rate at which each switch accepts cells arriving over input transmission paths.

Congestion control mechanisms come into play if the network, or some portion of it, becomes overloaded in spite of the flow control mechanisms. The principal technique used to control congestion in an ATM network is to discard cells.

Chapter 9 describes the functions performed in the ATM Adaptation layer.

The ATM Adaptation Layer

The *ATM Adaptation layer (AAL)* is the uppermost layer in the ATM architecture. As we introduced in Chapter 3, the ATM Adaptation layer provides the required interface between ATM user network software and the ATM network itself. The AAL is implemented only in ATM endpoint devices and is not used in ATM switches (see Fig. 9.1).

AAL SERVICE CLASSES

As we described in Chapter 2, an ATM network is capable of transporting a variety of different types of network traffic. Therefore, the ATM Adaptation layer (AAL) must be capable of handling all these different types of information. Specifically, the ATM Adaptation layer must be able to work with telephone voice information, packet data traffic, images,

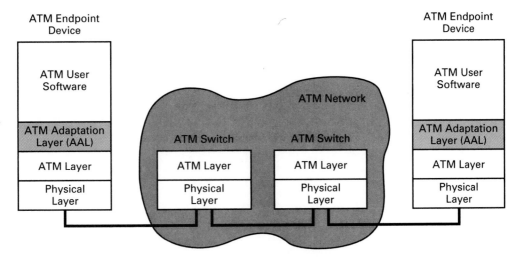

Figure 9.1 The ATM Adaptation layer of the ATM architecture.

audio, and video. In order to support these very different types of information, the ATM standards for the ATM Adaptation layer define four different classes of service: classes A, B, C, and D.

Class A Service—Circuit Emulation

Class A service is designed to have many of the same characteristics as the service provided by an analog channel in a conventional telecommunications network. The service is connection-oriented and requires that a connection be established between the sending and receiving ATM users before information can be exchanged between them. Class A service assumes that the sending ATM user provides input in the form of a continuous bit stream with a constant bit rate.

Class A service provides an isochronous delivery service, so the receiving ATM user is provided with a bit stream with the same constant bit rate as that transmitted by the sender. This class of service specifies mechanisms for clock synchronization used for matching the bit rates of the sender and receiver. Class A service is intended to support voice and video applications where information needs to be transmitted through the network at a constant rate.

Class B Service—Variable Bit Rate

Class B service is similar to class A. It is connection-oriented and assumes that the transmission takes the form of a continuous bit stream. Class B service is isochronous, and clock synchronization is provided for matching the receiver's bit rate with the transmitter's. However, with class B service, the bit stream can flow at a variable rate. Class B service is intended to support voice and video traffic that has been encoded and compressed, so the flow of the bit stream may vary from one point in the transmission to another.

Class C Service—Connection-Oriented Data

Class C service is intended to provide the type of service typically provided by a WAN link in a computer network or by a data link implemented in a packet-switched data network, such as one conforming to the ITU-T X.25 specification.

Class C service requires that a point-to-point connection be established between the sending and receiving users before data transfer can take place between them. After the connection has been established, the source user sends information into the network in the form of packets of varying sizes. These packets are eventually received by the destination ATM user software. With class C service, the arrival rate of packets at the destination ATM user may vary and may not match that of the transmitter.

Class D Service—Connectionless Data

Class D service is intended to provide the type of data transfer service associated with computer networks that have a connectionless style of operation, such as a typical local area network. Class D service also can also be used in place of the service provided by a connectionless wide area network, such as the Internet or a private WAN that implements the TCP/IP protocol family.

With class D service, the information to be carried through the ATM network takes the form of varying-size packets that may have a variable arrival rate. Unlike classes A, B, and C, class D service does not require that a connection be established between the sending and receiving ATM user software. Each packet the source ATM user software sends into the network must contain full source and destination network addresses and is transmitted independently of any other packets. Each packet can be sent to a single specified receiver, or it can be multicast to multiple receiving users.

AAL SUBLAYER STRUCTURE

The ATM Adaptation layer consists of two sublayers: the *Convergence sublayer (CS)* and the *Segmentation and Reassembly (SAR) sublayer.* The Convergence sublayer is itself subdivided into two sublayers: the *Service Specific Convergence sublayer (SSCS)* and the *Common Part Convergence sublayer (CPCS)* These layer and sublayer relationships are shown in Fig. 9.2.

Convergence Sublayer

The Convergence sublayer (CS) is responsible for providing functions needed for the particular type of service being provided. The Service Specific Convergence sublayer (SSCS)

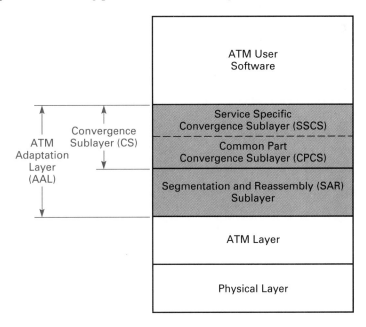

Figure 9.2   The ATM Adaptation layer (AAL) is divided into layers and sublayers.

functions are application-dependent, and in some cases, this part of the Convergence sublayer may be null. The Common Part Convergence sublayer (CPCS) provides functions required for all users of a particular type of service. These functions vary from one type of AAL service to another.

Segmentation and Reassembly Sublayer

The Segmentation and Reassembly (SAR) sublayer in a source ATM endpoint device is responsible for packaging into 48-octet Payload fields the data arriving from the Convergence sublayer. The SAR sublayer passes individual Payload fields down to the ATM layer for inclusion in cells for transmission. The SAR sublayer in a destination ATM endpoint device is responsible for accepting Payload fields from the ATM layer, reconstructing the information contained in cell Payload fields, and passing it up in its original form to the Convergence sublayer.

AAL SUBLAYER DATA UNITS

Figure 9.3 shows the names of the different types of data units involved in AAL processing. Following OSI model terminology, the user data unit, or *frame*, enters AAL as an AAL-SDU. (OSI protocol-data-units (PDUs) and service-data-units (SDUs) are described in Appendix C

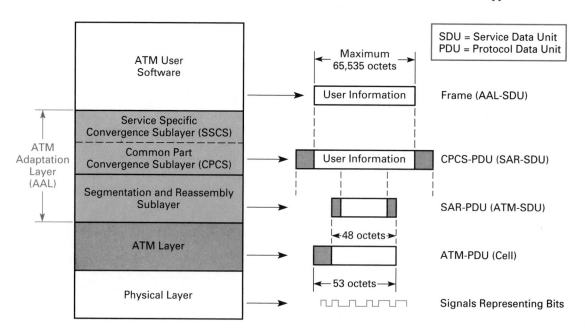

Figure 9.3   The ATM Adaptation Layer (AAL) consists of sublayers that may add protocol control information (PCI) in the form of headers and trailers to user data before passing it to the ATM layer for packaging into cells.

for those readers unfamiliar with OSI concepts and terminology.) The AAL-SDU can be of any size up to a maximum of 65,535 octets to support the protocols required to provide the class C connection-oriented and class D connectionless data transfer services.

CPCS adds header and trailer information to each AAL-SDU it receives, forming a CPCS-PDU. The CPCS-PDU enters the SAR sublayer as an SAR-SDU. The SAR sublayer divides the SAR-SDU into segments. Depending on the service class, the SAR sublayer may add an SAR header and trailer to each segment, forming an SAR-PDU.

Each SAR-PDU is 48 octets in length and enters the ATM layer as an ATM-SDU. The ATM layer adds a 5-octet cell header to the ATM-SDU to create the final 53-octet ATM-PDU, or cell.

AAL PROTOCOLS

The protocol control information contained in the 5-octet cell headers are used to control the operation of the ATM layer and the Physical layer. Protocol control information contained within the Payload fields of certain cells is used to control the functions required to provide the four types of AAL service.

A series of protocols are being defined that specify the formats of the cell payload fields used to carry AAL protocol control information and the procedures required to provide each class of AAL service. The various AAL protocols, which are referred to using numbers, are described in the following sections.

AAL TYPE 1 PROTOCOL

The *AAL type 1 protocol (AAL-1)* defines the cell Payload field formats and protocol procedures used to provide ATM users with AAL class A service. As described earlier, class A service is connection-oriented, has a constant bit rate, and supports a fixed timing relationship between the sending and receiving ATM users. With the AAL type 1 protocol, input to and output from an ATM user is in the form of a continuous bit stream with a constant bit rate.

Segmentation and Reassembly Sublayer Functions

As we saw earlier in this chapter, the SAR sublayer in a source ATM endpoint device is responsible for packaging bits from the input bit stream into 48-octet Payload fields for transport in cells through the ATM network. The SAR sublayer in the receiving ATM endpoint is responsible for constructing an output bit stream from the cells it receives. Box 9.1 illustrates the data format used for the 48-octet Payload field within the 53-octet cell when ATM endpoints are using the AAL-1 protocol.

As bits are received from the input bit stream, they are placed into a cell. When all 47 octets in the User Data field have been filled, the Sequence Number (SN) and Sequence Number Protection (SNP) values are calculated and added as the 48th octet. The

---

BOX 9.1   AAL type 1 Payload field format.

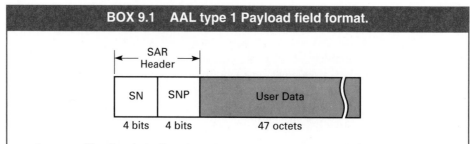

- **Sequence Number (SN).** Contains a 3-bit sequence number used to perform sequence checking to detect lost, misinserted, or damaged cells. The fourth bit, called the CS Indicator, is used for different purposes depending on the type of data being transferred.

- **Sequence Number Protection (SNP).** A 4-bit cyclic redundancy check value used for error detection and correction of the SN field.

- **User Data.** Data being sent from the source user to the destination user.

---

full 48 octets of data is then passed to the ATM layer for packaging in a cell for transmission. When handling slow-speed bit streams, the time it would take to fill a complete 47-octet User Data field might cause excessive transit delays. In such a case, the AAL-1 protocol in the sending and receiving endpoints might agree to use a User Data field smaller than 47 octets in each cell.

As data is received from the ATM layer, the Sequence Number field is used to detect lost, misinserted, and damaged cells. The Sequence Number Protection field allows for recovery of some bit errors. Errors that cannot be corrected cause an error indication to be passed to the Convergence sublayer.

Convergence Sublayer Functions

For the AAL-1 protocol, the Convergence sublayer performs the following functions:

- Smoothing jitter
- Handling lost, misinserted, or damaged cells
- Synchronizing clocks
- Supporting framed data transport

With AAL-1 the Convergence sublayer compensates for jitter (variations in transit delay) by buffering data as it is received. If variations in transit delay exceed the ability of the buffer to provide bits to the destination ATM user at a constant rate, the Convergence sublayer may insert extra bits when the buffer is empty or drop excess bits when the buffer overflows.

Handling lost, misinserted, or damaged cells may involve inserting dummy cells or discarding extra cells. In some cases, error-correction techniques may be used to reconstruct lost cells. In other cases, lost cells are replaced by cells with predetermined bit patterns in the payload field.

Clock Synchronization

The AAL-1 protocol is designed to provide the isochronous class A service by passing data to the destination ATM user at the same rate as the source ATM user delivers the data to its endpoint. In order to provide an isochronous service, the clocks that control processing in the source and destination endpoints must be synchronized. The two methods that can be used to provide this synchronization include the use of a synchronous residual time stamp and the use of an adaptive clock.

Synchronous Residual Time Stamp

The *Synchronous Residual Time Stamp (SRTS)* approach to clock synchronization assumes that each endpoint has its own clock and that there is also a networkwide reference clock available. The reference clock must be of lower resolution than the clocks used by the endpoints and thus must cycle much more slowly than the endpoint clocks. As the source endpoint processes the input bit stream, it keeps track of the number of its own clock cycles that occur in one cycle of the reference clock. The source endpoint periodically uses this value as a time stamp that it sends across the network to the destination endpoint. The destination endpoint uses the received time stamp and the reference clock to control the rate at which it receives bits from the network. Time stamps are calculated and sent at regular intervals to enable the two endpoints to stay in synchronization.

Adaptive Clock

The *Adaptive Clock (AC)* method of clock synchronization does not require a networkwide reference clock. This method requires that the receiving AAL-1 entity buffers the bits it receives. As the receiving AAL-1 entity receives bits from the ATM layer it stores them in a buffer before passing them up to the receiving ATM user. The AAL-1 entity removes bits from the buffer as it passes them to the ATM user and adds bits to the buffer as it receives them from the ATM layer. If the output bit stream is being processed at exactly the same rate as the input bit stream, the total number of bits in the buffer will remain the same. If the number of bits in the buffer falls below a certain level, the AAL-1 process causes that endpoint's clock to run more slowly. If the number of bits in the buffer increases above a certain level, the AAL-1 process speeds up the endpoint's clock.

The adaptive clock synchronization method is effective for smoothing out jitter. However, the time each bit spends in the buffer adds to the overall transit delay experienced by the two communicating ATM users.

Structured Data Transfer

Commonly used Physical layer protocols, such as SONET/SDH and PDH (see Chapter 7), use framed data transport. The *Structured Data Transfer (SDT)* protocol is used in conjunction with framed data transport in which a single transmission frame might be carried by a sequence of ATM cells. With SDT, the CS Indicator bit in the cell header is used to indicate that the first octet of the User Data field contains a pointer. The pointer specifies the location within the User Data field that begins a new physical transmission frame. Not every cell contains the start of a frame, so the pointer octet is used only when the cell contains the beginning of a new transmission frame.

AAL TYPE 2 PROTOCOL

The AAL type 2 protocol (AAL-2) defines the formats of cell Payload fields and the protocol procedures required to provide ATM users with AAL class B service. Class B service is connection-oriented and supports a variable bit rate.

At the time of writing, specifications for the AAL-2 protocol were still under discussion. Box 9.2 shows a likely cell Payload field format to be used to provide class B service. The lengths and uses of each field were not finalized at the time of writing.

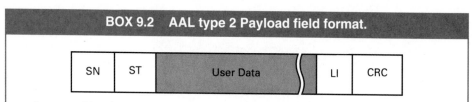

BOX 9.2   AAL type 2 Payload field format.

- **Sequence Number (SN).** A value used to perform sequence checking to detect lost or misinserted cells.

- **Segment Type (ST).** A value used to indicate that the cell contains the beginning, middle, or end of a message. This field is used for message segmentation and reassembly.

- **User Data.** Data being sent from the source user to the destination user.

- **Length Indicator (LI).** A value that indicates how much of the User Data field contains user data.

- **CRC.** A cyclic redundancy check value used for error detection and correction of the User Data field.

The Segment Type and Length Indicator fields allow input data in the form of logical units to be segmented into cells for transmission and then reassembled into logical units for the receiving ATM user. Since the size of logical units may not be exact multiples of the cell size, the last cell for the logical unit may be only partially filled. The Length Indicator field indicates how much data the last cell in a logical unit contains.

Class B service is intended to be used for variable bit rate voice and video applications, where data has been compressed by removing redundant information. Since there is less redundancy in the data being transmitted, there may be greater sensitivity to errors, and lost or damaged cells might be more noticeable to the ATM users. The Sequence Number field allows for detection of lost, misinserted or damaged cells, for some forms of bit error correction, and for cell insertion and deletion. Additionally, the CRC field allows for correction of some types of errors in damaged cells.

As with AAL-1, AAL-2 requires clock synchronization between the sending and receiving ATM users. Although the bit stream flows at a variable rate, the receiving user needs to accept data at a rate sufficiently close to that at which it was sent so that the audio or video information presented to a person at the final destination will appear continuous. Additionally, some applications may require the synchronization of separate bit streams. For example, when transmitting a video program, there may be separate bit streams for the audio and video components of the program, each with different variable bit rates.

The AAL-2 protocol to provide class B service has the challenge of providing a service that provides varying capacity as required for variable bit rates and that is still able to meet timing requirements for continuous delivery of information. Therefore, this protocol has been difficult to formulate and was still under development at the time of writing.

AAL TYPE 3/4 PROTOCOL

The AAL type 3/4 protocol (AAL-3/4) defines the cell Payload field formats and protocol procedures necessary to provide both class C and class D service used for the transport of computer network traffic. As we discussed earlier, class C service is connection-oriented, and class D is connectionless.

For these classes of service, input to the network takes the form of discrete packets of information that may be generated at a variable rate. It is not necessary to maintain a timing relationship between the sending and receiving ATM users in providing class C or class D service.

With the AAL-3/4 protocol, header and trailer information is added by both the CS and SAR sublayers. We will look at the control information for each of these sublayers separately.

The CPCS-PDU and SAR-SDU

After formatting the CPCS header and trailer fields and inserting the proper amount of padding to bring the PDU to a multiple of 4 octets, the CPCS sublayer passes the CPCS-PDU to the SAR sublayer as an SAR-SDU.

The CPCS-PDU and SAR-SDU format is shown in Box 9.3.

The SAR-PDU and ATM-SDU

The SAR sublayer divides the SAR-SDU into 44-octet segments. If necessary, it pads the last segment to bring in up to a total of 44 octets. The SAR sublayer then adds the SAR header and trailer fields to each segment to form an SAR-PDU. The SAR sublayer passes the SAR-PDU to the ATM layer as an ATM-SDU.

The SAR-PDU and ATM-SDU format is shown in Box 9.4.

Message Mode Versus Streaming Mode

The AAL-3/4 protocol can operate in either message mode or streaming mode. In *message mode*, input blocks can be fixed or varying in length. Each block is passed down to the Convergence sublayer, which transports the user data through the ATM network in the

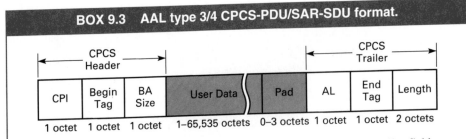

BOX 9.3   AAL type 3/4 CPCS-PDU/SAR-SDU format.

- **Common Part Indicator (CPI).** Defines how other CPCS header and trailer fields are coded.
- **Beginning Tag.** Contains a value that is incremented for each CPCS-PDU processed. The same value is placed in the Ending Tag field. On the receiving side, the two values are compared to provide an error check.
- **Buffer Allocation Size (BASize).** Specifies the buffer size required when the CPCS-PDU is received and reassembled.
- **User Data.** Contains the data unit passed down to the ATM Adaptation Layer by the ATM user software.
- **Pad.** Added to make the PDU length a multiple of 4 octets. This ensures that the CPCS trailer begins on a 32-bit boundary, making processing more efficient on some computers.
- **Alignment Field (AL).** Added to make the CPCS trailer 4 octets in length.
- **End Tag.** Contains the same value as the Beginning Tag, is used for error checking.
- **Length.** Contains a binary value specifying the length of the entire CPCS-PDU.

form of one or more CPCS-PDUS. In *streaming mode,* input blocks are fixed in length, and multiple input blocks may be combined in one CPCS-PDU with a single CS header and trailer. In either mode, each CPCS-PDU is segmented by the SAR sublayer so that each segment of a CPCS-PDU is contained in a separate cell.

Error-Handling Mechanisms

We stated earlier that ATM networks are designed to operate over highly reliable communication links. The ATM layer simply discards cells when occasional errors occur during transmission. The type 1 and type 2 protocols are designed for audio and video applications in which occasional errors have little or no effect on the two communicating ATM users. However, the type 3/4 protocol supplying class C and class D services is designed to support data transmission in computer networks. Computer network traffic is generally not as sensitive to timing as audio and video information, but computer data is very sensitive to errors. In general, computer data must be transported through the network in an essentially error-free manner. A change to even a single bit in a long transmission can affect the meaning of the information being transmitted.

To handle the requirement for an error-free data link, the AAL-3/4 protocol incorporates error handling procedures not defined for the class 1 and class 2 protocols. These

BOX 9.4 AAL type 3/3 SAR/PDU format.

- **Segment Type (ST).** A 2-bit value used to indicate that the cell contains the beginning, middle, or end of a message:
  — 10—beginning of message
  — 00—continuation of message
  — 01—end of message
  — 11—both beginning and end of a single segment message

  This field is used for message segmentation and reassembly.

- **Sequence Number (SN).** A 4-bit value used to perform sequence checking to detect lost or misinserted cells.

- **Multiplexer ID (MID).** A 10-bit value used to multiplex multiple user connections over a single physical ATM connection.

- **CPCS Segment.** A 44-octet portion of a CPCS-PDU containing control information and data being sent from the source user to the destination user.

- **Length Indicator (LI).** A 6-bit value that indicates how many octets of the User Data field contains user data.

- **CRC.** A cyclic redundancy check value used for error detection and correction of the CPCS Segment field.

procedures allow the ATM Adaptation layer to provide an error-free link by detecting and recovering missing information that results from cells the ATM layer discards when transmission errors occur.

Error-Detection Mechanisms

The AAL-3/4 protocol provides for several types of error checking to help ensure that no uncorrected errors occur during transmission. The following are error-handling mechanisms applied to each individual cell the SAR sublayer passes down to the ATM layer for transmission:

- A CRC check is made to detect cells that have been corrupted during transmission.

- A Sequence Number field is used to detect lost or misinserted cells.

- Multiplexing Identifier and Sequence Type fields are used to ensure that cells are properly reassembled into a CPCS-PDU.

- A Header Error Check field is used to detect errors in the cell header.

In addition to the error-handling mechanisms applied to each individual SAR-PDU cell, the Beginning Tag/End Tag fields and Length field that are part of a complete CPCS-PDU provide additional checks to ensure that all the cells making up a complete CPCS-PDU have been received and reassembled correctly.

Error-Recovery Mechanisms

In addition to mechanisms for detecting corrupted SAR-PDUs or CPCS-PDUs, the AAL-3/4 protocol specifies mechanisms for dealing with errors that are detected in a complete CPCS-PDU. The AAL-3/4 defines three separate modes of operation that differ by the mechanisms that are employed for error recovery in each mode:

- **Non-assured Operation with Discard.** With this mode of operation, retransmission is not attempted and the user information contained in corrupted CPCS-PDUs is not passed to the user.

- **Non-assured Operation with Delivery.** With this mode of operation, retransmission is not attempted, but the user information contained in corrupted CPCS-PDUs is passed to the user.

- **Assured Operation.** With this mode of operation, the ATM Adaptation layer handles the retransmission of corrupted CPCS-PDUs so the ATM user software perceives a completely error-free data link. Retransmission is a complex issue, since it may require acknowledgments and might involve retransmission of all the cells making up a complete CPCS-PDU. Detailed specifications for this mode of operation are still in development.

Providing Class C Connection-Oriented Service

As we have already discussed, the AAL-3/4 protocol supports both the connection-oriented class C service and the connectionless class D service. Since the basic operation of an ATM network is connection-oriented in nature, the ATM switched and semipermanent connections discussed in Chapter 8 can be used directly to provide the connections required to supply ATM users with class C service.

Providing Class D Connectionless Service

Class D service is connectionless and does not require that a connection be established between ATM users before data transmission takes place. Therefore, some discussion is needed to show how the connections required during ATM network operation are used to provide the class D connectionless data delivery service.

The class D connectionless service is intended to provide a transmission capability with the same characteristics as that offered by a shared-medium LAN data link or by a connectionless computer network like the Internet. However, as we have seen, the basic operational characteristics of an ATM network are connection-oriented. The VPI and VCI values in the ATM header used to route cells through the ATM network are based on the existence of virtual path connections (VPCs) and virtual channel connections (VCCs) between the sending and receiving ATM users.

Connectionless Servers

One approach to providing class D connectionless service that has received considerable attention is the use of network devices that play the role of *connectionless servers*. With the connectionless server approach, each end-user workstation might include a network interface card (NIC) and appropriate software to implement an ATM endpoint function. Each ATM workstation is connected via a virtual channel connection (VCC) to a device functioning as a connectionless server (see Fig. 9.4).

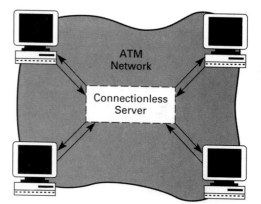

Figure 9.4 When a connectionless server function is used to provide class D connectionless service, each ATM user must have a direct VCC connection to the connectionless server.

With the connectionless server approach, ATM workstations transmit frames in the same manner as they would if connected to a conventional shared-medium LAN. The frames are segmented into cells by the ATM Adaptation layer in the workstation and sent over an ATM VCC to the connectionless server. The connectionless server analyzes the first cell of each frame to identify its destination address and to determine the best ATM connection required to reach that destination. The connectionless server then forwards all the cells making up that frame to their destination over the chosen ATM connection.

Multicasting Mechanisms

A key characteristic of connectionless computer networks is that they typically use multicasting mechanisms that allow a network user to send a message to two or more destinations in a single operation. On a connectionless LAN data link, every frame transmitted is received by every other station on the LAN. A receiving station uses the destination address value in the frame to determine whether it should accept and process the frame. To handle multicasting, certain destination address values are used to refer to groups of stations rather than to a single station. All stations in a given group are then directed to handle frames that contain the group address as well as frames addressed specifically to them.

Techniques used to provide a multicast capability in an ATM network are generally based on converting the physical structure of the ATM network into a logical tree structure. In the logical tree structure, the source ATM endpoint is the root of the tree and all other ATM endpoints in the network are leaves. Data sent from the ATM user at the root of the tree is delivered to all the leaves, as shown in Fig. 9.5.

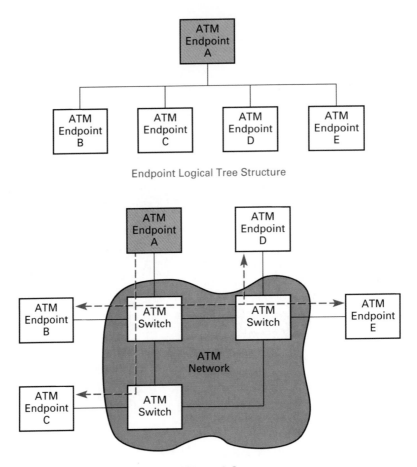

Figure 9.5   Multicasting is based on an ATM endpoint logical tree structure.

The type of connection created by generating a logical tree structure is called a *multipoint connection*. In implementing a multipoint connection, the appropriate ATM switches must make copies of the cells in question and must relay them over multiple transmission paths to implement the required multicast tree structure. The logical tree structure can be defined in advance by a network administrator through a network management action, or the tree structure can be defined dynamically and changed as required.

Notice that a multicast connection provides transmission from the root user to the leaves but does not support transmission from leaf to leaf. In order to support a complete broadcast facility among a set of ATM endpoints, a separate multicast tree must be defined for each endpoint.

Multicast operation in an ATM network has the following characteristics:

- Cells are copied as late as possible. In the example in Fig. 9.5, separate copies of the cells destined for endpoints D and E are created in the switch connected directly to endpoints D and E.

- VPI/VCI values are assigned and swapped as with any other type of connection. No special VPI/VCI values are reserved for multicasting.

Multiplexing Mechanisms

During operation of an ATM network, it is possible for more than one source ATM user to concurrently send frames to the same destination. When this occurs, multiple source ATM users all share a single ATM connection in reaching that destination. In a connectionless server environment, as illustrated in Fig. 9.6, this situation could lead to cells from different frames being intermixed on the same ATM connection. The AAL-3/4 protocol includes multiplexing mechanisms for allowing the cells associated with different ATM users to be distinguished from one another.

The Multiplexing Identification (MID) value in the SAR-PDU header (see Box 9.4) can be used to identify all the cells carrying data from a particular frame. All cells from a particular frame have the same MID value, which will be different from that used for any other frame. Therefore, the MID values in cells can be used in implementing a multiplexing mechanism that can be used to assign cells to their proper frames when they are being reassembled at the destination.

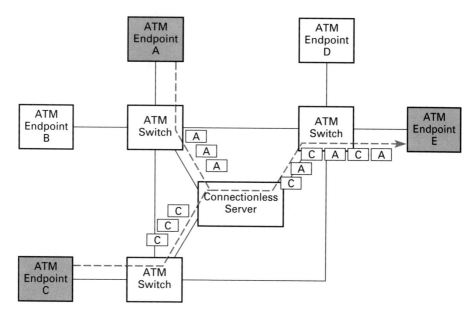

Figure 9.6   When a connectionless server is used to provide LAN-like services in an ATM network, cells from different CPCS-PDUs may be intermixed on the same connection.

Compatibility with IEEE 802.6

The use of the MID field for multiplexing provides compatibility with Switched Multimegabit Data Service (SMDS). SMDS, defined by the IEEE 802.6 Metropolitan Area Network (MAN) standard. An IEEE MAN standard describes a data link that provides connectionless LAN-type service over an entire metropolitan area. It uses the same 53-octet cell format as ATM and uses the MID identifier to allow cells from multiple frames to be multiplexed on the MAN.

AAL TYPE 5 PROTOCOL

The AAL type 5 protocol (AAL-5) is an alternative protocol that can also be used in providing class C and D services. The AAL-5 protocol is less complex than AAL-3/4 and can be used when a multicasting mechanism is required but when there is no need for multiplexing.

AAL-5 has been defined as an alternative to AAL-3/4 because of the complexity and protocol overhead associated with AAL-3/4. When AAL-3/4 is used to provide class C or class D service, 4 octets in each cell are occupied by an SAR header and trailer. In addition, 8 octets for the CPCS header and trailer are added to each frame that a user transmits, with up to 3 octets of padding also required.

With the AAL-5 protocol, CPCS adds an 8-octet trailer and sufficient padding to the entire CPCS-PDU and makes the resulting CPCS-PDU an even multiple of 48 octets. This allows the CPCS-PDU to be divided evenly into cells. The AAL-5 protocol requires no protocol control information in the individual cells, and all 48 payload octets can be used to carry user data. For frames larger than 80 octets, AAL-5 is more efficient in terms of payload usage than AAL-3/4. Box 9.5 shows the CPCS-PDU format for AAL type 5.

The SAR layer divides the CPCS-PDU into 48-octet segments and passes each segment to the ATM layer for transmission without having to add additional CPI to each cell. The SAR entity in the destination system reassembles the cells to create the original CPCS-PDU. After all the cells are received, the Convergence sublayer examines the information in the CPCS trailer to check that the CPCS-PDU has been received correctly. The user data portion is then passed up to the AAL entity in the destination system.

In order to reassemble the CPCS-PDU properly, the receiving AAL entity must be able to determine when it has received the last cell making up a complete CPCS-PDU. The sending SAR entity directs the ATM layer to flag the last cell in a CPCS-PDU by setting to 1 the last bit in the Payload Type field in the cell header. When the receiving entity receives a cell having that bit set to 1, it knows that the cell is the last cell in a CPCS-PDU.

The AAL-5 protocol offers basically the same service options as the AAL-3/4 protocol. Blocking and segmentation of data and other service-specific functions are performed at the SSCS level. For error checking, the CPCS trailer Length field assures that no cells have been lost, and the CRC value assures they have been received correctly. The same assured delivery and non-assured delivery options are available to the user. Multicasting is supported, but, since the AAL-5 protocol does not specify an MID field or its equivalent, AAL-5 does not support multiplexing.

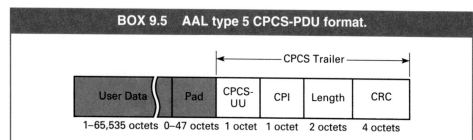

BOX 9.5   AAL type 5 CPCS-PDU format.

User Data	Pad	CPCS-UU	CPI	Length	CRC
1–65,535 octets	0–47 octets	1 octet	1 octet	2 octets	4 octets

CPCS Trailer

- **User Data.** Data being sent from the source user to the destination user.
- **Pad.** Padding octets added to make the CPCS-PDU a multiple of 48 octets.
- **CPCS User-to-User Indication (CPCS-UU).** Control information passed from the source CPCS to the destination CPCS.
- **Common Part Indicator (CPI).** Not currently used.
- **Length.** The length of the User Data field. Used by the receiving AAL entity to distinguish between user data and padding.
- **CRC.** A 32-bit cyclic redundancy check value used for error detection in the entire CPCS-PDU.

AAL TYPE 0 PROTOCOL

AAL type 0 defines a null service interface and a protocol that essentially does nothing. With the AAL-0 protocol, the ATM user software is required to break the user data into cells and completely format each cell's 5-octet header. The AAL entity performs no processing on the cells other than passing them down to the ATM layer for transmission. The type 0 protocol is defined for use by ATM users who wish to communicate using their own private protocol.

CONNECTION MANAGEMENT FUNCTIONS

The ATM Adaptation layer includes a *signaling* AAL service used to manage the establishment and termination of switched ATM connections. As we learned in Chapter 8, ATM connections can be either semipermanent or switched. A switched connection is often referred to as a *call*. Semipermanent connections are set up by ATM network management functions (see Chapter 10). If an ATM network fails and is later restarted, network management functions are automatically invoked to restore all semipermanent connections. If a switched connection is lost due to a network failure, the endpoints that were using the connection must request that another connection be established. ATM endpoints use the functions making up the AAL signaling service to establish switched connections.

ATM signaling includes three functions related to switched connections: call setup, call control, and call clearing.

Call Setup

The call setup procedure defines messages that are exchanged when an ATM endpoint requests that a connection be established. Figure 9.7 illustrates the message flow for establishing a connection. As part of connection establishment, VPI and VCI values to be used along the connection's path through the ATM network are determined. Quality-of-Service (QoS) parameters, included in the call setup messages, are also used to determine the type of service required for the connection.

Call Control

The Call Control function is used to check on the status of a connection and to change the parties included in a multipoint connection. Box 9.6 lists the messages used to perform the Call Control function.

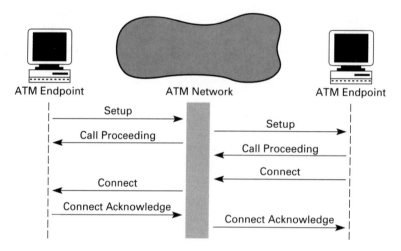

Figure 9.7   ATM switched circuit setup protocol message exchanges.

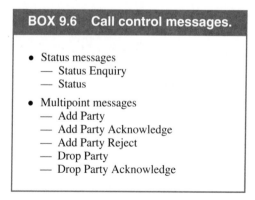

BOX 9.6   Call control messages.

- Status messages
  — Status Enquiry
  — Status
- Multipoint messages
  — Add Party
  — Add Party Acknowledge
  — Add Party Reject
  — Drop Party
  — Drop Party Acknowledge

Call Clearing

The Call Clearing function is used to terminate a connection. Figure 9.8 shows the message flow for call clearing.

Signaling Channels

Certain VCI and VPI values are reserved for use in implementing signaling channels. Signaling messages are exchanged using VCCs that are separate from the VCCs used to transfer data. In addition to these assigned values, *meta-signaling* allows an ATM endpoint to set up additional signaling channels. As with data transfer channels, signaling channels can be either point-to-point or multipoint.

Signaling AAL Protocol

The signaling AAL protocol defines the message formats used to perform signaling functions and the procedures governing the exchange of those messages. The signaling AAL protocol provides a reliable delivery service by handling error detection and retransmission of corrupted signaling messages. For the CPCS and SAR sublayers, the signaling AAL uses essentially the same procedures defined for the AAL-5 protocol.

Figure 9.9 shows how the Service Specific Convergence sublayer (SSCS) performs two major service specific functions in handling signaling functions: a Service Specific Coordination Function (SSCF) and a Service Specific Connection-Oriented Peer-to-Peer Protocol (SSCOP).

Service Specific Coordination Function (SSCF)

The Service Specific Coordination Function (SSCF) provides the interface between the ATM user and the Service Specific Connection-Oriented Peer-to-Peer Protocol (SSCOP).

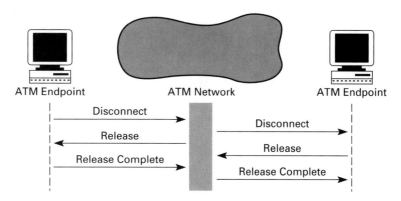

Figure 9.8 ATM switched circuit disconnect protocol message exchanges.

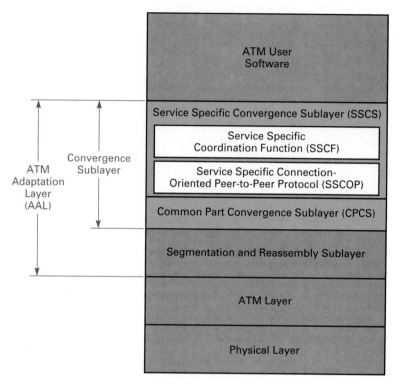

Figure 9.9   The Service Specific Convergence Sublayer of the ATM adaptation layer performs two major service specific functions to handle signaling: a Service Specific Coordination Function (SSCF) and a Service Specific Connection-Oriented Peer-to-Peer Protocol (SSCOP).

Service Specific Connection-Oriented Peer-to-Peer Protocol (SSCOP)

The Service Specific Connection-Oriented Peer-to-Peer Protocol (SSCOP) is responsible for the following functions:

- **Data Transfer.** Signaling messages are transmitted between endpoints, with the sequence of the messages preserved. Data transfer can be either assured or non-assured.

- **Error Detection and Correction.** As part of assured operation, a sequencing mechanism is used to detect missing or duplicate signaling messages. If a signaling message is not received correctly and acknowledged, it is retransmitted.

- **Flow Control.** A sliding window mechanism allows the receiver to control the rate at which the sender transmits data over a signaling connection.

- **Connection Management.** Signaling connections are established, maintained, released, and reset.

SUMMARY

The ATM Adaptation layer (AAL) is the uppermost layer in the ATM architecture and provides an interface between ATM user network software and the ATM network. In order to work with telephone voice information, packet data traffic, images, audio, and video, the ATM standards for the ATM Adaptation layer define four different classes of service: class A service is a circuit emulation service; class B service supports variable-bit-rate circuit services; class C service is designed for connection-oriented data transport; class D service supports connectionless data transfer.

The ATM Adaptation layer consists of two sublayers: the Convergence sublayer (CS) and the Segmentation and Reassembly (SAR) sublayer. The Convergence sublayer is itself subdivided into two sublayers: the Service Specific Convergence sublayer (SSCS) and the Common Part Convergence sublayer (CPCS).

The user data unit, or frame, enters AAL as a variable-length AAL-SDU. CPCS adds header and trailer information to AAL-SDUS to form CPCS-PDUs. The SAR sublayer may divide the SAR-SDU into segments and add an SAR header and trailer to each segment to form an SAR-PDU. The ATM layer then adds a 5-octet cell header to the ATM-SDU to create a 53-octet ATM-PDU, or cell.

The protocols for the ATM Adaptation layer include the AAL type 1 protocol to provide class A service. The type 1 protocol defines a segmentation and reassembly function to package bits from the input bit stream into 48-octet Payload fields for transport in cells. It also uses the Convergence sublayer for smoothing jitter; handling lost, misinserted, or damaged cells; synchronizing clocks; and supporting framed data transport.

The AAL type 2 protocol provides the class B service, which provides a variable bit rate for delivery of compressed voice and video applications. The type 2 protocol must be designed to provide the varying capacity needed to support variable bit rates and also meet the timing requirements required for continuous delivery of audio and video information.

The AAL Type 3/4 protocol (AAL-3/4) is used to provide both class C and class D service used for the transport of computer network traffic. The AAL-3/4 protocol can operate in either message mode or streaming mode. In message mode, input blocks can be fixed or varying in length. In streaming mode, input blocks are fixed in length. The AAL-3/4 protocol is designed for use in computer networks and specifies error handling procedures not specified by the type 1 and type 2 protocols. These procedures allow the ATM Adaptation layer to provide an error-free link by detecting and recovering missing information that results from discarded cells.

The AAL type 5 protocol (AAL-5) is a less complex protocol than AAL-3/4 that can alternatively be used to provide class C and class D services. The type 5 protocol can be used when a multicasting mechanism is required but when there is no need for multiplexing.

The AAL type 0 protocol defines a null service interface and a protocol that specifies no functions. AAL type 0 is used when two ATM users choose to use their own private protocol for communication.

The ATM Adaptation layer includes a signaling AAL service used to manage the establishment and termination of switched ATM connections. ATM signaling provides call setup, call control, and call clearing functions. The signaling AAL protocol provides a reliable delivery service that includes error detection and retransmission functions.

The next chapter describes some of the approaches to network management that are being used in ATM networks for controlling and monitoring the network.

Chapter 10

ATM Network Management

An important requirement for enterprise networking is the ability to manage large networks that consist of equipment purchased from many different vendors. This chapter discusses the fundamental techniques and strategies that are used to manage the operation of ATM networks.

Network management is generally concerned with monitoring the operation of components in the network, reporting on events that occur during network operation, and controlling the operational characteristics of the network and the components that make it up. The following are descriptions of these three categories of mechanisms that can be used in implementing network management functions:

- **Monitoring.** Monitoring involves determining the status and processing characteristics currently associated with different physical and logical components of the network. Depending on the type of component in question, monitoring can be done either by continuously checking the operation of the component, or it can be based on detecting the occurrence of extraordinary events during network operation.

- **Reporting.** The results of monitoring activities must be reported, or made available, either to a network administrator or to network management software operating in some machine on the network.

- **Controlling.** Based on the results of monitoring and reporting functions, the network administrator or the network management software should be able to modify the operational characteristics of the network and its components. These modifications should make it possible to resolve problems, to improve network performance, and to continue normal operation of the network.

NETWORK MANAGEMENT FUNCTIONAL AREAS

ISO has been active in the development of a series of standards relating to the management of all aspects of information processing systems. As part of this work, ISO has identified five major functional areas that need to be addressed as part of the management of communication networks that support information processing systems. Most of the approaches used today with network management architectures and software reflect the work done by ISO in this area.

The international standards that ISO is developing for the management of information processing systems divide management functions into five *specific management functional areas (SMFAS)*. These five functional areas, as they apply to the management of communication networks, are as follows:

- **Configuration Management.** Configuration management is concerned with the ability to identify the various components that make up the network configuration, to process additions, changes, or deletions to the configuration, to report on the status of components, and to start up or shut down all or any part of the network.

- **Fault Management.** Fault management is concerned with the ability to detect, isolate, and correct abnormal conditions that occur in the network environment.

- **Performance Management.** Performance management is concerned with the ability to evaluate activities of the network and to make adjustments to improve the network's performance.

- **Security Management.** Security management is concerned with the ability to monitor and control access to network resources.

- **Accounting Management.** Accounting management is concerned with the ability to identify costs and establish charges related to the use of network resources.

The following sections further describe each of these SMFAS.

Configuration Management

Configuration management is concerned with the continuous operation of the network on a day-to-day basis and with changes in the network configuration that occur over time. The system should maintain configuration information that reflects the physical and logical components that make up the network. As components are added, deleted, or changed in the way they operate or are interconnected, this should be reflected in the configuration information. The configuration information should also reflect the current status of the components.

Configuration management includes both data collection from network components, to identify them and determine their status, and data transmission to network resources, to implement desired changes in status. These changes in status may reflect normal start-up or shut-down operations or changes in configuration needed to improve performance or to bypass a failing component.

Fault Management

When problems occur during network operation, it is necessary to:

- Identify the cause of the problem.
- Determine how network operation can be continued until the fault is corrected.
- Make any changes required to continue operation with the failed component.
- Repair the failed component and make any changes required to return it to normal operation.

Fault management is concerned with the collection of data needed to identify and analyze failures in network operation. Appropriate status information should be generated in order to keep network users notified of changes in network service availability. Logs should also be maintained to provide problem tracking and control over time.

Performance Management

Performance management involves both monitoring and controlling network activities. Monitoring functions track service and resource usage levels and provide statistics on the responsiveness and reliability of the network. Performance management may also include corrective actions that need to be taken when service or usage levels reach a certain point, in order to keep performance within acceptable limits.

Security Management

Security management is responsible for controlling access to network resources. This involves:

- **Authentication.** Determining that the network user wishing to access network resources is, in fact, the person or process it claims to be.
- **Authorization.** Determining the access rights that an authenticated user has to a particular network resource.
- **Privacy.** Keeping unauthorized parties from being able to eavesdrop on network communications.

Authentication involves validating the claimed identity of an entity, which might be a person, an application program, or a system process. Authentication involves determining that you are who you say you are. This validation may be based on information supplied by the entity, such as a password, personal identification number (PIN), or secret phrase.

When the entity being authenticated is a person, authentication can also be based on the presentation of a physical object, such as a badge or card. For a person, it can also be based on a physical characteristic, such as a thumbprint, retinal scan, hand shape, or voice print. Different types of authentication information can be used in combination, as for example with an ATM card and its associated secret PIN value.

Authorization determines who can access a particular resource and what they can do with it. It is concerned with granting access rights to an authenticated user and with refusal of access to an unauthorized user.

Privacy is usually provided through the use of an encryption technique. Encryption involves the encoding and decoding of data based on a key. Two approaches to encryption are in common use today:

- **Data Encryption Standard (DES).** The Data Encryption Standard method of encryption is based on a single key, which must be used both to encrypt and decrypt the data. A consideration with this method is key management—how the key is provided to the recipient in order to decrypt the data without risk of the key being divulged to an unauthorized party.

- **Public/Private Key Encryption.** Public/private key encryption is based on work done by Ron Rivest, Adi Shamir, and Leonard Adelman, and is often referred to as RSA encryption. RSA encryption involves the use of a pair of keys. One key is used to encrypt the data; the other is required to decrypt it. One key is kept private, and the other is distributed publicly. Any user holding the public key can encrypt data and send it across the network. Only someone holding the private key is able to decrypt the data.

The public/private key system can be used to implement *digital signatures*. The holder of the private key uses the private key value to encrypt a name or other identifying information to be used as a signature. The recipient of the signature decrypts it with the public key. If the signature decrypts correctly, the recipient knows that the information must have been sent by the holder of the private key.

The public/private key system requires more processing power than the DES method. When large texts need to be encrypted, the two systems can be combined to provide a more efficient approach to encryption that is still sufficiently secure. The text is encrypted with the DES key. The DES key is then encrypted using the public key, and sent along with the encrypted text. The recipient decrypts the DES key with the private key and then uses the DES key to decrypt the text.

Accounting Management

A network is a shared resource that supports different users or groups of users. Different users often have widely varying requirements and consume varying amounts of network resources. Accounting management is concerned with recording information on the usage of network resources and then implementing a system for charging different network users for the resources they consume.

ATM MANAGEMENT STRUCTURE

Management of ATM networks involves the same basic mechanisms that are used in the management of other types of communication networks (see Fig. 10.1). Software entities called *access agents* are located throughout the network, in both hardware and software components. These agents monitor and control system elements in the devices in which the agents reside. Access agents running in a particular device are capable of communicating with each other and with a *node management* function also running in that device. The node management function monitors and controls each of the components making up an ATM device. The node management function is sometimes called *box management*. Network management software running in one or more systems in the network communicates with all the node management functions and provides centralized or distributed monitoring and control for the network as a whole.

OPERATIONS ADMINISTRATION AND MAINTENANCE

ATM management protocols are still in the process of being developed. One area where protocols have been specified is called *operations administration and maintenance*

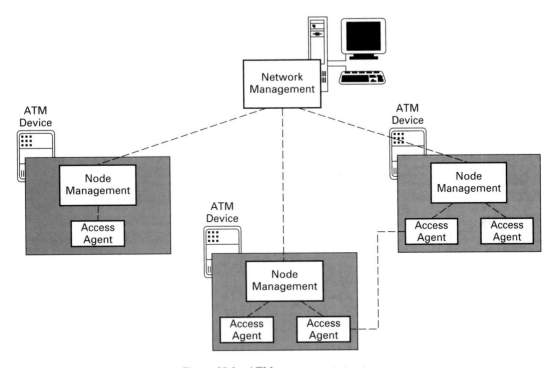

Figure 10.1   ATM management structure.

(OA&M). The ATM OA&M protocols that had been specified as of the time of writing address the following functions:

- **Performance Monitoring.** Monitoring of a managed entity by continuous or periodic checking of its functions. Results of the checking are reported to other management entities in the form of maintenance information.

- **Defect and Failure Detection.** Detection of malfunctions or predicted malfunctions based on continuous or periodic checking. Results are reported in the form of maintenance information or alarms.

- **System Protection.** Minimizing a fault in the system by deactivating a failed entity and switching to or activating an alternative component to bypass the failure.

- **Failure or Performance Reporting.** Reporting failure information, such as alarm indications, to other management entities, and responding to status report requests.

- **Fault Isolation.** Determining the cause of a fault through internal or external test mechanisms applied to a failed entity when failure information is not sufficient.

OA&M FUNCTIONAL LAYERS

The OA&M functions that have been defined for ATM have the layered structure shown in Fig. 10.2.

ATM Layer	F5	Virtual Channel (VC) Level	Virtual path links and virtual path connections
	F4	Virtual Path (VP) Level	Virtual channel links and virtual channel connections
Physical Layer	F3	Path Level	Portion of system between two elements that assemble/disassemble payload (cells)
	F2	Line Level	Portion of system between two elements that assemble/disassemble continuous bit streams
	F1	Section Level	Portion of line between two signal regenerators

Figure 10.2 Layered structure of Operations Administration and Maintenance (OA&M).

Physical Layer Functions

Levels F1, F2, and F3 in Fig. 10.2 are associated with the Physical layer of the ATM architecture. The exact functions of OA&M in these levels vary with the particular link protocol used. The Physical layer functions may include:

- **Performance Monitoring.** Evaluating and reporting on performance. Factors monitored include the rates of cell header errors, line errors, path errors, and section errors. Monitoring may be done continuously or on a periodic basis.

- **Fault Management.** Detecting, isolating, and correcting faults. Detection may be based on continuous monitoring or periodic testing. Fault conditions may include loss of cell rate decoupling (inclusion/deletion of idle cells), cell delineation, frame, signal, or pointers. Fault information is communicated in the form of messages that include the indicators listed in Box 10.1. Fault correction may involve deactivating the failed entity and switching to or activating an alternative component.

- **Facility Testing.** Verifying that the connection between path endpoints is active.

ATM Layer Functions

Levels 4 and 5 in Fig. 10.2 are associated with the ATM layer. Performance and availability monitoring is performed on virtual paths and virtual channels either on an end-to-end

---

BOX 10.1 Operations administration and management fault indicators.

- Alarm indication signal (AIS)
- Far-end remote failure (FERF)
- Remote alarm indication (RAI)
- Far-end block error (FEBE)
- Error frame indicator (EFI)

basis or on individual segments. Loopback testing is performed using cells that are dedicated to OA&M purposes and are identified by specific VPI or Payload Type values. Level 4 and 5 functions include:

- **Fault Management.** Detecting and reporting of faults. Fault detection includes detection of invalid VPI/VCI values and VP/VC availability checking. Availability checking is performed using continuity check cells, which are sent when no data cells are available to send. If no cells are received over a specific period of time, a fault is assumed to have occurred. AIS and FERF are used for fault notification.

- **Performance Management.** Inserting special performance management/reporting cells into a block of data cells. The cells are used to detect or measure error blocks, lost or damaged cells, cell delay, and so on.

- **Activation/Deactivation.** Activating and deactivating entities may be done in response to degraded performance or unavailability of a resource.

SIMPLE NETWORK MANAGEMENT PROTOCOL

An *Interim Local Management Interface (ILMI)* is a temporary network management interface that has been defined for use in ATM networks until the full ATM management standard has been completed. The ILMI is based on a protocol for network management called *Simple Network Management Protocol (SNMP)*. SNMP was originally designed to provide an easy-to-implement, but comprehensive, approach to network management in the TCP/IP environment. SNMP is now being applied in networks that conform to many other network architectures and is the network management approach currently used in ATM networks that implement ILMI.

SNMP Components

Figure 10.3 shows the overall architectural structure of the network management components associated with SNMP. The following are brief descriptions of each of the SNMP architectural components:

- **Network Management Station.** A *Network Management Station (NMS)*, or *manager*, is a system running one or more network management applications that allow a network administrator to monitor and control the network or a portion of it. A manager sends a request for information or directives to take actions to agents. SNMP allows network administrators to use their NMSs to communicate with each other in a hierarchical structure.

- **Management Agent.** A *Management Agent (MA)*, or *agent*, is a program running in a network component responsible for performing the network management functions requested by a manager. This might include responding to requests for information and to action directives received from a manager.

- **Management Information Base.** A *Management Information Base (MIB)* is a database of information on all managed entities in a network. An agent stores information in the MIB for all objects in the network for which it is responsible and on which it can operate. Managers maintain portions of the MIB that reflect all components in their particular portion of the network.

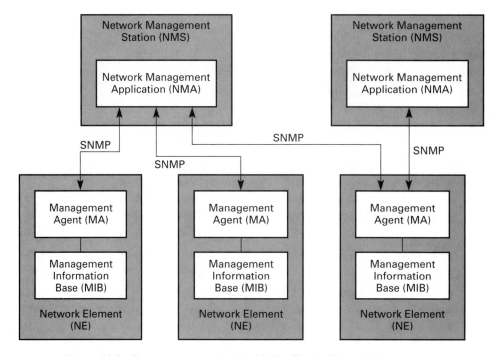

Figure 10.3 Components associated with the Simple Network Management Protocol (SNMP).

Managers and agents communicate using SNMP messages. SNMP defines the formats of a set of network management messages and the rules by which those messages are exchanged.

SNMP Protocol Functions

The SNMP protocol defines three operations for acting on the variable values that make up an MIB:

- **Get.** Used by a management station to retrieve a variable value from an agent.
- **Set.** Used by a management station to update a variable value in an agent.
- **Trap.** Used by an agent to send an unsolicited variable value to a management station.

The three types of SNMP operations are implemented through an exchange of request and response messages. SNMP also defines the formats of the messages exchanged among management stations and agents.

INTERIM LOCAL MANAGEMENT INTERFACE

The Interim Local Management Interface (ILMI) defined for ATM networks defines information to be collected by access agents called *User/Network-Interface Management Entities (UMEs)*. The ILMI also defines a method for exchanging management information

between peer UMEs. The information that UMEs use is stored in an SNMP MIB, with the structure shown in Box 10.2.

SUMMARY

Network management is concerned with monitoring the operation of components in the network, reporting on events that occur during network operation, and controlling the operational characteristics of the network and its components. International standards for

---

BOX 10.2　ILMI Management Information Base structure.

Physical Layer Information

- Interface address
- Transmission type
- Media type
- Operational status

ATM Layer Information

- Maximum number of VPCs/VCCs
- Number of configured VPCs/VCCs
- UNI type (public/private)
- VPI/VCI address field size

ATM Layer Statistics

- Number of ATM cells received
- Number of ATM cells dropped on the receive side
- Number of ATM cells transmitted

Virtual Path Connection (VPC) Information (for Each VPC Value)

- Send and receive side traffic descriptors, including specified peak cell rate, average cell rate, and cell delay variation tolerance
- Operational status
- Send and receive side Quality-of-Service class

Virtual Channel Connection (VCC) Information (for Each VCC Value)

- Send and receive side traffic descriptors, including specified peak cell rate, average cell rate, and cell delay variation tolerance
- Operational status and receive side Quality-of-Service class

the management of information processing systems divide management functions into five specific management functional areas (SMFAS): configuration management, fault management, performance management, security management, and accounting management.

Management of ATM networks involve access agents that manage system elements in ATM devices and a node management function that manages each of the components making up an ATM device. Network management software running in one or more systems in the network communicates with ATM node management functions.

ATM management protocols for operations administration and maintenance (OA&M) define functions for performance monitoring, defect and failure detection, system protection, failure and performance reporting, and fault isolation. ATM OA&M functions have a layered structure defining levels F1, F2, F3, F4, and F5. Level F1, F2, and F3 functions are associated with the ATM Physical layer and include functions for performance monitoring, fault management, and facility testing. Levels 4 and 5 are associated with the ATM layer and include functions for fault management, performance management, activation, and deactivation.

An Interim Local Management Interface (ILMI) is a temporary network management interface that has been defined for use in ATM networks until the full ATM management standard has been completed. The ILMI is based on the Simple Network Management Protocol (SNMP) originally defined for the TCP/IP environment.

Chapter **11**

ATM Switch Architectures

As we have already seen, an ATM switch is typically connected to a number of physical communication circuits each of which implements a transmission path (TP). A switch receives cells on incoming TPs and transmits cells on outgoing TPs. The switching mechanism in the ATM switch must be capable of performing the following four functions:

1. Receiving a cell over any incoming transmission path.
2. Determining the output transmission path on which it should be sent.
3. Storing appropriate values in the VPI and VCI fields of the cell's header.
4. Transmitting the cell on the selected outgoing transmission path.

The physical communication circuits that implement the transmission paths connected to an ATM switch are typically full-duplex circuits that implement one inbound TP and one outbound TP, as illustrated in Fig. 11.1. An ATM switch, however, views each unidirectional TP as logically separate from all the others.

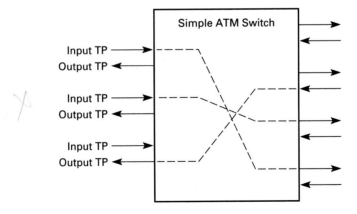

Figure 11.1 An ATM switch views each transmission path as logically separate from all the others.

ARCHITECTURAL APPROACHES TO SWITCH DESIGN

A number of different approaches have been used in designing ATM switches. Issues that need to be addressed as part of ATM switch design include the following:

- **Throughput.** Throughput measures the rate at which data passes through the switch. It reflects the switch's internal processing and transmission rates, as well as the degree of parallelism within the switch. ATM switches may be designed to process cells at state-of-the-art speed, at the time of writing in the neighborhood of 2 Gbps. It is interesting to note that at a data rate of 2 Gbps, the switch needs to be capable of receiving and transmitting cells at the rate of 4 million cells per second over each active transmission path.

- **Contention Resolution.** With every switch design, there are places where contention for resources may occur. Buffers can be used to hold cells until the contention is resolved, but at times buffer capacity can be exceeded. Switch design includes the size and placement of buffers, as well as methods for avoiding or handling congestion.

- **Scalability.** Some switch designs work well with lower numbers of transmission paths but may not retain acceptable levels of performance or cost when the number of transmission paths becomes large.

- **Cost.** Complexity of design and the relative cost of different technologies employed in implementing a switch can affect its overall cost.

The following four design approaches have been the focus in recent work done on the research and development of ATM switches:

- Crosspoint switch architecture
- Shared transmission medium switch architecture
- Shared memory switch architecture
- Multi-stage switch architecture

These four approaches are described in the following sections.

CROSSPOINT SWITCH ARCHITECTURE

Crosspoint switch technology was developed primarily to support telephone applications, and crosspoint switches are still used extensively in conventional telephone networks. A crosspoint switch implements a form of multiplexing called *space-division multiplexing,* and a crosspoint switch is sometimes called a space-division switch.

Crosspoint switches use parallel data paths to connect input and output transmission paths. The parallel paths help reduce congestion and increase throughput by allowing multiple cells to flow through the switch in parallel. Typically, a crosspoint switch consists of a matrix of data paths connecting input and output transmission paths, as shown in Fig. 11.2.

Each input transmission path is connected by some number of parallel data paths to the output transmission paths. The paths may be constructed so that any input transmission path can reach any output transmission path. At each intersection, or crosspoint, of

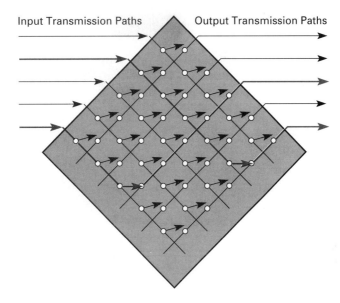

Figure 11.2   Crosspoint switch. The bold lines show two currently active paths through the switch.

the matrix, there is a switch. An input transmission path is connected to an output transmission path by setting the appropriate intersection, or crosspoint, switch. A central control function is responsible for determining the output transmission path to be used and for setting the appropriate switch to set up the path to that transmission path. An input transmission path can be connected to multiple output transmission paths; however, only one input transmission path can be connected to a given output transmission path at a particular time.

The switch shown in Fig. 11.2 has a separate data path for each output transmission path. This means that data could potentially flow in parallel over all the data paths without any blocking occurring due to contention for data path resources. However, blocking could still occur if two input transmission paths need to transmit data at the same time over the same output transmission path.

The parallel data paths make crosspoint switches efficient, and their relatively simple structure makes them relatively inexpensive to construct. However, problems can arise when the number of transmission paths attached to the switch is very large. For the fully meshed configuration shown in Fig. 11.2, the number of crosspoints needed in the switch is equal to the square of the number of data paths the switch supports. This can cause the size and cost of the switch to increase rapidly as the number of transmission paths increases. For a large number of transmission paths, there can also be problems with contention for the central control function that handles setting the individual crosspoint switch elements.

Crosspoint switches can be designed with partially shared data paths and fewer crosspoints. With this type of design, the shared data paths can be a source of increased contention. Buffers can be used to hold cells when contention occurs. They can be located at the input transmission path, at the intersections of the matrix, or at the output transmission path.

SHARED TRANSMISSION MEDIUM SWITCH ARCHITECTURE

Another form of switch architecture uses transmission paths that are interconnected by a shared transmission medium. The shared transmission medium can take the form of a bus or backplane, or it can take the form of a ring. Both bus/backplane and ring switches are illustrated in Fig. 11.3. Cells arriving from input transmission paths are transmitted over the shared transmission medium. The cells are then copied and sent out over the appropriate output transmission paths.

Figure 11.3 uses diagrams of switches to show the flow of data through the switch, but an actual shared-medium switch would not use physical switches to control the data flow. Instead, each cell placed on the shared medium has an address associated with it that specifies the output transmission path to be used to transmit it. Each transmission path examines the cell's associated address as the cell passes by. If the cell's destination address matches the address of the transmission path, that transmission path copies the cell and transmits it.

Broadcast/multicast operations can be handled in a shared-medium switch by placing on the shared medium multiple copies of the cell, each of which has different output transmission path addresses associated with it. Alternatively, addresses can be used that refer to groups of output transmission paths. To avoid contention for the shared medium, the transmission capacity of the shared medium must be as great as the sum of the transmission capacities of all input transmission paths.

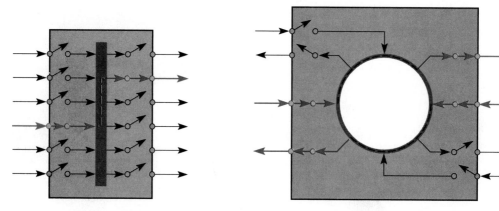

Bus/Backplane Configuration   Ring Configuration

Figure 11.3 An ATM switch that implements a shared transmission medium can use a bus/backplane or a ring configuration.

If there is minimal contention for the shared medium, input transmission paths require minimal buffering, since cells can be placed on the medium as quickly as they arrive. However, it is possible for cells from multiple input transmission paths to be switched to the same output transmission path. Therefore, output transmission paths typically require sufficient buffers to hold multiple cells until they can be transmitted.

With the shared medium switch architecture, each transmission path typically implements its own control function, so there is no contention for a central control function.

SHARED MEMORY SWITCH ARCHITECTURE

Transmission paths can also be interconnected using a shared buffer memory, as shown in Fig. 11.4. With a shared memory switch, cells arriving over input transmission paths are temporarily written to the shared memory. Cells are then accepted from the shared memory for transmission over output transmission paths.

When a cell arrives over an input transmission path, the output transmission path to be used is determined and the cell is placed in an output queue for that transmission path. The output queue might contain an actual copy of the cell, or the queue might consist of pointers to the actual locations of cells in memory. Memory used for output queues may be partitioned, with an equal amount assigned to each output transmission path, or all the memory may be shared, with each transmission path given as much queue space as it needs as cells arrive.

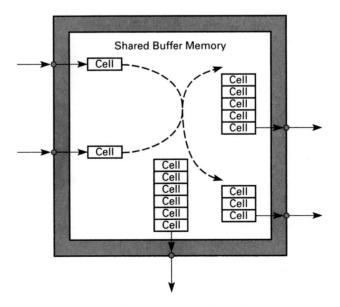

Figure 11.4 Shared memory switch architecture.

MULTISTAGE SWITCH ARCHITECTURE

A form of switching well suited to ATM is multistage, or serial stage-by-stage switching. With multistage switching, the switch consists of a number of individual switching elements that are connected by internal transmission paths. A cell passes through a series of these switching elements to reach its intended output transmission path based on an address associated with that transmission path. This process is illustrated in Box 11.1.

A switch conforming to the general architecture illustrated in Box 11.1 is sometimes called a *Banyan switch*. Each switching element in the switch has two inputs and two outputs. The interconnections between the switching elements form a structure such

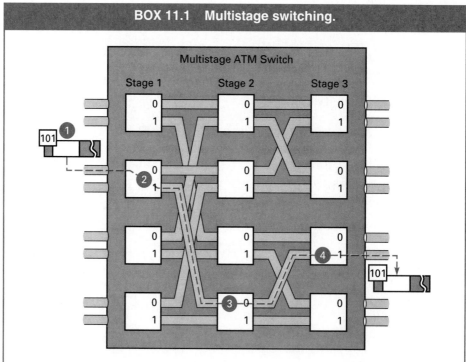

BOX 11.1   Multistage switching.

1. At the time the cell enters the switch, the identifier, or address, assigned to the output transmission path (010) to be used is determined and associated with the cell during its trip through the switch.

2. The switching element in stage 1 sends the cell out based on the first bit of the address (1).

3. The switching element in stage 2 sends the cell out based on the second bit of the address (0).

4. The switching element in stage 3 sends the cell to the appropriate output transmission path based on the third bit of the address (1).

that every output transmission path can be reached from each input transmission path. With this design, it is possible to have collisions, where two cells enter a switching element and both need the same output transmission path from that element. The internal blocking resulting from collisions can be eliminated by sorting cells based on their output transmission path addresses before sending them through the switching elements.

With multistage designs, the individual switching elements are simple and low in cost to produce. Multistage switches can support a large number of input and output transmission paths without sacrificing performance or cost.

SUMMARY

The functions of an ATM switch are to receive a cell over any incoming transmission path, determine the output transmission path on which it should be sent, store appropriate values in the VPI and VCI fields of the cell's header, and transmit the cell on the selected outgoing transmission path. Approaches that have been used in designing ATM switches typically address the issues of throughput, contention resolution, scalability, and cost.

Crosspoint switch technology was developed primarily to support telephone applications. A crosspoint switch, sometimes called a space-division switch, uses parallel data paths to connect input and output transmission paths. The parallel data paths make crosspoint switches efficient, and their relatively simple structure makes them relatively inexpensive to construct. However, problems in scalability can arise when the number of transmission paths attached to the switch is very large.

ATM switches using a shared transmission medium architecture often take the form of a backplane or ring structure. Cells arriving from input transmission paths are transmitted over a shared transmission medium and are then sent out over the appropriate output transmission paths. Broadcast/multicast operations can be handled in a shared-medium switch by placing on the shared medium multiple copies of the cell, each of which has different output transmission path addresses associated with it.

With a shared memory switch architecture, cells arriving over input transmission paths are temporarily written to a shared memory. Cells are then accepted from the shared memory for transmission over output transmission paths. The shared memory implements output queues in which cells are temporarily held until the switch can transmit them.

A multistage switch, often called a Banyan switch, consists of a number of individual switching elements that are connected by internal transmission paths. A cell passes through a series of these switching elements to reach its intended output transmission path based on an address associated with that transmission path. Each switching element has two inputs and two outputs, and the interconnections between the switching elements form a structure such that every output transmission path can be reached from each input transmission path.

Chapter 12 in Part IV concludes the text. This final chapter discusses how the ATM standards are being implemented by vendors and service providers and how ATM technology can be used in an enterprise network.

PART IV

ATM IMPLEMENTATION

Chapter **12**

ATM in the Enterprise Network

Many information systems hardware and software vendors use the term *enterprise computing* in referring to the type of networking employed by their largest customers. Enterprise computing typically refers to an information technology environment that has the following characteristics:

- **Any-to-any Connectivity.** Any person or application program in the organization can reach and communicate with any other person or program, in that organization or in the organization's trading partners around the world.

- **Data Highways.** A user can have access to myriad sources of data, both internal and external to the organization and can transport those data over the network to where they are needed.

- **Distributed Environment.** All forms of processing capabilities are accessible from any location on the network.

- **Multimedia Applications.** The organization can create applications that use image processing, digitized sound, animation, and full motion video.

- **Flexibility.** Network users can rapidly respond to changing business requirements.

- **Economy.** Small, inexpensive processors can handle the organization's information processing and share expensive data transmission facilities.

Providing such an information technology environment is not an easy task, and no single vendor can provide what is needed to build a true enterprise computing solution.

Today, moving in the direction of enterprise computing is not just a question of installing a particular set of hardware and software systems. Typically, the move to enterprise computing involves the integration of a wide range of existing computing facilities, different types of networks, different operating systems, and an array of different applications. To build an enterprise computing environment, the organization must develop a framework within which each of the separate different pieces can fit and effectively interoperate with each other.

ENTERPRISE NETWORKS

Enterprise computing requires the firm footing of an effective networking infrastructure on which to build. The networking infrastructure comprises an *enterprise network* that provides the underlying connectivity and distributability required for enterprise computing applications. In this chapter, we introduce some of the requirements associated with the networking infrastructure required to make an enterprise computing environment a reality, and we see how ATM technology can help make true enterprise networking a reality.

ATM IN THE ENTERPRISE

As we pointed out in Chapter 1, ATM technology has the potential for serving as a transmission alternative for both WAN and LAN data links in enterprise networks. Since ATM networks are designed to handle the transmission of all types of data, including voice and video, ATM technology can be used to create integrated networks that satisfy all of an organization's telecommunications requirements. This assumes, of course, that ATM products and services become available that offer all the required types of ATM service, and that these are competitive in terms of cost and performance. In this chapter we examine some of the issues involved for ATM to become widely used in enterprise networks.

REPLACING WAN DATA LINKS

As we have seen, ATM data links can often be used as a direct replacement for other types of WAN data links, such as voice line modem links, high-speed leased T1 and T3 digital connections, X.25 PSDN virtual circuits, point-to-point protocol (PPP) TCP/IP links, and frame relay connections. ATM services can be implemented that provide an equivalent level of service as conventional telecommunications links, in terms of data rates, transit delay, delay variation, error rates, timing, and availability of permanent and switched virtual circuits.

In order to be appropriate for use in enterprise networks, ATM products and services must offer compatible interfaces to commonly used high-level transport protocols so that the ATM can be used without needing to make major changes to existing network software subsystems and application programs.

ATM and Standard Telephone Service

The class A service of ATM, supported by the AAL type 1 protocol, is designed to provide the same type of service as a conventional, connection-oriented telecommunications facility, such as an ordinary analog voice line or a high-speed digital T1 or T3 circuit. Class A service is connection-oriented, maintains a constant bit rate, and supports timing-dependent (isochronous) traffic. Quality of Service (QoS) parameters for class A specify delay, jitter, and bit error rates that conform to the requirements of acceptable voice or video transmission requiring a constant bit rate.

Many early implementations of class A service, typically offered as part of common carrier ISDN services, provide 64-Kbps fixed-bandwidth channels, comparable to the circuit-switched line used in standard telephone service. Some ISDN providers also provide services based on collections of individual 64-Kbps channels that provide a total bandwidth up to 1.544 Mbps, the same capacity as a conventional T1 line. Some initial implementations of class A ATM service have offered access only to semipermanent connections.

The next phase of ISDN service likely to be offered by telecommunications service providers is called *broadband-ISDN (B-ISDN)*. B-ISDN services will initially provide class A service over both switched and semipermanent ATM connections that offer bandwidths up to about 45 Mbps.

ATM and Conventional Computer Network Data Links

As we saw in Chapter 9, ATM class C service is intended to provide data transfer capabilities similar to that provided by connection-oriented data networks such as an X.25 PSDN or a long-distance PPP link in a TCP/IP network. Class C service is used to transfer variable-length frames of data over a virtual circuit between pairs of ATM service users.

With an X.25 virtual circuit or a PPP data link, the data link layer implements error detection and recovery procedures using sequence numbers and acknowledgments. These procedures handle the automatic retransmission of corrupted frames. Network software subsystems typically used in enterprise networks also provide additional end-to-end error detection and recovery procedures using mechanisms operating in the Network and Transport layers.

As we have seen, ATM transmission services are based on a highly reliable transmission medium with a very low bit error rate. Many class C ATM services will be based on protocol mechanisms that provide only the nonassured delivery modes supported by the class C service. The two nonassured modes of class C service either discard frames that have been corrupted during transmission or pass the corrupted frames to the user with an error indication (see Chapter 9). Use of an ATM data link service that does not provide assured delivery places heavy reliance on the error detection and recovery mechanisms implemented in the Network and Transport layers of the network software subsystem.

As we discussed in Chapter 9, the ATM-3/4 protocol specifies an assured operational mode that provides guaranteed error-free delivery using error detection and retransmission in the Data Link layer. The assured-mode error recovery procedures operate much like the recovery mechanisms provided by an X.25 virtual circuit or PPP TCP/IP data link. However, at the time of writing, the protocol mechanisms for providing the assured delivery mode of operation in the ATM Adaptation layer has not yet been specified in detail. Therefore, current ATM products and services typically use the nonassured modes of operation when providing class C service.

ATM and Frame Relay Data Links

Frame relay data links provide a high-speed alternative to data links based on X.25 virtual circuits. The virtual circuits provided by frame relay data links are similar in operation to X.25 virtual circuits, but the frame relay protocols are optimized for higher-speed data links. The following are some of the similarities between ATM class C service and the service provided by a frame relay data link:

- Both offer switched and permanent virtual connections.
- Both allow virtual connections to be multiplexed on a single physical link.
- Both provide bandwidth-on-demand transmission facility.
- They carry routing information with only local, or link-by-link, significance.
- Both implement priority indicators and congestion indicators to help in managing congestion when it occurs.
- Both typically rely on the higher layers of network software handling error detection and recovery mechanisms.

The primary difference between a frame relay data link and an ATM data link is in the size of the data unit transmitted over the physical links. A frame relay data link transmits data over a physical circuit in the form of variable-size frames, and an ATM data link transfers data in fixed-length cells.

The many similarities between frame relay data links and ATM data links allow them to be used for the same purposes and also allows them to interoperate with one another easily in the same enterprise network.

ATM class C service using the AAL type 5 protocol in message mode with nonassured delivery provides an identical data transmission service as a frame relay data link. Therefore, a telecommunications service provider might actually use ATM technology to implement a frame relay data transmission service. For example, the service provider might simply accept frame relay transmission frames and transparently transport them using the AAL type 5 protocol.

Alternatively, the service provider might implement a Frame Relay Service-Specific Convergence Sublayer (FR-SSCS) in the ATM Adaptation layer that is specifically designed to accept frames in the format specified for a frame relay data link. An FR-SSCS implementation performs the basic functions that have been defined as core functions in the Frame Relay protocol, including:

- Routing based on DCLI values
- Frame delineation
- Frame multiplexing
- Error detection
- Congestion control

The FR-SSCS implementation accepts frame relay transmission frames and transports them in the ATM layer in the form of ATM cells. Figure 12.1 compares the frame relay transmission frame format with the CPCS-PDU format for ATM class C service.

The FR-SSCS implementation removes the Flag and Frame Check Sequence fields from the frame relay transmission frame, since equivalent frame-level error detection will be performed using the ATM CPCS trailer. The frame is then passed to CPCS for further pro-

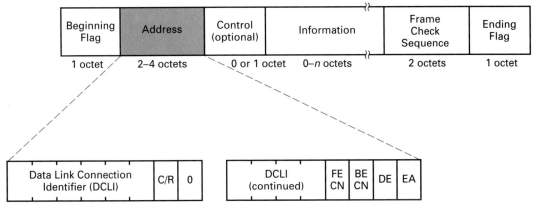

Frame Relay Transmission Frame Format

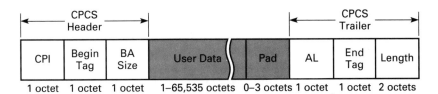

CPCS-PDU Format for Class C Service Using the AAL-3/4 Protocol

Figure 12.1 The frame relay transmission frame and the ATM CPCS-PDU.

cessing. Additionally, the frame relay Discard Eligibility (DE) and Forward and Backward Explicit Congestion Notification (FECN and BECN) fields are mapped to their counterparts in the ATM cell header.

REPLACING LAN DATA LINKS

Many enterprises are experiencing a need for increased bandwidth in their local networks. These needs are largely driven by a move toward supporting more users and more applications. New multimedia applications that use combinations of text, image, audio, and video require especially large amounts of network bandwidth. The need for higher bandwidths in local area networks has led to the development of technologies such as Fast Ethernet, 100VG-AnyLAN, and FDDI, that support data transfer in the 100 Mbps range. ATM technology offers promise as an alternative to conventional shared-medium LANs for providing higher bandwidths. The challenge for ATM is to provide a service that is equivalent to existing LAN data link protocols, and is usable with existing LAN network operating systems and applications.

Since most LAN network software is designed to be used with a variety of different data link types at the MAC level (Ethernet, Token Ring, FDDI, etc.), the simplest way to maintain compatibility with existing network software is to implement ATM functions in the Medium Access Control that provide the same services to the LLC sublayer as do the existing LAN MAC protocols.

LAN Data Link Characteristics

All LAN data links operate as multiaccess links. Each user workstation on the LAN implements a LAN station using an appropriate network interface card (NIC) and network software. All stations on the LAN share access to the transmission medium, and a frame transmitted on the link is received by all stations on the LAN. LAN software typically provides only connectionless service at the LLC level, and no connections are required between source and destination users. A source station transmits a frame on the transmission medium, and the addressed destination workstation recognizes that it should process the frame from the destination and accepts the frame from the transmission medium. Multicast operations are provided by designating certain destination addresses that correspond to a particular group of destination stations. Since all stations receive all the frames, all destinations can be reached with a single transmission.

ATM Connectionless Service

As we saw in Chapter 9, ATM class D service provides ATM users with a connectionless data transfer service. However, the ATM network operates in a connection-oriented manner in the ATM and Physical layers. To appropriately deliver frames in an ATM network that is providing LAN-like services, the ATM network must be able to determine, from the destination address in the frame, which virtual channel connection (VCC) to use to reach the destination user. For a multicast group address, an appropriate multipoint VCC or a group of point-to-point VCCs must be identified. The source ATM endpoint can then use either the AAL type 3/4 or AAL type 5 protocol to actually transfer the data over the selected VCCs.

Two approaches have been defined for providing the connectionless service. The first approach is based on using direct VCCs, and the second on using a connectionless server (CLS) function.

The Direct VCC Approach

With the direct VCC approach, a virtual path connection is established between the source user and the destination user, and the VCC is then used to transfer data between them. The VCC used can be either a switched or semipermanent connection. A multicast delivery service can be provided by using an appropriate multipoint VCC or by sending the frame out over multiple VCCs. This approach requires an ATM function that translates between the destination address contained in each transmission frame and the VCC or VCCs to use to reach the destination stations.

The direct VCC approach is illustrated in Fig. 12.2. In order for an ATM network using the direct VCC approach to provide connectionless service, every ATM endpoint must be able to establish a VCC to every other endpoint in the network. (Since VCCs are unidirectional, there must be a VCC in each direction.)

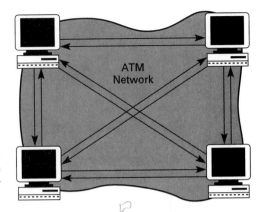

Figure 12.2   To provide any-to-any connectivity using direct VCCs, two VCCs must be established between each user and all other users.

As the number of LAN users increases, it may become difficult for the ATM switches to store the information required to implement the many VCCs that are required. If switched connections are used, information needs to be stored only for active connections, which reduces the ATM switch resource requirements. However, with switched connections, the delay resulting from establishing and terminating connections may be a consideration. Connections must be established quickly enough so that higher layers do not cause retransmissions to occur because acknowledgments do not arrive in time.

The Connectionless Server Approach

Chapter 9 introduced the connectionless server (CLS) approach to providing LAN-like services (see Fig. 12.3). With the connectionless server approach, each LAN user implements an ATM endpoint function using an appropriate network interface card (NIC) and network software. Each ATM endpoint then has a direct VCC connecting the endpoint to a connec-

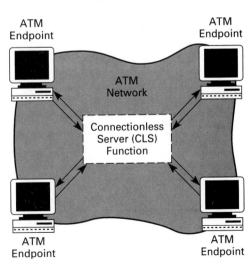

Figure 12.3   When a connectionless server (CLS) function is used to provide LAN connectivity, each LAN user implements an ATM endpoint that has a direct virtual channel connection (VCC) to the connectionless server.

tionless server function operating within the ATM network. Note that each VCC to the CLS function may be physically implemented by many transmission paths using many ATM switches; the transmission paths and ATM switches are not shown in Fig. 12.3. Also, the CLS function may be distributed among many devices in the network, possibly in specially designed ATM switches designed to provide class D service.

With the connectionless server approach, when a source endpoint has a frame to send, the endpoint sends the frame over its direct VCC to the CLS function. The CLS function then determines, based on the destination address contained in the frame, where to send the frame. For a frame destined for a destination endpoint, the CLS function sends the frame out over the VCC that leads to the destination endpoint. For a multicast frame, the CLS function sends the frame out over an appropriate multipoint VCC or over multiple point-to-point VCCs.

The connectionless server approach requires fewer VCCs than the direct VCC approach. However, with the connectionless server approach, the CLS function becomes a critical component. If the CLS function is implemented in a single device, the device becomes a single point of failure that can bring the entire network down. This is because all communication functions in the entire LAN are lost if the connectionless server malfunctions. The connectionless server must also provide sufficient processing power to handle the total throughput requirements for all concurrent users in the LAN.

Virtual LANs

With conventional LAN data links, LAN stations belong to LANs based on the physical links that connect them. As described in Chapter 6, LAN switching equipment is now available that allows virtual LANs to be created by grouping LAN stations and isolating the LAN traffic associated with each group to certain transmission medium segments.

An ATM network that is providing LAN-like communication services can also easily be used to create virtual LANs. Virtual LANs are created in an ATM by using VCCs to define different groups of users, each of which appears to use a different logical connectionless server function for communication. Each virtual LAN is made up of a different collection of users. Groups can be defined without respect to their physical locations, as long as they are part of the same physical ATM network. This is shown in Fig. 12.4. As workstations are added or removed from the ATM network, information maintained by the different logical CLS functions describing virtual-LAN workgroup membership must be updated.

Simulating a Bridge Function

In a conventional LAN, communication between virtual LANs can be implemented by using a bridge or router to interconnect different groups of transmission medium segments. This is discussed in Chapter 6. An ATM network that simulates two or more virtual LANs can implement a logical bridge or logical router function to permit communication between virtual LANs. This can be done, as shown in Fig. 12.5, by using additional VCCs to forward frames from one CLS function to another.

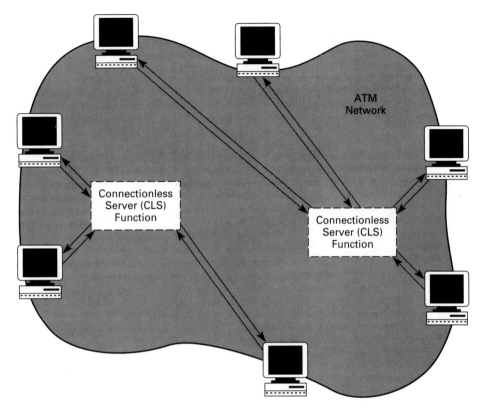

Figure 12.4 With the virtual LAN approach, multiple workgroups can be defined, without regard to the physical locations of workstations, by implementing multiple logical connectionless server functions in the ATM network.

Simulating a Backbone Network

With conventional LAN equipment, a LAN data link is sometimes used as a *backbone* LAN that serves as a communication medium used to interconnect other LAN subnetworks. The functions of a backbone LAN can be simulated in an ATM network by using a set of VCCs that provide a function equivalent to a backbone LAN. This is shown in Fig. 12.6.

SUMMARY

ATM technology has the potential for serving as a transmission alternative for both WAN and LAN data links in enterprise networks. Since ATM networks are designed to handle the transmission of all types of data, including voice and video, ATM technology can be used to create integrated networks that satisfy all of an organization's telecommunications requirements.

The class A service of ATM, supported by the AAL type 1 protocol, is designed to provide the same type of service as a conventional, connection-oriented telecommunica-

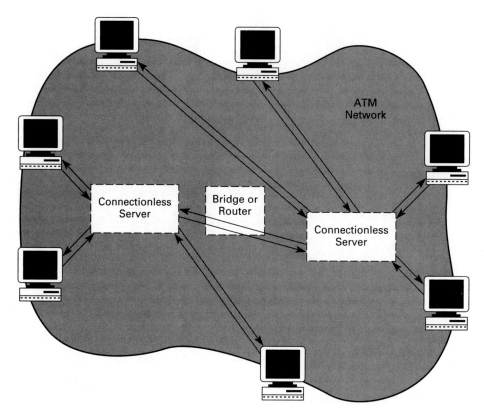

Figure 12.5   Communication between virtual LANs can be provided by using VCCs to implement the function of a bridge or router between connectionless servers.

tions facility, such as an ordinary analog voice line or a high-speed digital T1 or T3 circuit. ATM class C service is intended to provide data transfer capabilities similar to that provided by connection-oriented data networks such as an X.25 PSDN or a long-distance PPP link in a TCP/IP network. Current ATM products and services typically use the nonassured modes of operation when providing class C service and expect higher layers of network software to handle error detection and retransmission functions. Frame relay data links provide a high-speed alternative to data links based on X.25 virtual circuits. The many similarities between frame relay data links and ATM data links allow them to be used for the same purposes and also allow them to interoperate with one another easily in the same enterprise network.

ATM technology offers promise as an alternative to conventional shared-medium LANs for providing higher bandwidths. ATM class D service provides ATM users with a connectionless data transfer service. Two approaches have been defined for providing the connectionless service: using direct VCCs between users and using a connectionless server (CLS) function. An ATM network providing LAN-like communication services can be used

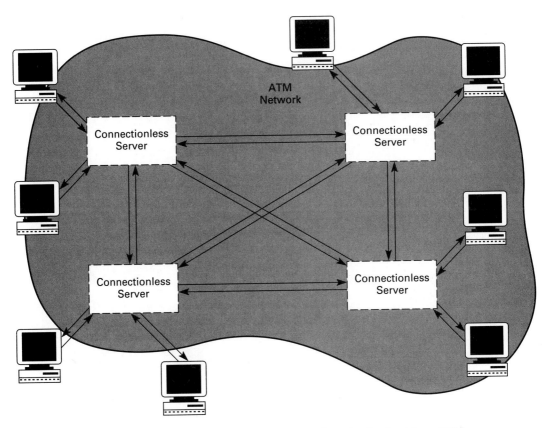

Figure 12.6   The function of a backbone network can be simulated in an ATM network by establishing VCCs between multiple connectionless server functions.

to create virtual LANs in which different groups of users can communicate among one another as if they were connected to a physical LAN. An ATM network that simulates two or more virtual LANs can implement a logical bridge or logical router function to permit communication between virtual LANs. The functions of a backbone LAN can also be simulated in an ATM network by using a set of VCCs that provide a function equivalent to a backbone LAN.

PART V

Appendices

Appendix **A**

International Standards Organizations

A number of organizations around the world are actively involved in developing standards and architectures for data communications and computer networking. Four important standards organizations for the computer networking industries are ISO, IEEE, ANSI, and ITU-T, all of which we discuss in this appendix. Other important standards organizations and standards terminology are also briefly described.

INTERNATIONAL ORGANIZATION FOR STANDARDIZATION (ISO)

A prominent standards organization is the *International Organization for Standardization (ISO)*, the largest standards organization in the world. ISO produces large numbers of standards on nearly every subject, from humane animal traps to screw threads. It is also the dominant information technology standardization organization in the world. The members of ISO are individual national standards organizations; only national positions—positions representing an entire country—are discussed in ISO. The ISO member organization from the United States is the American National Standards Institute (ANSI); every major industrialized country has a similar standards organization that represents its national interests in ISO. ISO technical meetings take place at various locations around the world.

ISO Organizational Structure

The Secretariat of ISO, located in Geneva, Switzerland, is the organization charged with running the day-to-day affairs of ISO, including keeping track of its numerous technical committees (TCs) and publishing the standards the technical committees produce. The technical committees—which not only create the standards but also determine what standards to produce—are composed of thousands of volunteers from computer manufacturers, suppliers of communication products, major computer users, governments, and consulting organizations.

To participate, these delegates operate under the aegis of the national body. For example, a delegate from the United States not only brings technical expertise to the committee but also represents his or her sponsoring organization (ANSI, described later) and the United States itself. A TC is ordinarily divided into subcommittees (SCs) and working groups (WGs), which write the standards. The standards then receive the approval of the technical committee as a whole before they finally become accepted as international standards.

International Electrotechnical Commission

Closely associated with ISO is the *International Electrotechnical Commission (IEC)*. IEC has a role similar to that of ISO but is restricted to electrical and electronic matters. There is an agreement between ISO and IEC to ensure that their work does not overlap. In the field of communications standards, IEC's role is limited to Physical layer aspects, such as electrical safety.

Joint Technical Committee 1

ISO and IEC have recently merged their technical committees working on information technology into a single organization, called ISO/IEC Joint Technical Committee 1 (JTC1), to ensure and improve continued close cooperation.

JTC1 is the ISO/IEC technical committee that oversees a particularly important framework for a computer network architecture called the *Reference Model for Open Systems Interconnection* or the *OSI model* for short. JTC1 is also publishing a comprehensive set of standards for the various functional layers defined by the OSI model. The OSI model is described in Chapter 2 and discussed further in Appendix C.

The ISO Standardization Process

There are four major steps in the standardization process. A standard begins its journey through the standardization process as a *working document*. After the working group or subcommittee agrees that the working document should be developed into an international standard, it becomes a *committee draft*, at which time ISO/IEC assigns a unique number to it. At this stage, the standard is referred to with the letters "CD," such as ISO CD 12345. (A committee draft was formerly called a *draft proposal* and was abbreviated DP.)

After the subcommittee or working group agrees that the standard is close to being accepted as an international standard, it is given *draft international standard* status and is referred to using its number and the letters DIS, such as ISO DIS 12345.

A standard may go through multiple revisions at both the committee draft and draft international standard phases. A standard that has made it all the way through the standardization process and has been accepted by ISO is called an *international standard* and is referred to only by its number, such as ISO 12345.

ISO also sometimes produces documents called *technical reports* when support cannot be obtained for the publication of a standard, when a subject is still under technical development, or when a technical committee has collected information of a different kind from that normally published as a standard. The identification number of a technical report is preceded by the letters TR, such as ISO TR 12345.

Amendments

ISO also produces amendments to international standards as changes are required. Like the international standards themselves, amendments go through four phases. An amendment to an international standard begins as a *working draft* and then progresses to a *committee draft amendment (CDAM)*, goes on to become a *draft amendment (DAM)*, and finally becomes an *amendment (AM)* when it is approved. Generally, amendments are eventually incorporated into the text of their associated standards after the amendment is accepted. Amendments were formerly called *Addenda (ADS)*, draft amendments were called *Draft Addenda (DADS)*, and committee draft amendments were *proposed draft addenda (PDADS)*.

Sources for ISO Standards

ISO/IEC standards documents and technical reports can be obtained in the United States from ANSI, Inc., 1430 Broadway, New York, NY 10018. Global Engineering Documents, 2805 McGaw Avenue, Ervine, CA 92714, telephone (800) 854-7179 also stocks copies of ISO standards.

INTERNATIONAL TELECOMMUNICATION UNION-TELECOMMUNICATIONS (ITU-T)

The *International Telecommunication Union (ITU)* has existed since around the early 1900s and is the leading organization involved in the development of standards relating to telephone and other telecommunications services. The ITU is a body of the United Nations, and the delegation to the ITU from the United States is the Department of State. In other countries, the ITU delegation is often the governmentally controlled Postal, Telephone, and Telegraph (PTT) organization.

The Telecommunications sector of the ITU (ITU-T) publishes important standards relating to computer networking. ITU-T standards for the information technology standards were formerly known as CCITT standards for the *International Telegraph and Telephone Consultative Committee*, the old name for ITU-T.

ITU-T Areas of Standardization

The ITU-T deals with standards for interconnecting the world's telephone networks and for the signaling systems used by modems in sending computer data over telephone lines. The ITU-T calls the standards it produces recommendations, which have such names as Recommendation X.25 and Recommendation X.400. It was a natural outgrowth of the data aspects of telephone service that ITU-T should become involved in information system standards, particularly those directly related to public data networks.

In the last decade, ITU-T has also been involved in a major effort to define standards for a worldwide *Integrated Services Digital Network (ISDN)* for providing unified public voice and data communication services.

ITU-T Organizational Structure

The principal contributors to ITU-T are individuals representing the public and private telecommunications organizations, although nonvoting memberships are also open to industrial organizations. The ITU-T maintains a secretariat in Geneva, where most of the meetings take place. However, representation is international. As with ISO, all of the technical contribution comes from individual volunteers drawn primarily from telephone companies and other companies that supply telecommunications products and services. Again, membership is limited to national body representation—it is the State Department, not U.S. common carriers, that represents the U.S. national position.

ITU-T Publication Process

ITU-T recommendations are published at four-year intervals, with the color of the covers changed with each new edition. Although the recommendations are newly published every four years, each new version represents evolutionary change from the previous version; many of the recommendations change little from one version of the recommendations to another. Each set of ITU-T recommendations is published in the form of a series of volumes, each of which is divided into separately bound *fascicles*. Each fascicle can be ordered separately.

ISO/IEC/ITU-T Cooperation

ISO, IEC, and ITU-T cooperate quite closely. ISO and ITU-T, in particular, have a strong interest in aligning their standards and thus try not to duplicate work between them. (Unfortunately, duplication of effort still sometimes occurs.) Standards of mutual interest typically are developed in one organization and then published by both. For example, the OSI model was developed principally by a subcommittee of ISO and is documented in ISO 7498; ITU-T also publishes the OSI model as Recommendation X.200. Similarly, ITU-T has developed Recommendation X.400, which standardizes electronic mail facilities. Recommendation X.400 has been adopted by ISO, which publishes it as ISO 10021. The technical people participating in committees of ISO are very often the same people on ITU-T committees, and the technical development activities associated with information systems standardization are often undertaken jointly by ISO and ITU-T.

Sources for ITU-T Standards

ITU-T recommendations can be obtained from the United States Department of Commerce, National Technical Information Service, 5285 Port Royal Road, Springfield, VA 22161. They can also be obtained from Global Engineering Documents, whose address was given previously.

INSTITUTE OF ELECTRICAL AND ELECTRONICS ENGINEERS (IEEE)

The *Institute of Electrical and Electronics Engineers (IEEE)* is a professional society whose members are individual engineers rather than companies. The IEEE operates under ANSI guidelines when it develops standards and ordinarily concentrates on product standards.

The IEEE Computer Society Local Network Committee (Project 802) has focused on standards related to local area networks, and has produced a set of LAN standards. The IEEE LAN standards have been accepted by ISO as international standards and are published by ISO as well as by IEEE. ANSI standards for local area networks also conform to the IEEE Project 802 LAN architecture.

AMERICAN NATIONAL STANDARDS INSTITUTE (ANSI)

Virtually every country in the world has a national standards organization responsible for publishing standards to guide that nation's industries. In the United States, this organization is the *American National Standards Institute (ANSI)*. ANSI is a nonprofit organization that writes the rules for standards bodies to follow and publishes standards produced under its rules of consensus. ANSI accredits standards committees to write standards in areas of their expertise. The major accredited standards committees (ASCs) in the information technology arena are:

- **JTC1 TAG.** This is the U.S. *technical advisory group (TAG)* for the ISO/IEC JTC1. This group provides U.S. positions on JTC1 standards and is the single interface to ISO/IEC JTC1 in the United States.
- **ASC X3.** This committee produces approximately 90 percent of the standards for U.S. information technology and provides the technical expertise for a majority of U.S. technical advisory groups to the subcommittees and working groups in ISO/IEC JTC1. A subcommittee of ANSI X3 is responsible for standardizing the Fiber Distributed Data Interface (FDDI) LAN data link technology.
- **ASC T1.** This group is the voluntary standards-making body for the U.S. telecommunications industry and sets U.S. national telecommunications standards. T1 helps the State Department with ITU-T positions.
- **ASC X12.** This group is responsible for standards relating to electronic data interchange (EDI) in the United States. It acts to set national positions for the United Nations EDIFACT group, which is establishing EDI standards worldwide.

ANSI has a small secretariat located in New York City whose function is organizational and administrative rather than technical. ANSI is not a government organization; it is funded by its members and through the sale of standards.

National standards organizations from other countries include:

- **France.** Association Française de Normalisation (AFNOR).
- **United Kingdom.** British Standards Institute (BSI).
- **Canada.** Canadian Standards Association (CSA).

- **Germany.** Deutsches Institut für Normung e.V. (DIN).
- **Japan.** Japanese Industrial Standards Committee (JISC).

These standards organizations have the same general role and organization as ANSI and provide a discussion forum for individuals. Some of those individuals then participate in international meetings and represent the agreed views of their countries. It is the national bodies that vote in the formal approval process for standards.

OTHER STANDARDS ORGANIZATIONS

There are a number of other organizations that participate in information systems standardization. The following sections provide brief descriptions of some of the more prominent ones.

Open Software Foundation (OSF)

OSF is a nonprofit organization established by a number of computer manufacturers to develop a common foundation for open computing. It is not directly concerned with standards but rather with the development of an agreed collection of software around a UNIX-like operating system kernel. OSF has its own permanent technical staff and depends on the participation of its members. Particularly important in the NAS environment is the Distributed Computing Environment (DCE) that OSF has defined.

European Computer Manufacturers Association (ECMA)

ECMA was originally formed by a group of European companies. Since then, its membership has grown to become international and includes representatives from such organizations as IBM, Digital, AT&T, British Telecom, and Toshiba. ECMA is considered a regional standards organization and develops information technology standards for the European region. ECMA standards are often forwarded to ISO/IEC JTC1 for development as international standards. Such cooperation between organizations can result in a faster standards development process, since consensus has already been demonstrated. ECMA has a small secretariat in Geneva, and its members meet in various places throughout Europe.

Comité Européen de Normalisation (CEN) and Comité Européen de Normalisation dans le domain Electrique (CENELEC)

CEN and its associated organization CENELEC have a relationship similar to that between ISO and IEC. They are concerned with the adoption of standards by the countries of the European Economic Community (EEC) and other European countries. Standards adopted

by CEN/CENELEC are called European Norms (ENS) and are binding for procurement purposes on the CEN's member countries. CEN normally does not develop its own standards but instead relies heavily on standards developed by other organizations, especially ISO. Where there is no ISO or IEC standard, however, CEN will develop its own standard and forward it to ISO for development as an international standard.

National Institute for Science and Technology (NIST)

NIST (formerly known as the National Bureau of Standards) is a U.S. government organization. ISO standards often cover broad ranges of function and allow many choices to be made by individual implementors. The NIST has taken a leadership role in creating *profiles* that define preferred groups of choices from among the many options documented in ISO standards. Initially this was done in an informal workshop that developed *implementors' agreements*. As the importance of these profiles has increased and other organizations have started similar work internationally, the NIST workshop has become more formally organized. NIST is one of the three major international contributors to the development of Internationally Standardized Profiles (ISPS), which are the profiles formally ratified by ISO.

European Workshop on Open Systems (EWOS)

EWOS has the same role in Europe as the NIST workshop has in the United States. EWOS was started primarily by members of SPAG (see below) to ensure that Europe had a voice in the development of profiles. It also serves as the technical committee to support the technical activity of CEN. EWOS and NIST work closely together to achieve and maintain harmonization of their profiles. EWOS is located in Brussels.

Promotion of OSI/Asia and Oceania Workshop (POSI/AOW)

AOW is another organization that contributes to the international adoption of profiles. POSI is a Japanese organization concerned with promoting the adoption of ISO standards for the OSI model, while AOW is an open workshop that includes Australia and other Pacific countries as well as Japan.

Corporation for Open Systems (COS)

COS was initiated as a consortium of computer manufacturers and others to encourage the adoption of ISO information systems standards. It has initially directed its efforts toward the development of testing procedures to allow vendors to demonstrate conformance to ISO standards. COS operates as a nonprofit organization funded by its members. It does not produce standards nor does it contribute to the development of standards. COS is located in McLean, VA.

Standards Promotion and Application Group (SPAG)

SPAG was initially a private consortium of European companies, set up with objectives similar to those of the COS. Like COS, it has now directed its efforts primarily toward the development of testing procedures, and it cooperates closely with COS in that regard. Membership in SPAG is now open, and many U.S. companies are members.

Electrical Industries Association (EIA)

EIA is an association of companies involved in electrical and related industries. EIA undertakes some standardization projects and operates in that capacity as an accredited organization (AO) under the rules of consensus standards formulated by ANSI. The standards developed by the EIA are concerned primarily with physical communication interfaces and electrical signaling. A well-known EIA standard is RS-232-D, which documents the way in which a terminal or computer is attached to a modem.

Conference of European PTTs (CEPT)

CEPT was established by the European PTTs primarily to develop technical standards that could be used in Europe prior to the development of corresponding ITU-T standards. With the establishment of ETSI (see below), CEPT remains a closed forum concerned mainly with marketing and lobbying.

European Telecommunications Standards Institute (ETSI)

ETSI was established by the European Economic Commission to formalize many of the activities formerly undertaken by CEPT. Membership is open to suppliers of telecommunications equipment and services, PTTs, and other industrial organizations, with formal voting on a national basis. ETSI develops European telecommunications standards (ETSs). Some of these are intended as a basis for the provision of services and as a foundation for ITU-T work, while others are oriented toward permission to connect testing for the attachment of equipment to public networks. ETSI is based in Sophie Antipolis, France. It has its own permanent technical staff and depends on the participation of its members.

X/Open

X/Open was set up by European computer manufacturers to develop a consistent UNIX-like suite of application programming interfaces to permit application portability. Membership is open and worldwide.

ADDITIONAL STANDARDS TERMINOLOGY

A number of additional terms making up the alphabet soup of information technology standardization are defined below:

- **Manufacturing Automation Protocol (MAP).** A project started in the United States by General Motors to develop a single standard for communication between devices in a factory automation environment. Its work has been based on U.S. national and ISO standards and also defines additional standards specific to factory automation applications.

- **Technical and Office Protocols (TOP).** A complementary project to MAP started by Boeing to extend the applicability of MAP into other environments, such as office information systems and computer-aided design.

- **Government Open Systems Interconnection Profile (GOSIP).** A name for procurement-oriented standard profiles specifying how ISO standards will be used for U.S. government computing. The acronym GOSIP has been adopted by other countries to describe their own government procurement specifications.

- **European Procurement Handbook for Open Systems (EPHOS).** A project similar to GOSIP for government computing throughout Europe.

- **Open Distributed Processing (ODP).** A project started within ISO to develop standards for a heterogeneous distributed computing environment. It is defining an overall reference model for distributed computing that goes beyond the OSI model.

- **POSIX.** A standard developed by IEEE under its Project 1003 that defines a UNIX-like interface to basic operating system functions to provide for application portability.

Appendix **B**

TCP/IP Technology

Networking software that implements the major TCP/IP protocols is available on a wide range of computing systems, from the largest mainframes to the smallest personal computers. It is included as an integral part of many variants of the UNIX operating system. It can be used in conjunction with IBM's MVS, VM, OS/400, OS/2, and AIX operating systems and with Microsoft's MS-DOS, Windows, Windows 95, and Windows NT system software. Digital Equipment Corporation's OpenVMS and Ultrix operating systems provide TCP/IP communication support, and TCP/IP communication software is also available for use on Apple computer equipment. Many network operating systems for personal computers, such as NetWare, LAN Manager, LAN Server, and PATHWORKS incorporate support for the TCP/IP protocols as well as support for their own native communication protocols.

This appendix provides an overview of the characteristics of the TCP/IP protocol suite.

TCP/IP ARCHITECTURE AND FUNCTIONAL LAYERS

Figure B.1 illustrates the architecture that underlies TCP/IP, shows its relationship to the OSI model, and lists the major protocols making up the TCP/IP protocol suite.

The Network Interface Layer

The main function of the Network Interface layer is to handle hardware-dependent functions and to present a standardized interface to the Internet layer of TCP/IP. The Hardware layer, shown with dashed lines, is considered to operate outside the scope of the TCP/IP architecture. The Network Interface layer of TCP/IP is responsible for accepting messages from the Internet layer and preparing them for transmission across any desired type of data link technology.

An individual TCP/IP network may be a local area network, using LAN data link protocols such as Ethernet, Token Ring, or FDDI. An individual TCP/IP network may also be

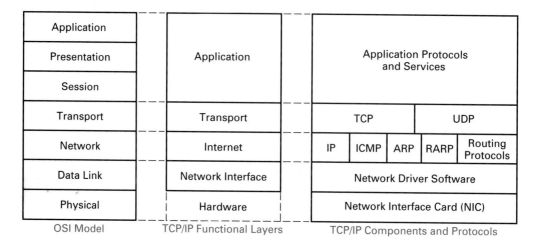

OSI Model	TCP/IP Functional Layers	TCP/IP Components and Protocols
Application		
Presentation	Application	Application Protocols and Services
Session		
Transport	Transport	TCP · UDP
Network	Internet	IP · ICMP · ARP · RARP · Routing Protocols
Data Link	Network Interface	Network Driver Software
Physical	Hardware	Network Interface Card (NIC)

TCP	= Transmission Control Protocol	ICMP	= Internet Control Message Protocol
UDP	= User Datagram Protocol	ARP	= Address Resolution Protocol
IP	= Internet Protocol	RARP	= Reverse Address Resolution Protocol

Figure B.1   Comparison of the OSI model and the TCP/IP architectural layers and protocols.

implemented using a wide area network data link technology, such as a point-to-point leased or dial-up line, satellite link, or specialized digital circuit. One of the reasons TCP/IP has become widely used is that it can be used in conjunction with almost any type of underlying physical circuit and data link technology.

The Internet Layer

The TCP/IP Internet layer provides routing and relaying functions for carrying packets of data from a source system to a destination system through a network. At this layer routing decisions are made that determine the path over which each packet travels.

The following TCP/IP protocols operate in the Internet layer:

- **Internet Protocol.** The *Internet Protocol (IP)* is the core protocol of the TCP/IP protocol suite. It provides a connectionless, best-efforts data delivery service used in moving packets from one system to another through the network.

- **Internet Control Message Protocol.** The *Internet Control Message Protocol (ICMP)* employs the services of IP to allow systems to report on error conditions and to provide information about unexpected circumstances.

- **Address Resolution Protocol.** The *Address Resolution Protocol (ARP)* helps a source system deliver data directly to a destination system when the two systems are on the same physical network. It allows the source system to determine the destination system's physical hardware address given the destination system's network address, called its *internet address.* TCP/IP internet addresses are discussed later in this appendix.

- **Reverse Address Resolution Protocol.** The *Reverse Address Resolution Protocol (RARP)* allows a system that does not yet have its internet address to obtain it. RARP is typically used to support workstations and intelligent terminals that do not have their own disk storage.

- **Routing Protocols.** The basic routing function in a TCP/IP network is performed by IP. However, in networks that employ routers, the routers often run additional routing protocols that allow them to exchange routing information with each other.

The Transport Layer

The Transport layer provides an end-to-end data delivery service that application programs use to exchange messages over the network. Protocols operating in the Transport layer use the services of IP to deliver messages.

The following are descriptions of the two major TCP/IP Transport layer protocols:

- **User Datagram Protocol.** The *User Datagram Protocol (UDP)* is the simpler of the two transport protocols. It is a best-effort, connectionless data transport protocol that adds little to the underlying IP datagram delivery service.
- **Transmission Control Protocol.** The *Transmission Control Protocol (TCP)* is a connection-oriented data transport protocol that provides for reliable, sequenced, stream data delivery.

An application program can use either UDP or TCP to request data transfer services. The protocol that an application developer chooses to use depends on whether the application requires only a best-efforts, datagram data delivery service or whether it requires the reliability controls provided by a connection-oriented data transfer service.

The Application Layer

TCP/IP defines a wide range of application layer protocols that provide services to network users, including remote login, file copying and sharing, electronic mail, directory services, and network management facilities. Some application protocols are widely used; others are employed only for specialized purposes. Box B.1 introduces some of the most widely used TCP/IP application protocols and services.

TCP/IP ADDRESSING

Each system attached to a TCP/IP network (host or router) is assigned at least one unique 32-bit *internet address* value used as the system's network address. A system, such as an end-user system, that implements a single network interface card (NIC) has one internet address. A system, such as a router, that implements multiple NICs, has multiple internet addresses, one for each NIC.

The general format of an internet address is shown in Fig. B.2. The initial bits of the internet address identify the internet address type and describe how the 32-bit address is divided between a *Network Identifier* field and a *Host Identifier* field. The Network Identifier field identifies the individual physical subnetwork on which the source or destination is located; the Host Identifier field identifies a particular system on that subnetwork.

End-User Services

- **Ping Connectivity Testing.** *Ping*, which is short for *Packet InterNet Groper*, can be used to test for connectivity between any two systems in the internet. Ping uses an Internet layer protocol called the *Internet Control Message Protocol (ICMP)* in performing its functions. In using Ping, a user typically executes a program named **ping** that sends an ICMP Echo Request message to another host. When a host receives an ICMP Echo Request message, it sends an ICMP Echo Reply message back to the original sender. For each Echo Reply message that it receives, Ping calculates the amount of time elapsed since it sent the original Echo Request message. This provides the Ping user with an estimate of the round-trip delay that is being experienced in exchanging data with the specified host.

- **Telnet Remote Login.** Telnet allows a user to login to some other host in the internet. The Telnet protocol establishes a client/server relationship between the local Telnet software (the client) and the remote Telnet software (the server). Telnet handles the data transfers that are required between the host implementing the client and the host implementing the server. These data transfers make it appear as if the user is logged into the remote host directly, even though the user is actually employing the user interface device to communicate with the local host.

- **Rlogin Remote Login.** The Rlogin service is a service that is related to Telnet but is typically provided only by variations of the UNIX operating systems. Telnet allows a user at any type of TCP/IP host to login to any other type of TCP/IP host. The local host and remote host may be running entirely different operating systems. The Rlogin service is normally used when a user at a local UNIX host wants to login to a remote UNIX host. For the UNIX user, Rlogin is somewhat easier to use than Telnet and provides a few additional services.

- **Rsh Remote Execution.** The *Rsh* remote execution service allows the user to issue, at the local host, a command to request an operating system function or to request the execution of an application program on some other host in the internet. When using the Rsh service, the user enters a command at the local host, and the command is then sent to and executed on the remote host. The results of the command or the results of the application program execution are then returned to the user at the local host. A similar service to Rsh called *Rexec* is available on some TCP/IP hosts as well.

- **FTP File Transfer.** The *File Transfer Protocol (FTP)* implements a user-oriented file transfer service. FTP allows the user to transfer data in both directions between the local host and a remote host. FTP can be used to transfer files that contain either binary data or ASCII text. Certain versions of FTP also allow for the transfer of files containing EBCDIC data. Files can be transferred one at a time, or a single request can cause multiple files to be transferred. FTP also provides ancillary functions, such as listing the contents of remote directories, changing the current remote directory, and creating and removing remote directories. FTP typically uses a connection-oriented Transport layer protocol, such as TCP, in providing its services.

- **NFS Remote File Access.** The *Network File System (NFS)* implements a number of high-level services that provide authorized users with access to files located on remote hosts. System administrators generally designate one or more hosts in the internet to play the role of NFS file servers. These hosts run NFS server software that make certain designated directories on their disk storage devices available to other hosts. A user accesses an NFS-mounted directory in the same manner as accessing a directory on a local disk. The fact that a directory is an NFS-mounted directory on a remote host is typically transparent to the user of the local host.

Support Services

- **TFTP File Transfer.** The *Trivial File Transfer Protocol (TFTP)* is a simple file transfer facility that also provides the ability to transfer data in both directions between the local host and a remote host. TFTP is generally used only by system software that performs such functions as downline loading of program code and is not intended to be employed directly by end users. TFTP implements its own reliability controls and can run on top of any type of transport service. Most implementations of TFTP use the connectionless UDP Transport layer protocol.

- **DNS Name Resolution.** Each host attached to a TCP/IP internet has at least one 32-bit internet address assigned to it. Each host also typically has a unique name to make it possible for users to easily refer to the host without knowing its internet address. Since the underlying TCP/IP protocols all refer to individual hosts using their internet addresses, each host must implement a *name resolution* function that translates between host names and internet addresses. In small TCP/IP internets, the function of translating between a host name and the internet address associated with that host can be performed by the host itself through a configuration file typically named **hosts**. In a large internet, it is unwieldy to try to maintain name-to-address mappings for each individual host in local **hosts** files. The *Domain Name System (DNS)* is a directory service that can be used to maintain the mappings between names and internet addresses in a limited number of places in the internet rather than at the location of each host.

- **SMTP Electronic Mail.** The *Simple Mail Transfer Protocol (SMTP)* is a protocol used for the transfer of electronic mail messages. SMTP is designed to be used by electronic mail software that provides the user with access to messaging facilities; it is not designed to be employed by end users directly. Mail facilities allow the user to send messages and files to a user connected to the local network, to a user connected to some other network in the internet, or to a user connected to a non-TCP/IP network that has a connection to the TCP/IP internet. Many types of electronic mail systems have been implemented for the TCP/IP environment, some of which can be interconnected with the electronic messaging systems of other types of networks, such as PROFS and DISOSS in the IBM environment, and with public electronic mail services, such as MCI Mail and CompuServe.

- **X Window System Presentation.** The *X Window System* is a set of distributed graphical presentation services that implement a windowing system on a graphics display. It implements a client/server relationship between an application program (the client) and the windowing software in a workstation or terminal that controls a window on the graphical display (the server). The client and server can be running in different computing systems or in the same computing system. The X Window

(Continued)

BOX B.1 *(Continued)*

System allows a user at a graphics workstation to have multiple windows open on the screen, each of which might be controlled by a separate client application program. The X Window System defines a protocol that is used to transmit information between the client application program and the server windowing software.

- **Kerberos Security.** Kerberos is an encryption-based security system that provides mutual authentication between a client component and a server component in a distributed computing environment. It also provides services that can be used to control which clients are authorized to access which servers. In the Kerberos system, each client component and each server component is called a *principal* and has a unique *principal identifier* assigned to it. These principal identifiers allow clients and servers to identify themselves to each other to prevent fraudulent exchanges of information. Authorization of a client to access a particular server can be implemented independently from the authentication service.

- **Remote Procedure Call.** *Remote procedure call (RPC)* mechanisms allow a process running in the local host to call a procedure that is running in a remote host. Procedure argument and results values are transferred across the internet in a transparent fashion.

- NTP **Distributed Time.** The *Network Time Protocol (NTP)* implements algorithms that permit networked computing systems to maintain common, correct values for the date and time of day.

- SNMP **Network Management.** Network management services are typically provided in a TCP/IP internet through software that implements the *Simple Network Management Protocol (SNMP)*. SNMP defines a *Management Information Base (MIB)*, which is a database that defines all the objects that can be managed in the internet. SNMP also defines the formats of a set of network management messages and the rules by which the messages are exchanged. The network management messages are used to make requests for performing network management functions and to report on events that occur in the network.

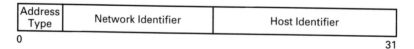

Address Type	Network Identifier	Host Identifier

0   31

Figure B.2   TCP/IP internet address structure.

Internet addresses are distinct from the physical hardware addresses of the NICs installed in systems. Each type of data link technology used to implement a particular network in a TCP/IP network may define its own physical hardware addressing scheme. For example, as we have seen, a network implemented using a local area network technology may employ IEEE/ISO/ANSI 48-bit station addresses (MAC addresses) as physical hardware addresses. The TCP/IP *Address Resolution Protocol (ARP)* and *Reverse Address Resolution Protocol (RARP)*, described later in this appendix, provide mechanisms for converting between 32-bit internet addresses and the physical hardware addresses used on a particular data link.

Internet Address Formats

In a TCP/IP internet address, the initial bits of the Network Identifier field of the address identify a particular *address class*. The formats of the internet addresses for four commonly used address classes are shown in Fig. B.3. The following are descriptions of each of these four classes of internet addresses:

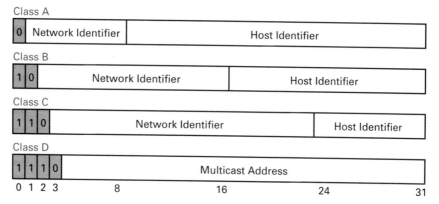

Figure B.3   Four primary formats for TCP/IP internet addresses.

- **Class A Addresses.** An address whose first bit is set to 0 is a class A address. A class A address provides 7 bits to identify the physical network and 24 bits to identify systems on that network. In any network there can be up to 126 networks that use class A addresses. Since a class A address provides 24 bits for uniquely identifying systems, a class A network can, for practical purposes, contain an almost unlimited number of systems.

- **Class B Addresses.** An address whose first two bits are set to 10 is a class B address. A class B address provides 14 bits to identify the network and 16 bits to identify systems. A class B address allows for up to $2^{14}-2$ different physical networks and up to $2^{16}-2$ different systems on each network.

- **Class C addresses.** An address whose first three bits are set to 110 is a class C address. A class C address provides 21 bits to identify the network and 8 bits to identify systems. A class C address allows for up to $2^{21}-2$ different physical networks but only up to 254 different systems on each network.

- **Class D Addresses.** An address whose first four bits are set to 1110 is a class D address. A class D address is used to implement a form of multicasting in which an address refers to some collection of systems in a network, all of which receive the data units having the specified multicast address.

The internet addressing scheme allows for relatively few class A networks. For example, in the Internet, only very few class A addresses still remain unallocated, and it is no longer possible for an individual organization to get a class A address assignment. Class B and class C addresses are the only types of addresses available for assignment to individual organizations.

In order to ensure that network identifiers are unique across the entire Internet, a central authority assigns address classes and ranges of internet address values to be used by individual organizations when their networks connect to the Internet.

Extended IP Addressing

At the time of writing, the Internet, the world's largest TCP/IP network, is rapidly running out of unique addresses that can be assigned to new users. In order to allow the Internet to accommodate future growth, an effort is underway to expand the IP address structure beyond its current 32-bit limitation. Several different methods for providing more possible unique address values are under investigation.

The current version of IP is called IP Version 4 (IPv4); and it is likely that the next version of IP will be called IP Version 6 (IPv6). The version of IPv6 that currently has the highest probability of succeeding IPv4 specifies a 320-bit address (40 octets), which will allow almost unlimited growth.

Subnets

TCP/IP network administrators can use a single network identifier in multiple networks by defining TCP/IP *subnetworks*, or *subnets*. When using subnetting, some of the high-order bits in the host identifier portion of the address are used to identify individual subnets. A value called a *subnet mask* must be used by each system to identify how the internet address bits should be interpreted in a particular network.

Dotted-Decimal Notation

When writing down internet addresses, or when software displays them to human users, a form of notation called *dotted-decimal notation* is typically used to represent 32-bit TCP/IP internet addresses. For example, assume a system has the following internet address:

```
10000010 00001111 00000100 00000001
```

The above internet address would be written down or displayed in dotted-decimal notation as follows: 130.15.4.1.

A separate decimal number is used to represent the value of each individual octet of the address.

Ports

A computing system can typically support multiple independent programs that all execute concurrently. Each of the concurrently executing programs may be communicating with active programs running in other computing systems in the network. An individual active program within a computing system is represented by a data structure called a *port*. Each application program running in a TCP/IP system is assigned a 16-bit *port number* to uniquely identify it within that system. Each application program using TCP/IP communication services is assigned one or more ports on its system.

When a source application program sends data to a destination application program, it must provide three pieces of information:

- The data to be sent.
- The internet address of the host on which the destination application program is running.
- The number of the port on the destination host assigned to the destination application program.

TRANSPORT LAYER PROTOCOLS

TCP/IP Transport layer protocols provide application programs with end-to-end data transfer services. The following sections describe the operation of the two major data transport protocols that operate in the Transport layer of the TCP/IP architecture. The two protocols described here are the User Datagram Protocol (UDP) and the Transmission Control Protocol (TCP).

User Datagram Protocol (UDP)

The *User Datagram Protocol (UDP)* permits packets to be sent with a minimum of protocol overhead. With UDP, delivery is not guaranteed. There is no checking for missing, out-of-sequence, or duplicate packets, and no acknowledgments are sent. UDP datagrams are often called *user datagrams* to distinguish them from IP datagrams. UDP datagrams are carried through the network encapsulated within IP datagrams.

The only error checking provided by UDP is via a Checksum field carried within the UDP packet. If the checksum value calculated by the receiving station does not agree with the checksum contained in the user datagram, the receiving system discards the user datagram. It is possible for UDP to lose user datagrams, to deliver them in a sequence different from that in which they were sent, or to duplicate them. Because it is possible for these errors to occur, UDP cannot be considered a reliable data delivery service. The application itself must implement any required reliability controls when it uses the UDP Transport layer protocol.

Transmission Control Protocol (TCP)

The *Transmission Control Protocol (TCP)* also operates in the TCP/IP Transport layer. TCP provides a connection-oriented, reliable data transfer service used to transmit an unstructured stream of octets from a port in the source system to a port in the destination system. Before data delivery can begin, the TCP user at one end requests a connection, both the protocol itself and the TCP user at the other end agree, and TCP establishes the connection.

TCP provides a full-duplex data delivery service. The source and destination TCP processes use the services of the underlying IP protocol to exchange messages called *segments*. Segments are encapsulated in IP datagrams for transmission using the services of IP. TCP itself does not impose any structure on the data being transmitted, and segments are transparent to the two TCP users, who can view the transmitted data as a continuous stream.

TCP segments can be of any desired size. Octets transferred from one TCP user to another appear at the destination system in the same sequence in which they were sent.

With TCP, either an identical copy of the data stream appears at the destination, or the connection is released and the two TCP users are informed that a failure has occurred.

INTERNET LAYER PROTOCOLS

The protocols that operate in the TCP/IP Internet layer provide services to the Transport layer protocols. The protocols that operate in the Internet layer are the Internet Protocol (IP), the Internet Control Message Protocol (ICMP), the Address Resolution Protocol (ARP), and the Reverse Address Resolution Protocol (RARP).

Internet Protocol (IP)

The *Internet Protocol*, generally referred to by its acronym IP, operates in the TCP/IP Internet layer. IP routes packets across interconnected networks and performs packet segmentation and reassembly functions. Other protocols operating in the TCP/IP Internet layer provide support to the basic IP routing function. IP packets are often called *IP datagrams*.
   IP performs two primary functions:

- Determining a route and relaying packets across the network.
- Segmenting a packet, if necessary, to accommodate a network that has a small maximum packet size and then reassembling the packet when it reaches its destination.

Internet Control Message Protocol (ICMP)

The *Internet Control Message Protocol (ICMP)* is another protocol that operates in the Internet layer. Its purpose is to allow end systems and routers to report on error conditions and to provide information about unexpected circumstances. Although ICMP is viewed as residing in the Internet layer, ICMP packets travel through a network in the form of IP datagrams. ICMP uses the IP best-efforts delivery service in a similar manner to a Transport layer protocol in moving ICMP packets through a network. Fields in the header information of an IP datagram identify a packet as being an ICMP packet.
   The following are some of the most common purposes for which ICMP is used:

- A system can determine whether a destination system is currently reachable.
- A router can inform a system that there is a better route that it can use in sending subsequent IP datagrams to a particular destination network.
- A system can tell a router that IP datagrams are arriving too fast for the system to process them.
- A system can tell a router that it has received a bad IP datagram, such as one that has exceeded the amount of time it is allowed to exist in a network or one that has incorrect parameter information in its header.
- Systems can exchange packets used to synchronize their clocks.
- Systems can exchange packets that contain subnet mask values that inform each other of the specific formats of their internet addresses, indicating how many bits are used to identify a subnetwork and how many are used to identify individual systems.

Address Resolution Protocol (ARP)

The *Address Resolution Protocol (ARP)* is a protocol used by IP in helping it to route IP datagrams to the correct destination system. It can be used by IP in a source system to help it deliver an IP datagram to a system or router on the same physical network as the source system.

Internet Addresses

As we discussed earlier in this appendix, the network identifier field of a system's internet address uniquely identifies the physical network to which the system is attached. Therefore, the IP process running in a system can examine the destination internet address in an IP datagram and can easily determine the identity of the individual physical network to which the packet should be sent. However, the host identifier field of a system's internet address may have no direct relationship to the system's physical hardware address on its physical subnetwork. When the IP process running in one system wishes to deliver data to another system on its own network, it may know the internet address of the destination system, but it may not yet know the system's physical hardware address. The system's physical hardware address is needed by the Data Link layer for transmission over a data link.

Mapping Internet Addresses
to Physical Hardware Addresses

In some cases, it is possible to provide each system on a network with a table that maps the internet addresses of all the systems and routers on that network to their associated physical hardware addresses. However, most LANs use a 48-bit MAC address as a physical hardware address and permit a great many devices to be attached to an individual LAN. Such a LAN may be constantly changing as some users turn their machines off or remove them from the LAN and as other users attach new systems to the LAN. For such a situation, a dynamic scheme is required that allows systems to automatically maintain tables used to convert internet addresses into their associated physical hardware addresses. This is the function of ARP.

ARP Operation

ARP in each system maintains an *ARP cache* containing the mappings of internet addresses to physical hardware addresses for the systems on its own network that it currently knows about. When the IP process running in a system needs to deliver an IP datagram to a system on its own network, it looks up the system's internet address in its ARP cache. If the cache has an entry for that internet address, IP retrieves the associated physical hardware address in that ARP cache entry and delivers the IP datagram to the NIC with that address.

When a system is first powered up, its ARP cache is empty. Assume that the IP process in system A is attempting to deliver an IP datagram to system B but that system B's internet address is not yet in system A's ARP cache. IP uses ARP to determine system B's physical hardware address.

System A performs the following steps to determine system B's physical hardware address:

1. The ARP process running in system A broadcasts an ARP packet on the LAN containing system B's internet address.

2. The ARP processes running in all the systems on the LAN receive this broadcast packet.

3. System B recognizes its own internet address in the broadcast packet and replies to the system that sent the broadcast packet with a packet containing system B's physical hardware address.

4. When system A receives the reply from system B, system A stores system B's internet address to physical hardware address mapping in its ARP cache.

5. The IP process running in system A can now use the information in the new ARP cache entry to determine system B's physical hardware address and can directly deliver the IP datagram destined for system B.

There is an additional refinement to ARP that reduces the network traffic associated with running the protocol. This refinement is based on the assumption that it is likely that when system A has data to send to system B, system B will later need to send data back to system A. In anticipation of this likelihood, when the ARP process running in system A sends an ARP broadcast packet asking for system B's physical hardware address, system A also places into that ARP packet its own internet address to physical hardware address mapping. When system B receives system A's ARP broadcast packet, system B adds system A's internet address to physical hardware address mapping to its own ARP cache. This eliminates the need for the IP process in system B to run ARP should it later have to send data back to system A.

Reverse Address Resolution Protocol (RARP)

A protocol related to ARP , but used for the opposite purpose, is the *Reverse Address Resolution Protocol (RARP)*. RARP allows a system that knows only its physical hardware address to obtain the internet address that it should use in communicating with other systems. RARP is typically of use only to systems on a LAN data link that do not implement disk storage, often called *diskless workstations*. Terminals that implement the X Windows protocols—sometimes called *X Terminals*—may also use RARP to obtain their internet addresses.

In order for RARP to operate, at least one system on the LAN must be designated as a *RARP server*. A diskless workstation obtains an internet address by broadcasting on the LAN a RARP packet giving the workstation's physical hardware address. The RARP packet asks any RARP server on the LAN to reply with the internet address associated with that physical hardware address.

A RARP server maintains a table that maps the physical hardware addresses of the diskless workstations it serves to the internet addresses that those diskless workstations should use. When a RARP server receives a broadcast packet from a diskless workstation asking for an internet address, it looks up the physical hardware address in its table, obtains the internet address corresponding to that physical hardware address, and replies with the internet address that the diskless workstation should use.

TCP/IP ROUTING

The routing function in a TCP/IP network has the responsibility of determining the path over which each IP datagram should travel from a source system to a destination system. Each end system and router maintains a routing table that it uses to determine the best next destination for each datagram it processes that must be sent to some other physical network. An end system's routing table must have at least one entry: an entry containing the address of a *default router*. An end system's default router is typically assigned when the TCP/IP communication software is configured for that system.

TCP/IP assumes the source system is able to send an IP datagram directly to the destination system if both are on the same network. When a source system has an IP datagram to deliver to a destination system in another network, it consults its routing table to see if has an entry matching the address of the destination network. If the routing table has no entry corresponding to the destination network, the source system sends the datagram to the default router. If the default router is not the most direct route for a particular destination, the router returns an ICMP Redirect packet to the source system, giving it the address of the router it should use for subsequent datagrams destined for that destination network. The source system updates its routing table and directs future datagrams for that destination to the specified router.

Routing Protocols

The basic routing function is handled in a TCP/IP network by IP, and many small TCP/IP networks operate using only basic IP routing facilities. In larger networks, additional routing protocols are used by routers to exchange routing information with each other. There are many different routing protocols that routers can employ. The choice of the routing protocols used in any given TCP/IP network is generally based on the size and the structure of the network.

Autonomous Systems and Gateways

A TCP/IP network is made up of one or more *autonomous systems*. An autonomous system consists of a set of computer systems and data links making up one or more physical networks administered by a single authority. An authority might be, for example, a university, a corporation, or a government agency.

Routers are often referred to as *gateways* in TCP/IP literature. Routers used only within a single autonomous system are called *interior gateways*. Routers that connect one autonomous system to another are called *exterior gateways*. Outside of TCP/IP, the term gateway generally is used to refer to a system that interconnects networks that use different network protocol families. To avoid confusion, we use the term router throughout this book when referring to a system that performs routing and relaying functions.

INTERIOR GATEWAY PROTOCOLS

The routers within an autonomous system are free to use any desired interior gateway protocol in communicating among themselves. A number of interior gateway protocols are in common use in TCP/IP networks. The following sections describe the more common of these.

Routing Information Protocol

The *Routing Information Protocol (RIP)* is run by a routing program called **routed**. **Routed** and RIP were developed as part of the UNIX operating system developed by the University of California at Berkeley. This variation of UNIX is called *BSD UNIX*. (The BSD acronym stands for *Berkeley Software Distribution*.) The program was developed and distributed as part of 4.3BSD UNIX and became quite widely used without actually being defined in a formal specification.

RIP uses a distance-vector routing algorithm that employs hop counts as distance measurements. With RIP, routers periodically send out routing information, and both routers and end systems use the routing information to update their routing tables.

Periodically, every router running RIP sends out a message reflecting the information in its routing table. The message is sent to all systems on networks to which the router is directly attached. Routers and end systems use the information in the message to update their routing tables. A table is updated to reflect an alternate route to a given destination only if the alternate route is shorter. Routers also send out routing information messages if a change occurs to the information in its routing table.

When a router installs a route in its table, it starts a time for that route. The timer is restarted whenever a message is received that shows the same route. If the timer expires, the route is considered no longer available.

Hello Protocol

The *Hello* protocol is similar to RIP except that it measures distance based on estimated delays rather than hop counts. Hello includes a mechanism for synchronizing clocks in different systems and uses timestamps on packets sent between systems to estimate routing delays.

Open Shortest Path First Protocol

The *Open Shortest Path First Protocol (OSPF)* uses an algorithm called a link-state routing algorithm. Routers exchange information about their own data links and then use that information to develop a map of the network topology. Routes are calculated based on the topology. Periodically, routers test neighbor availability, and broadcast status information about links. A router can also request information about specific links. OSPF allows for multiple routes to a destination based on different types of service, such as low delay or high throughput.

With OSPF, an autonomous system can be divided into areas, where each area is self-contained in terms of topology and routing. A router within a given area will have complete information on links and systems within that area, and will be able to calculate routes within that area. Area border routers can route packets to other areas within an autonomous system. Autonomous system border routers can route packets to other autonomous systems. Routers within an area receive information on destinations outside the area in summary form that enables them to route a packet to the appropriate border router.

OSPF is better suited than RIP or Hello to larger autonomous systems. The OSPF specification is available in the published literature and is an open standard that many router vendors have implemented.

EXTERIOR GATEWAY PROTOCOLS

In order for data to flow between two autonomous systems in a large TCP/IP network, a router in one autonomous system must be able to communicate with a router in the other autonomous system. Protocols used for communicating between routers in different autonomous systems are called *exterior gateway protocols (EGPs)*. One commonly used routing protocol that allows routers in different autonomous systems to communicate is the *Exterior Gateway Protocol (EGP)*. Another exterior gateway protocol sometimes used for communicating between autonomous systems is the *Border Gateway Protocol (BGP)*.

This section describes the operation of the more commonly used of the two exterior gateway protocols: the Exterior Gateway Protocol. EGP is defined by a TCP/IP RFC and is implemented by many different router vendors.

Exterior Gateway Protocol Functions

EGP packets are used to perform three functions:

- Agreeing to exchange routing information with another autonomous system.
- Checking that a router in another autonomous system is still responding.
- Obtaining routing information from another autonomous system.

Each of these functions is described in the following sections.

Neighbor Acquisition

The process of agreeing to exchange information with another autonomous system is called *neighbor acquisition*. When a router functioning in the role of an exterior gateway wishes to exchange information with a router in another autonomous system, it sends an EGP Acquisition Request packet to that router. The other router responds with either an Acquisition Confirm or Acquisition Refuse packet. Assuming the response is positive, the two routers are then able to exchange routing information and the two gateways are then known as *exterior neighbors*.

As part of the acquisition packet exchange, the two routers agree on how frequently each router will be tested to see if it is still responding and how frequently requests for routing information can be sent. If, at a later time, a router no longer wishes to be available to its neighbor, it sends an EGP Cease request. The neighbor responds with an EGP Cease Confirm.

Neighbor Reachability

Periodically, each router operating in the role of an exterior gateway checks its exterior neighbors by sending them EGP Hello packets. The neighbors respond with EGP I Heard

You packets. If a neighbor does not respond after a certain number of tries, it is considered to be down and is no longer available for routing.

Routing Information Updating

When a router functioning as an exterior gateway wants to receive routing information from an exterior neighbor, it sends an EGP Poll Request packet. This packet identifies a *source network* common to the two exterior neighbor routers. The exterior neighbor router returns routing information in an EGP Poll Response. Only destinations part of the autonomous system providing the information are included in the information in the Poll Response. The distances shown for reaching the different destination networks are based on entering the autonomous system via the specified source network.

EGP implements a distance-vector form of routing protocol. However, the measure used for distance is not defined as part of the EGP specification. Each autonomous system defines its own distance measure. This means that distance values included in a Poll Response are comparable from route to route with an autonomous system, but they may not be comparable from one autonomous system to another.

Appendix C

OSI Technology

During the time that today's network architectures and communication protocols were being developed, an ambitious project was underway in ISO to develop a single international standard set of communication protocols that could be used in a communication network. By 1984, ISO had defined the *Reference Model for Open Systems Interconnection (OSI model)*, a generalized model of system interconnection described in international standard ISO 7498 and in ITU-T Recommendation X.200.

PURPOSE OF THE OSI MODEL

The OSI model is designed to provide a common basis for the coordination of standards development for the purpose of interconnecting *open systems*. The term *open* in this context means systems open to one another by virtue of their mutual use of applicable standards.

The OSI model describes how machines can communicate with one another in a standardized and highly flexible way by defining the functional layers that should be incorporated into each communicating machine. The OSI model does not define the networking software itself, nor does it define detailed standards for that software; it simply defines the broad categories of function each layer should perform.

THE OSI NETWORK ARCHITECTURE

ISO has also developed a comprehensive set of standards for the various layers of the OSI model. These standards together make up the *OSI architecture* for computer networking.

The standards making up the OSI architecture are not today widely implemented in commercial products for computer networking, nor does it appear that they will be widely implemented in the forseeable future. However, the OSI model is still important. Many of the concepts and terminology associated with the OSI model have become generally accepted as a basis for discussing and describing network architectures. The layering structure of the OSI model is also often used in categorizing the various communication protocols in common use today and in comparing one network architecture with another.

The remainder of this appendix introduces the seven functional layers defined by the OSI model.

OSI MODEL FUNCTIONAL LAYERS

The OSI model defines the seven functional layers shown in Fig. C.1. Each layer performs a different set of functions, and the intent was to make each layer as independent as possible from all the others. The following sections briefly describe each of the seven layers of the OSI model, working from the bottom up.

| Application Layer |
| Presentation Layer |
| Session Layer |
| Transport Layer |
| Network Layer |
| Data Link Layer |
| Physical Layer |

Figure C.1   OSI model functional layers.

The Physical Layer

The *Physical* layer is responsible for the actual transmission of a bit stream across a physical circuit. It allows signals, such as electrical signals, optical signals, or radio signals, to be exchanged among communicating machines. The Physical layer, shown in Fig. C.2, typically consists of hardware permanently installed in the communicating devices. The Physical layer also addresses the cables, connectors, modems, and other devices used to permit machines to communicate physically.

Physical layer mechanisms in each of the communicating machines typically control the generation and detection of signals interpreted as 0 bits and 1 bits. The Physical

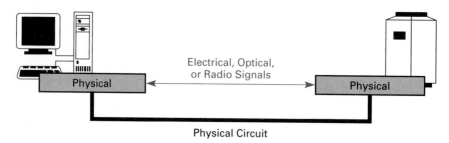

Figure C.2   The Physical layer is concerned with sending and receiving signals over a communications medium.

layer does not assign any significance to the bits. For example, it is not concerned with how many bits make up each unit of data, nor is it concerned with the meaning of the data being transmitted. In the Physical layer, the sender simply transmits a signal and the receiver detects it.

The Data Link Layer

The *Data Link* layer is responsible for providing data transmission over a single connection from one system to another. Control mechanisms in the Data Link layer handle the transmission of data units, often called *frames*, over a physical circuit. Functions operating in the Data Link layer allow data to be transmitted, in a relatively error-free fashion, over a sometimes error-prone physical circuit (see Fig. C.3). This layer is concerned with how bits are grouped into frames and performs synchronization functions with respect to failures occurring in the Physical layer. The Data Link layer implements error-detection mechanisms that identify transmission errors. With some types of data links, the Data Link layer may also perform procedures for flow control, frame sequencing, and recovering from transmission errors.

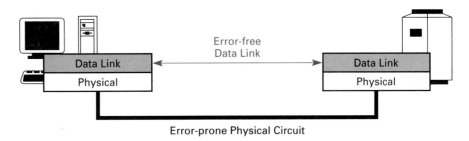

Figure C.3 The Data Link layer is responsible for the transmission of data units over a physical circuit.

The Network Layer

The *Network* layer is concerned with making routing decisions and with relaying data from one device to another through the network. The OSI model classifies each system in the network as one of two types: *end systems* act as the source or the final destination of data, and *intermediate systems* perform routing and relaying functions (see Fig. C.4).

The facilities provided by the Network layer supply a service that higher layers employ for moving data units, often called *packets*, from one end system to another, where the packets may flow through any number of intermediate systems. End systems generally implement all seven layers of the OSI model, allowing application programs to exchange information with each other. It is possible for intermediate systems performing *only* routing and relaying functions to implement only the bottom three layers of the OSI model.

In a complex network, the path between any two systems may at one instant be via a number of data links. The application programs running in two end systems that wish to

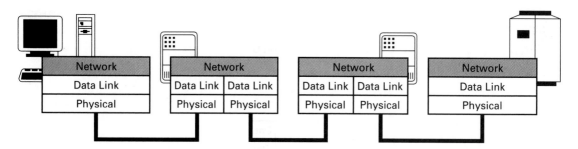

Figure C.4   The Network layer allows communication across multiple data links.

communicate should not need to be concerned with the route packets take nor with how many data links they must cross. The Network layer functions operating in end systems and in intermediate systems together handle these routing and relaying functions.

Whereas the Data Link layer provides for the transmission of frames between *adjacent* systems across a single data link, the Network layer provides for the much more complex task of transmitting packets between *any* two end systems in the network, regardless of how many data links may need to be traversed.

The Transport Layer

The *Transport* layer builds on the services of the Network layer and the layers below it to form the uppermost layer of a reliable end-to-end *data transport service*. The Transport layer hides from the higher layers all the details concerning the actual moving of packets and frames from one computer to another. The Network layer shields network users from the complexities of network operation.

The lowest three layers of the OSI model implement a common physical network that many machines can share independently of one another, just as many independent users share the postal service. It is possible for the postal service to occasionally lose a letter. To detect the loss of a letter, two users of the postal service might apply their own end-to-end controls, such as sequentially numbering their letters. The functions performed in the Transport layer can include similar end-to-end integrity controls to recover from lost, out-of-sequence, or duplicate messages.

Transport layer functions handle addressing of the processes, such as application programs, that use the network for communication. The Transport layer can also control the rate at which messages flow through the network to prevent and control congestion. Whereas the Network layer is concerned with the interface between network systems and operates in end systems and intermediate systems, the Transport layer provides an end-to-end service that programs can use for moving data back and forth between them.

The Transport layer is the lowest layer required *only* in the computers running the programs that use the network for communication (see Fig. C.5). The Transport layer need not be implemented in intermediate systems that perform only routing and relaying functions.

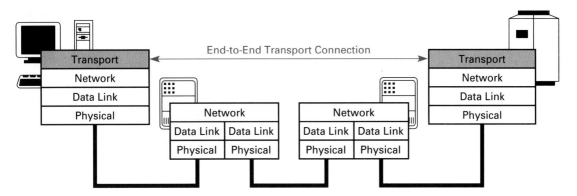

Figure C.5 The Transport layer is the lowest layer required only in the communicating end systems.

The Session Layer

There is a fundamental difference in orientation between the bottom four layers and the top three. The bottom four layers are concerned more with the network itself and provide a general data transport service useful to any application. The top three layers are more concerned with services oriented to the application programs themselves (see Fig. C.6).

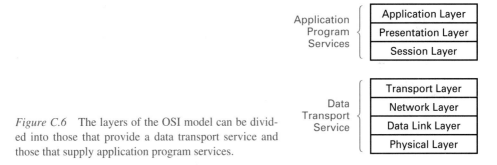

Figure C.6 The layers of the OSI model can be divided into those that provide a data transport service and those that supply application program services.

The *Session* layer is the lowest of the layers associated with the application programs. It is responsible for organizing the dialog between two application programs and for managing the data exchanges between them. To do this, the Session layer imposes a structure on the interaction between two communicating programs (see Fig. C.7).

The Session layer defines three types of dialogs: two-way simultaneous interaction, where both programs can send and receive concurrently; two-way alternate interaction, where the programs take turns sending and receiving; and one-way interaction, where one program sends and the other only receives. In addition to organizing the dialog, the Session layer services include establishing synchronization points within the dialog, allowing a dialog to be interrupted, and resuming a dialog from a synchronization point.

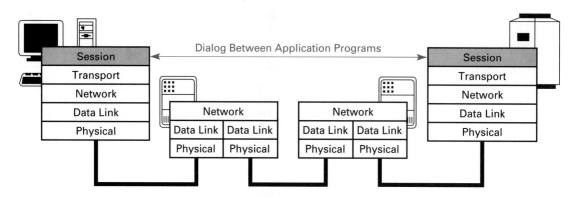

Figure C.7   The Session layer organizes the dialog between two application processes.

The Presentation Layer

The five layers below the *Presentation* layer are all concerned with the orderly movement of a stream of bits from one program to another. The Presentation layer is the lowest layer interested in the *meaning* of those bits. It deals with preserving the *information content* of data transmitted over the network (see Fig. C.8).

The Presentation layer is concerned with three types of *data syntax* that can be used for describing and representing data:

- **Abstract Syntax.** An *abstract syntax* consists of a formal definition of the information content of the data two programs exchange. An abstract syntax is concerned only with information content and not with how that information content is represented in a computer or how it is encoded for transmission. For example, an abstract syntax might define a data type called AccountNumber, values of which consist of integers. ISO 8824 *Abstract Syntax Notation One (ASN.1)* defines an international standard notation often used in practice to define abstract syntaxes in information technology standards.

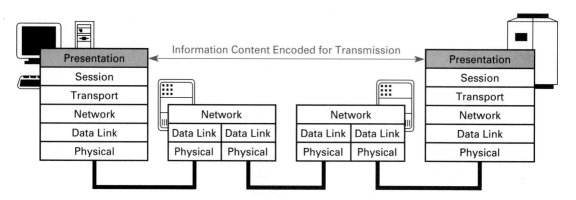

Figure C.8   The Presentation layer is responsible for preserving the information content of the data transmitted over the network.

- **Transfer Syntax.** A *transfer syntax* defines how the information content of data is encoded for transmission over the network. A value of the AccountNumber type might be transferred over the network using some form of encoding scheme that identifies the value as being of the AccountNumber type, specifies that it consists of an integer, and encodes that integer's value using a minimum number of bits.

- **Local Concrete Syntax.** A *local concrete syntax* defines how the information content of data is actually represented in a computing system. Two communicating systems might use different local concrete syntaxes. For example, one system might represent the integers in an account number in the form of a binary number using 2's complement notation; another system might use a string of decimal digits. The OSI model is not concerned with the local concrete syntax, and programs are free to represent data internally in any desired way.

The OSI model defines two major functions for the Presentation layer. First, the Presentation layer in the two communicating systems must negotiate a common transfer syntax to be used to transfer the messages defined by a particular abstract syntax. Second, the Presentation layer must ensure that one system does not need to care what local concrete syntax the other system is using. If the local concrete syntaxes in the two communicating systems are different, an implementation of the Presentation layer is responsible for transforming from the local concrete syntax to the transfer syntax in the sending system and from the transfer syntax to the local concrete syntax in the receiving system.

If both computers are running C programs in personal computers that use Intel microprocessors, the Presentation layer has little to do, since both programs use the same local concrete syntax. However, if a Pascal program running in a VAX is communicating with a FORTRAN program running in an IBM mainframe, the Presentation layer becomes more important. The FORTRAN program may represent an integer in decimal using a variable-length field; the Pascal program may represent an integer in binary using a 32-bit word. The Presentation layer performs the necessary conversions that allow each program to work with data in its own preferred format without having to be aware of the data formats that its partner uses.

The Application Layer

The topmost layer, the one user processes plug into, is the *Application* layer (see Fig. C.9). The Application layer is concerned with high-level functions that provide support to the application programs using the network for communication. The Application layer provides a means for application programs to access the system interconnection facilities to exchange information. It provides all functions related to communication between systems not provided by the lower layers.

The Application layer provides a means for application programs to exchange information with each other. Communication services provided by the Application layer hide the complexity of the layers below from the communicating programs. As far as the Application layer is concerned, a program running in one computer sends a message, and a program running in some other computer receives it. The Application layer is not concerned with any of the details concerning how the message gets from the source computer to the destination computer.

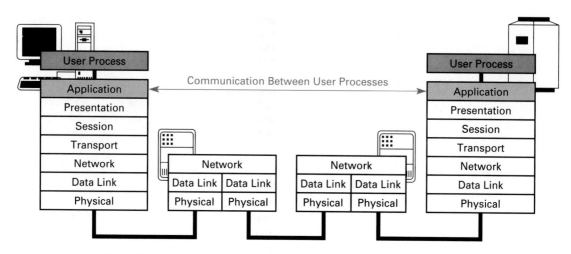

Figure C.9   The Application layer is the topmost layer into which user processes plug.

The Application layer is more open ended than the layers below. Due to the wide variety of applications that will ultimately use networks for communication, many standards for the Application layer have been developed, and many new ones will eventually be required.

OSI CONCEPTS

Many information technology standards for computer networking are based on the OSI model and use much of the terminology that ISO has adopted in documenting communication services and protocols. In order to understand the wide variety of standards important to enterprise networking, it is useful to understand some of the concepts underlying the OSI model.

The OSI model is concerned with the interconnection of systems—the way in which they exchange information—and not the internal functions performed by a given system. In OSI terminology, a system is defined as follows:

> A *system* is a set of one or more computers, the associated software, peripherals, terminals, human operators, physical processes, transfer means, etc., that forms an autonomous whole capable of performing information processing and/or information transfer.

The OSI model provides a generalized view of a layered architecture. With the broad definition given for a system, the architecture can apply to a very simple system, such as a point-to-point connection between two computers, or to a very complex system, such as the interconnection of two entire computer networks.

Entities and Service Access Points

The notions of entities and service access points are important to understanding how interactions take place between layers in communicating systems.

- **Entity.** An active element within a layer. Two communicating entities within the same layer, but in different network systems, are called *peer entities*. Entities in the Application layer are called *Application entities*, entities in the Presentation layer are called *Presentation entities*, and so on. A particular layer provides services to entities running in the layer above.

- **Service-Access-Point (SAP).** The point at which the services of a layer are provided. Each layer defines service-access-points at which entities in the layer above request the services of that layer. Each service-access-point has a *SAP address*, by which the particular entity employing a layer service can be differentiated from all other entities that might also be able to concurrently use that layer service.

Abstract Interfaces

The OSI model defines an interface between any two pairs of adjacent layers in the same system. At any point in the architecture, layer n can be viewed as a *service provider*, and layer $n + 1$ can be viewed as the *service requester* or *service user* (see Fig. C.10). An entity in layer n provides a set of services to entities running in layer $n + 1$ via layer n's service-access-point. The set of services provided by layer n defines the *abstract interface* between layer n and layer $n + 1$.

An abstract interface describes the semantics of the interactions that can occur between two architectural layers. An abstract interface does not specify implementation details, nor does it describe the syntax that must be used to implement the interface. The interactions between two adjacent layers are described only in terms of an abstract set of services that layer n provides to layer $n + 1$.

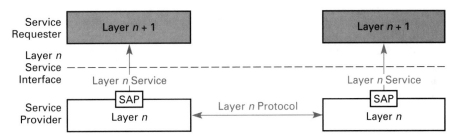

Figure C.10   A service provider provides a defined set of services to a service requester via a service-access-point (SAP). The set of services provided by layer n defines an abstract interface between layer n and layer $n + 1$.

Concrete Interfaces

In addition to abstract interfaces, *concrete interfaces* are also important at some points in the architecture, especially in the Physical layer and at points where application programming interfaces (APIS) must be specified. A concrete interface might describe a point in the architecture at which a physical connector is used, for example, to connect a device to a cable. A concrete interface might provide electrical and mechanical specifications for the cables and connectors that must be used to properly implement the architecture. A concrete interface might also define an application programming interface a programmer must adhere to in writing programs to request the services of a layer.

Services and Protocols

The ISO standards for the OSI model define for each layer a single service definition and one or more protocol specifications. A *service definition* defines the specific services a layer provides to the layer above it. A service definition specifically *does not* say anything about how those services are to be provided. A *protocol specification* describes the formats of the data units exchanged and specifies the procedures a layer must perform in exchanging those data units in providing the services of that layer.

The relationship between the services layer *n* provides and the protocol governing its operation are shown in Fig. C.11. As shown here, the layer *n* protocol uses the services of layer *n* − 1 to provide a defined set of services to layer *n* + 1 above it.

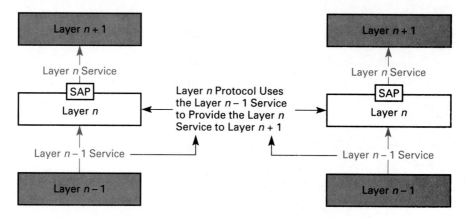

Figure C.11   Relationship between a layer's service definition and its protocol specification.

Some layer services are intended to be used to transmit units of data from a layer entity in one system to a peer layer entity in another system. A layer does this by issuing a data transfer request to the layer below and passing the data unit to be transferred as a parameter of the request. Data units passed from a service requester to a service provider are called *service-data-units (SDUs)*.

The name of the SDU passed from a layer to the layer below begins with the name of the layer to which the SDU is passed. For example, the SDUs passed from the Transport layer to the Network layer are called *network-service-data-units (NSDUs)*, the SDUs passed from the Network layer to the Data Link layer are called *data-link-service-data-units (DLSDUs)*, and so on.

Protocol Specifications

Another principle of the OSI model is that when two network systems are communicating with one another, an entity in each layer in the first system communicates with its peer entity in the second system using a *protocol*. Figure C.12 illustrates protocols operating in each of the seven layers of the OSI model.

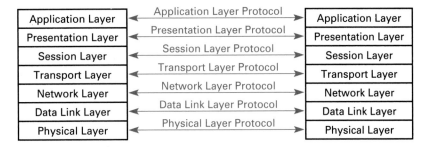

Figure C.12 A separate protocol controls the operation of each layer in the OSI model.

A protocol specification for layer *n* defines the following:

- The formats of the data units exchanged between peer layer *n* entities.

- The interactions that occur between peer layer *n* entities in exchanging data units.

- The way in which layer *n* and layer *n* + 1 interact in exchanging the service requests and responses defined in the service definition for layer *n*.

- The way in which the layer *n* and layer *n* − 1 interact in exchanging the service requests and responses defined in the service definition for layer *n* − 1.

Protocol-Data-Units

Data units sent from a layer entity in one system to a peer layer entity in another system are called *protocol-data-units (PDUs)*. PDUs appear to flow from a layer *n* + 1 entity in the sending system to a layer *n* + 1 entity in the receiving system using the layer *n* + 1 protocol. From this perspective, functions performed in layer *n* and below are hidden from layer *n* + 1.

Protocol Control Information

A layer constructs a protocol-data-unit from the service-data-unit passed down from the layer above by adding *protocol-control-information (PCI)* to it (see Fig. C.13). Some of the information making up the protocol information may be passed down from layer *n* + 1 to layer *n* in the form of service request parameters. The PCI is used to control the operation of the protocol in a particular layer. Protocol-control-information is carried in the form of a header (and, in the case of the Data Link layer, also a trailer) added to the SDU.

Segmentation and Blocking

In some cases, a layer might implement a *segmentation* facility in which a single SDU is used to create a number of individual PDUs. It is also possible for a layer to implement a *blocking* facility that allows multiple SDUs to be grouped together and transported across the network in a single PDU.

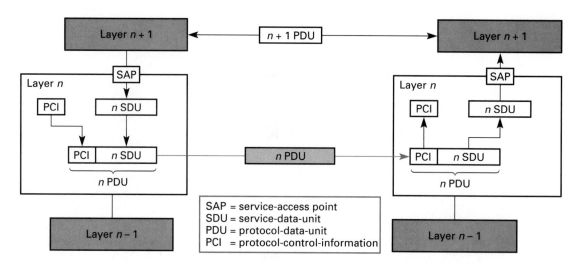

Figure C.13   A layer entity in one machine accepts a service-data-unit (SDU) from the layer above via its service-access-point (SAP). The layer entity then adds protocol-control-information (PCI) to the SDU to create a protocol-data-unit (PDU) and sends that PDU to its peer layer entity in another machine.

Generated PDUs

A layer *n* entity can also itself generate PDUs apart from the PDUs it creates from the SDUs it receives from layer *n* + 1. Such generated PDUs are typically transmitted between peer layer *n* entities to control the operation of the layer *n* protocol. The layer *n* + 1 service requester is not directly aware of the existence of these PDUs.

Appendix **D**

OSI Network Addressing Standards

Access to Network layer services, as in other layers, is through a service-access-point. Network-service-access-point (NSAP) addresses are the network addresses that provide unique identification of the end systems and intermediate systems in an OSI network. This appendix examines the structure of the NSAP address and discusses how NSAP address values are assigned. The structure of the NSAP address used in OSI networks is defined in ISO 8348—*Network Service Definition, Addendum 2: Network Layer Addressing* and in ISO 10589—*Intermediate System to Intermediate System Intra-Domain Routing Exchange Protocol for use in Conjunction with the Protocol for Providing the Connectionless-Mode Network Service.*

GLOBALLY UNIQUE ADDRESSES

The role of the OSI network addressing scheme is an ambitious one. It undertakes to provide a unique identifier for each end system and each router in what might someday become a single, global computer network. Therefore, it is not enough in the OSI environment to ensure that an end system or router has a unique NSAP address within a single organization's network. Instead, the OSI addressing scheme must provide a means for assigning the NSAP address of each end system and each router in an organization's network so that it is guaranteed to be different from the NSAP address of any other end system or router, anywhere in the world.

The OSI addressing scheme does this by defining a method for assigning values to the initial octets of NSAP addresses so that all the network addresses an individual organization generates are guaranteed to be different from any of the NSAP addresses assigned by any other organization in the world.

There are two ways in which we can view the OSI NSAP address. First, we can look at it from the viewpoint of a router that must interpret the NSAP address in making routing decisions. Second, we can look at it from the viewpoint of the ISO Network layer addressing standards that concern addressing authorities and network managers who make NSAP address assignments.

ROUTER ADDRESS INTERPRETATION

A router that is running the OSI routing protocol defined by ISO 10589 interprets an NSAP address as shown in Fig. D.1. The entire NSAP address must be at least 10 octets in length and can be no longer than 20 octets. This is quite a departure from the 16-bit or 24-bit addresses typically used in SNA networks and the 32-bit addresses typically used in TCP/IP networks. The fields that make up the NSAP address are described next.

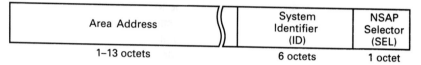

Area Address	System Identifier (ID)	NSAP Selector (SEL)
1–13 octets	6 octets	1 octet

Figure D.1   Router view of an OSI NSAP address.

Area Address

Large OSI networks can be structured hierarchically by dividing the network into collections of systems called *areas*. The division of a large OSI computer network into areas is similar to the way in which the telephone network in North America is partitioned using a system of area codes. However, the system used to divide an OSI computer network into areas need not be strictly geographic. The collections of systems making up each area are determined by network administrators and not by international standards.

The value assigned to the initial octets of an NSAP address constitutes an area address. The value assigned to an area address is a combination of octets containing a value assigned by an addressing authority and octets containing a value set by the organization administering the network. The way in which these values are set is of no concern to routers. Later in this appendix we examine the way values of the area address are administered.

System Identifier

The System Identifier (ID) field contains a six-octet value that uniquely identifies a system within its area. ID field values must be unique within an individual area. In actual practice, the ID field value is ordinarily assigned using the IEEE/ISO local area network addressing standard and corresponds to the station address of the LAN adapter used to attach the system to the OSI network. Therefore, the ID field itself is also globally unique in most cases. In many OSI implementations, a system that does not implement a LAN adapter, such as a system that attaches to an OSI network using a packet-switched data network or a point-to-point link, is still assigned an address using the IEEE/ISO LAN addressing plan. However, the ISO 10589 routing protocol requires only that ID field values be unique within an individual area.

NSAP Selector

The NSAP Selector (SEL) field is always the final octet of the address. It contains a one-octet value that acts as a selector to define the particular type of Transport layer entity that is to receive the packet. The SEL field values are not defined by the addressing standards and are set by the sending Transport layer entity.

Network-Entity-Title

The OSI addressing standards define a unique identifier called the *network-entity-title (NET)* that uniquely identifies an end system or a router. The NET for a system has a format identical to that of the system's NSAP address. The only difference between an NET and an NSAP address is in the interpretation of the NSAP Selector field value. The NSAP Selector field within an NSAP address identifies an entity within the system itself, and so an NSAP Selector field value is not required to uniquely identify a system. Therefore, the NET is defined as consisting of the entire NSAP address, including an NSAP Selector field value of 0. Assuming an NSAP Selector field value of 0 in the NET avoids any confusion that might result from having multiple network-entity-title values associated with the same system, each having a different NSAP Selector field value.

ADDRESSING AUTHORITY DEPENDENT OCTETS

Although the way in which area address values are assigned is of no concern to routers, it is of concern to network administrators who must make address assignments. The format of the initial octets of the NSAP address is defined by an addressing authority responsible for the assignment of values for the initial octets of area addresses. The assignment of values to the initial octets of the area address is the mechanism by which NSAP addresses are guaranteed to be globally unique.

Amendment 2 to ISO 8348, Network Layer Addressing defines methods by which the initial octets of NSAP addresses can be assigned so that all the network-entity-titles an organization generates are guaranteed to be globally unique.

ADDRESS SEMANTICS VERSUS SYNTAX

ISO 8348, Amendment 2 makes a clear distinction among three concepts, illustrated in Fig. D.2, that are associated with describing the semantics and syntax of a network address:

- **Abstract Syntax.** The abstract syntax of network addresses is the means employed in ISO 8348 Amendment 2 to define the hierarchical structure of a network address and is used by addressing authorities to allocate and assign network address values. An abstract syntax defines information content without specifying how that information content is represented in a computer or encoded for transmission. The standard allows the meaning of a network address value to be expressed in either decimal or binary form.

- **Encoding.** Encoding refers to the way in which a network address value is represented in the protocol-control-information attached to a packet and conveyed between systems during Network layer protocol operation. The way in which address values are encoded has no relation to the abstract syntax that defines how address values are allocated and assigned. For example, the abstract syntax might specify that address values are assigned in the form of decimal digits. An address whose value is assigned using a decimal digit

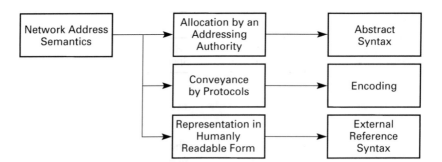

Figure D.2   Network addressing concepts associated with address semantics and syntax.

abstract syntax might well be encoded using a single binary number. Alternatively, some scheme might be used to individually encode each decimal digit of the address value. According to ISO 8348 Amendment 2, addresses can be encoded in any desired way, but the standard recommends certain preferred encoding methods. Other ISO standards for the OSI model specify that NSAP addresses be encoded using the ISO preferred binary encoding scheme, in which each digit of a decimal address is represented in a 4-bit semi-octet.

- **External Reference Syntax.** This is the syntax of a network address as it might be displayed in human-readable form in a printed report or on a display screen. The way a network address is externally represented can be different from both the abstract syntax and the encoding method. For example, the abstract syntax might specify that address values are assigned in the form of decimal digits, the encoding method might be the preferred binary encoding scheme, and the external reference syntax might use decimal numbers with punctuation added to separate the various fields of the address for ease of reading.

ADDRESSING AUTHORITY NSAP ADDRESS FORMAT

ISO 8348 Amendment 2 is concerned only with the abstract syntax of network addresses and with allocating and assigning address values. The ISO standard addressing scheme defines a hierarchical address with the top level of the hierarchy being a number of addressing domains, each of which is associated with an addressing authority. An addressing authority can itself allocate addresses within its own domain, or it can further subdivide its domain and assign an authority to each subdomain it creates. This process can be continued to an arbitrary extent, limited only by the 20-octet maximum length of an NSAP address. The uniqueness of addresses within a particular addressing domain must be ensured by the authority responsible for allocating addresses in that domain.

The addressing authority and network management view of an OSI NSAP address is illustrated in Fig. D.3. According to ISO 8348, Amendment 2, the NSAP address is divided into two major parts, the Initial Domain Part (IDP) and the Domain Specific Part (DSP). ISO 8348 does not define the format of the DSP, but Fig. D.3 shows the format of the DSP for addresses used in conjunction with the ISO 10589 routing protocol. We have already

Initial Domain Part (IDP)		Domain Specific Part (DSP)		
Authority and Format Identifier (AFI)	Initial Domain Identifier (IDI)	High Order Domain Specific Part (HO-DSP)	System Identifier (ID)	NSAP Selector (SEL)
1 octet	Variable	Variable	6 octets	1 octet

Figure D.3   Addressing authority and network manager view of an OSI NSAP address.

described the seven low-order octets of the DSP, containing the System Identifier and NSAP Selector fields, used by the OSI routing protocol.

INITIAL DOMAIN PART

The IDP makes up the beginning of an ISO network address and is further divided into an Authority and Format Identifier (AFI) and an Initial Domain Identifier (IDI). The abstract syntax of the IDP specifies that IDP values must be allocated in the form of decimal digits. This does not require, however, that the IDP must be encoded as decimal digits. It only indicates that addressing authorities must allocate and assign IDP values in the form of decimal digits. We next describe the AFI and IDI fields.

Authority and Format Identifier (AFI)

The AFI contains a two-digit decimal number that defines the addressing authority responsible for allocating IDI values, defines the format of the IDI, and specifies whether the abstract syntax of the domain specific part (DSP) of the address is binary or decimal. DSP address values can be allocated and assigned using either values expressed as decimal numbers or values expressed as binary numbers.

Initial Domain Identifier (IDI)

Specific AFI values determine the format of the IDI. For example, AFI value 48 for a decimal DSP and AFI value 49 for a binary DSP specify that the IDI is a null value and is 0 decimal digits in length. With this IDP value, the entire address is contained in the domain specific part (DSP). These are called local AFI values, and NSAP address values allocated using them cannot be guaranteed to be globally unique.

ADDRESS ADMINISTRATION PLANS

The other AFI values thus far defined can be divided into two categories: those associated with ISO-administered addressing plans and those associated with ITU-T-administered addressing plans. As we will see, the addressing scheme defined in ISO 8348, Amendment 2 goes far beyond the requirements of OSI computer networks. The network addresses assigned to end systems and routers in OSI computer networks represent only a subset of a much more all-encompassing ISO/ITU-T addressing scheme.

ISO Address Administration

With ISO address administration, each IDP value identifies a particular country or an international organization. An addressing authority in each country assigns one or more unique values for the initial octets of the DSP field to each organization applying for them. That organization then ensures that the remaining octets of the DSP field for each network address it creates contains one of the values the addressing authority assigned it.

Unique AFI values are assigned to each of the ISO-administered addressing plans described in Box D.1. The ISO 3166 DCC addressing scheme is the addressing scheme typically used to assign values to the high-order octets of network addresses in OSI computer networks administered by commercial and government organizations.

BOX D.1   Addressing schemes administered by ISO.

- **ISO 3166 DCC.** With this scheme, the IDI consists of a 3-digit code allocated according to ISO 3166. This is an ISO-defined geographically oriented addressing plan that assigns IDI values to countries and national areas independent of public data networks.
- **ISO 6523 ICD.** The IDI consists of a 4-digit International Code Designator (ICD) allocated according to ISO 6523. This is an ISO-defined nongeographic addressing plan that assigns values for the high-order octets in the network addresses used by certain types of international organizations, such as the United Nations, the Red Cross, and certain types of maritime and avionics networks that are nongeographical or multinational in scope.

ITU-T Address Administration

With ITU-T address administration, the values contained in the initial domain part identifies not an entire country but an individual subscriber, such as an individual telephone number. Therefore, the domain specific part of such addresses is often null in an ITU-T-administered address. Unique AFI values are assigned to each of the ITU-T-administered addressing plans described in Box D.2.

DOMAIN SPECIFIC PART

As we have already described, ISO 8348, Amendment 2 does not specify a specific format for the DSP. Different addressing schemes use different DSP formats, and the DSP is null with some addressing schemes, such as those administered by ITU-T. However, as we have seen, the DSP format used in conjunction with the OSI routing protocol is defined in ISO 10589, the ISO standard for OSI routing.

ISO 10589 defines a High Order Domain Specific Part (HO-DSP) field that contains the final octets of the area address. At the time of writing, ISO 10589 does not specify how the HO-DSP field is to be administered. However, the standard recommends that the initial octets of the HO-DSP be set by an addressing authority and that the final octets, preferably the last 2 octets, be allowed to be set by the organization administering the net-

---

BOX D.2   Addressing schemes administered by ITU-T.

- **ITU-T X.121.** With this scheme, the IDI consists of a sequence of up to 14 decimal digits defined by ITU-T Recommendation X.121. This is an ITU-T-defined addressing plan that assigns addresses to individual DTEs in X.21 and X.25 networks.

- **ITU-T F.69.** The IDI consists of a sequence of up to 8 decimal digits defined by ITU-T Recommendation F.69. This is the ITU-T-defined addressing plan for the international telex network.

- **ITU-T E.163.** The IDI consists of a sequence of up to 12 decimal digits defined by ITU-T Recommendation E.163. This is the ITU-T-defined addressing plan for the global telephone network.

- **ITU-T E.164.** The IDI consists of a sequence of up to 15 decimal digits defined by ITU-T Recommendation E.164. This is the ITU-T-defined addressing plan for the global integrated services digital network (ISDN).

---

work. By allowing the individual organization to set the value of the last 2 octets of the HO-DSP field, an organization can partition a network into as many as 65,535 areas before having to apply to the addressing authority for additional values for the initial octets of the HO-DSP field.

Some subset of the initial octets of the address can be used to define address prefixes in order to group areas into collections called routing domains. A routing domain is defined as a collection of areas that all run the same routing algorithm. In a network implementing OSI routing, this would be the routing algorithm defined in ISO 10589. However, the actual lengths of address prefixes and the way in which areas are grouped into routing domains are strictly a matter of policy and are determined by network managers. According to the international standards, address prefixes can be administered in any desired way.

The large number of octets that can be used to uniquely define an area theoretically permits building an individual routing domain with an almost unlimited number of areas. But implementation considerations will typically limit the number of areas a routing domain can contain. A large network can still have an almost unlimited number of areas by dividing the network into multiple routing domains.

AUTOMATIC CONFIGURATION OF END SYSTEMS

The OSI addressing standards are designed so that addresses can be assigned to end systems in an OSI network with little or no human intervention. The process of assigning an end system's NSAP address, and thus its network-entity-title, begins by determining the end system's area address.

A network manager is responsible for assigning the area address of a router before the router is attached to the network. A network management action is required to set a value for a router's area address (the IDP and the HO-DSP field of the DSP). This is because the way in which a network is divided into areas is inherently a policy matter that must be controlled by the network managers of a given organization's network.

When an end system that supports the ISO 9042 ES-IS protocol is attached to an OSI router, the end system gets the value of its area address from a router to which it is attached. It then typically gets its System Identifier (ID) field value from an internal identifier value that the system itself maintains. Each ID field value must be unique within the end system's area. However, as described earlier, ID field values are often assigned using the IEEE/ISO LAN addressing standard and are themselves globally unique. The SEL field value used in the address fields in a packet's PCI is then assigned by the entity creating the packet. An end system supporting the ISO 9042 ES-IS protocol is typically capable of generating its own complete NSAP address, and therefore, its own network-entity-title, when it is attached to the network. Thus, the complete NSAP address assignment procedure for an end system can be performed automatically without requiring human intervention.

An end system that does not support the ISO 9042 ES-IS protocol must be configured manually into the network using system definition procedures when it is attached to a router.

Index

Information Technology Management and Strategy	Methodologies for Building Systems	Analysis and Design	CASE
AN INFORMATION SYSTEMS MANIFESTO	STRATEGIC INFORMATION PLANNING METHODOLOGIES (second edition)	STRUCTURED TECHNIQUES: THE BASIS FOR CASE (revised edition)	STRUCTURED TECHNIQUES: THE BASIS FOR CASE (revised edition)
INFORMATION ENGINEERING (Book I: Introduction)	INFORMATION ENGINEERING (Book I: Introduction)	DATABASE ANALYSIS AND DESIGN	INFORMATION ENGINEERING (Book I: Introduction)
INFORMATION ENGINEERING (Book II:Planning and Analysis)	INFORMATION ENGINEERING (Book II:Planning and Analysis)	DESIGN OF MAN-COMPUTER DIALOGUES	**Languages and Programming**
STRATEGIC INFORMATION PLANNING METHODOLOGIES (second edition)	INFORMATION ENGINEERING (Book III: Design and Construction)	DESIGN OF REAL-TIME COMPUTER SYSTEMS	APPLICATION DEVELOPMENT WITHOUT PROGRAMMERS
SOFTWARE MAINTENANCE: THE PROBLEM AND ITS SOLUTION	STRUCTURED TECHNIQUES: THE BASIS FOR CASE (revised edition)	DATA COMMUNICATIONS DESIGN TECHNIQUES	FOURTH-GENERATION LANGUAGES (Volume I: Principles)
DESIGN AND STRATEGY FOR DISTRIBUTED DATA PROCESSING	**Object-Oriented Programming**	DESIGN AND STRATEGY FOR DISTRIBUTED DATA PROCESSING	FOURTH-GENERATION LANGUAGES (Volume II: Representative 4GLs)
Expert Systems	OBJECT-ORIENTED ANALYSIS AND DESIGN	SOFTWARE MAINTENANCE: THE PROBLEM AND ITS SOLUTION	FOURTH-GENERATION LANGUAGES (Volume III: 4GLs from IBM)
BUILDING EXPERT SYSTEMS: A TUTORIAL	PRINCIPLES OF OBJECT-ORIENTED ANALYSIS AND DESIGN	SYSTEM DESIGN FROM PROVABLY CORRECT CONSTRUCTS	**Diagramming Techniques**
	OBJECT-ORIENTED METHODS: A FOUNDATION	INFORMATION ENGINEERING (Book II:Planning and Analysis)	DIAGRAMMING TECHNIQUES FOR ANALYSTS AND PROGRAMMERS
	OBJECT-ORIENTED METHODS: THE PRAGMATICS	INFORMATION ENGINEERING (Book III: Design and Construction)	RECOMMENDED DIAGRAMMING STANDARDS FOR ANALYSTS AND PROGRAMMERS
	OBJECT-ORIENTED TOOLS		ACTION DIAGRAMS: CLEARLY STRUCTURED SPECIFICATIONS PROGRAMS, AND PROCEDURES (second edition)